Adobe Illustrator® 3 Complete

Sharyn Venit
Diane Burns
David Smith
Bruce Fraser

Addison-Wesley Publishing Company, Inc.
Reading, Massachusetts   Menlo Park, California   New York
Don Mills, Ontario   Wokingham, England   Amsterdam   Bonn
Sydney   Singapore   Tokyo   Madrid   San Juan
Paris   Seoul   Milan   Mexico City   Taipei

Many of the designations used by manufacturers and sellers to distinguish their products are claimed as trademarks. Where those designations appear in this book and Addison-Wesley was aware of a trademark claim, the designations have been printed in initial capital letters or all capital letters.

Artwork on the following pages
Copyright © 1987-1988 Adobe Systems Incorporated:
9, 10, 11, 21, 23, 24, 25, 26, 27, 29, 31, 32, 34, 35, 37,
39, 40, 41, 43, 45, 48, 71, 83, 116, 146

Copyright © 1991 Sharyn Venit, Diane Burns, David Smith, and Bruce Fraser

All rights reserved. No part of this publication may be reproduced, stored in a retrieval system, or transmitted, in any form or by any means, electronic, mechanical, photocopying, recording, or otherwise, without the prior written permission of the publisher. Printed in the United States of America. Published simultaneously in Canada.

Set in 11-point Palatino by Impressions, Madison, WI

Sponsoring Editor: Carole McClendon
Project Editors: Elizabeth Rogalin and Deborah McKenna
Technical Reviewer: Gregory Wasson
Cover design: Hannus Design Associates
Text design: Joyce Weston

ISBN 0-201-57756-9
1 2 3 4 5 6 7 8 9-MW-9594939291
First printing, June 1991

Contents

Acknowledgments *v*

Introduction *vii*

Part I: Tools 1

Part II: Commands 53

Part III: Techniques 161

Part IV: Applications 301

Introduction to Appendixes 355

Appendix A: Converting PICT Files with DrawOver 356

Appendix B: Printing Color Separations with Adobe Separator 3.0 360

Appendix C: Calculating Color Blends in Adobe Illustrator 3.0 370

Appendix D: Adobe Illustrator Color Trapping 372

Appendix E: Using the EPSF Riders File 374

Glossary 387

Indexes 403

Acknowledgments

First and foremost, thanks are due to the people at Adobe Systems who helped us gather some of the information, figures, and tips used in both the first and second editions of this book; they include John Warnock, John Kunze, Russell Brown, Jennifer Cohan, Luanne Cohen, and Yvonne Perry. Thanks also to John Van Pelt (Detroit Free Press), and EarthSurface Graphics (Sherman Oaks, California) for contributing examples of their work for Part IV, and to Laurie Miller (Redondo Beach, California) for her careful editing of the manuscript.

Special thanks to David Healy and Jennette Fuschini for their careful readings of the first edition manuscript, and to the readers of the second edition manuscript, Jane M. Kilgore (copy editor) and Gregory Wasson (technical editor), contributing editor to *MacUser* magazine.

Finally, thanks to the first edition editors and staff at Addison-Wesley (Carole McClendon, Rachel Guichard, Perry McIntosh, and Tanya Kucak) for their patience and flexibility in adapting the design of this book to meet the special needs of a graphics program, and to the second edition editors (Elizabeth Rogalin, Debbie McKenna) and production coordinator (Beth Burleigh).

This book was typeset by Impressions, Madison, WI, using Macintosh computers and a Linotronic 300 typesetter. Software used in production included Adobe Illustrator 3.0, Microsoft Word 4.0, SuperPaint, and PageMaker 4.0.

Introduction

Adobe Illustrator® 3 Complete is a complete reference designed to answer your questions about all Adobe Illustrator commands, tools, and techniques. The book includes expert advice about all Adobe Illustrator features, tips for increasing speed and productivity, and specific techniques to create special effects.

The beginning user will quickly learn how to use a tool or command without reading volumes of text. The intermediate user will learn new and valuable techniques for customizing designs. The advanced user will glean expert tips on how to use Illustrator more effectively and gain insight into how experienced artists create complex, layered art with Adobe Illustrator.

We have organized this book in four parts.

Part I: Tools is a reference to all of the tools in Adobe Illustrator. You will find an introduction to basic mouse operations and an overview of the toolbox, followed by detailed descriptions of all of the Illustrator tools listed as they appear on your Macintosh screen.

Part II: Commands is a reference to all of the commands in Adobe Illustrator. The introduction to this section provides a general description of how commands are selected and how to work with dialog box entries, as well as an overview of all the menus. The rest of Part II contains the Illustrator commands organized alphabetically for easy reference.

Part III: Techniques presents a listing of design effects available with Adobe Illustrator. In this section we give step-by-step descriptions of specific techniques that can be used to accomplish design tasks in the following areas:

- Alignment
- Text Manipulation
- Fills and Patterns
- Layering
- Lines
- Shapes (Closed Paths)
- Three-Dimensional Effects

Part IV: Applications contains examples of complex finished art created with Adobe Illustrator. With each example you will find detailed descriptions of how the artist conceptualized and completed the final art.

Included at the end of the book are Appendixes and a Glossary of special terms. Appendix A and Appendix B describe how to use two applications that come with Adobe Illustrator 3.0: DrawOver™, to convert PICT files, and Adobe Separator, to print color separations. Appendix C describes how to calculate an appropriate number of blends to prevent banding, and Appendix D explains color trapping. Appendix E describes how you can use the EPSF Riders file to change the default flatness setting, line screen, or screen angle at the time of printing, and how to add a standard line of text (such as a copyright line or a credit) at the bottom of all pages printed from Illustrator or Separator.

Each command and tool description in Part I and Part II is divided into an Overview and a Procedure subsection and sometimes contains a Warnings and/or a Tips subsection. Warnings and Tips also appear in the descriptions of techniques (Part III) and applications (Part IV). The subsections work as follows:

Overview   This section describes what the tool or command does. If you have forgotten a tool's or command's function, or if you want simply to learn about unfamiliar commands, the overviews in Parts I and II will be helpful.

Procedure   This section gives step-by-step directions on how to use the tool or command most effectively.

Warnings   This section offers guidelines on when not to use a particular tool, command, or technique, or describes some of the trade-offs that must be weighed in applying them (such as slower speed and larger file size in exchange for complex artwork).

Tips   This section will make the most interesting reading for users who want to rapidly increase their expertise with Adobe Illustrator. Hints, tricks, and insights included in this section will enhance your productivity.

This book is much more than descriptions and examples of tools and commands in Adobe Illustrator. It also contains a wealth of information experts have gleaned from using and teaching Adobe Illustrator since it was first released. We hope you will find it a useful information source that serves you long and well.

Part I:
Tools

Introduction to Tools

Basic Mouse Operations

This part of the book presents all of the tools available in Adobe Illustrator as they appear in the toolbox. You can easily find each tool by referring to the icons at the top corner of each page.

In order to use these tools, you must become familiar with two mouse operations. First, position the mouse pointer on the screen, and then (1) click the mouse button once or twice or (2) drag the mouse while holding down the mouse button. You will use each of these operations in working with Adobe Illustrator, sometimes combining these operations with holding the Shift key, Option key, Command key, or Spacebar. The terms used to define these actions are summarized below.

ACTION	DESCRIPTION
Click	First move the mouse without holding any keys or the mouse button in order to position the pointer over an object, then press the mouse button once and release it immediately.
Double-click	First move the mouse without holding any keys or the mouse button in order to position the pointer over an object, then press the mouse button twice, quickly.
Drag	First move the mouse without holding any keys or the mouse button in order to position the pointer over an object, then hold down the mouse button and move the mouse to a new position, then release the mouse button.
Shift-click	Click the mouse button while holding the Shift key down.
Option-click	Click the mouse button while holding the Option key down.
Control-click	Click the mouse button while holding the Control key down.
Shift-Option-click	Click the mouse button while holding both the Shift key and the Option key down.
Shift-Control-click	Click the mouse button while holding both the Shift key and the Control key down.
Shift-drag	Drag the mouse button while holding the Shift key down.
Option-drag	Drag the mouse button while holding the Option key down.
Shift-Option-drag	Drag the mouse button while holding both the Shift key and the Option key down.

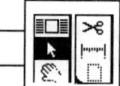

PART I

Illustrator Toolbox

Overview   Like other Macintosh graphics applications, the Illustrator toolbox is a palette, located vertically along the left side of the Illustrator screen, that contains icons for the various tools you use to create, select, and modify objects, and to adjust views of your files. The following figure shows what the Illustrator toolbox looks like with all of the pop-out tool options.

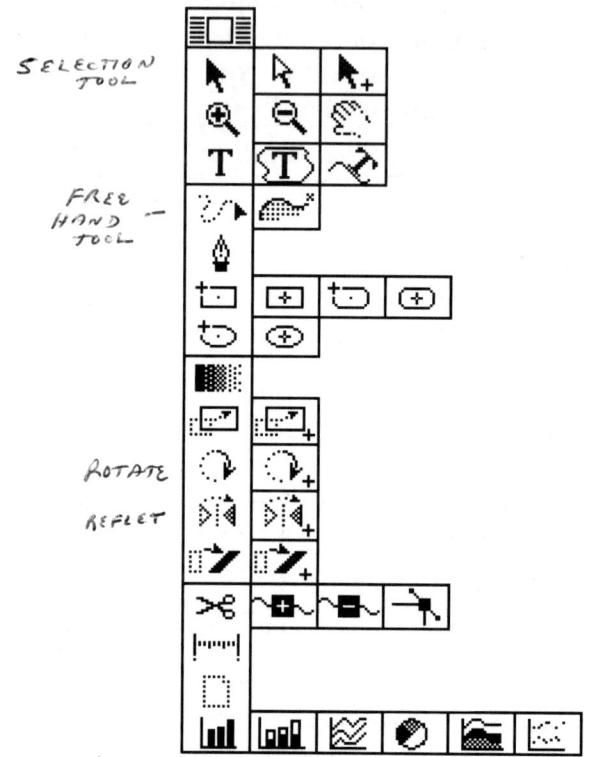

The Illustrator toolbox

You will often find yourself accessing the tools in Adobe Illustrator using a two-handed approach—with one hand on the mouse and the other on the keyboard. Becoming familiar with this two-handed approach is the key to attaining fluency in Illustrator, be-

TOOLS

cause many of the activities you perform in Illustrator require a combination of keyboard strokes and mouse movements. Although the number of combinations might at first seem daunting, you will find that there is a pattern to the way the keys combine with the various mouse tools. The result is an easy-to-learn set of powerful and flexible tools—once you learn how to activate and use one, you can readily apply the same or a similar technique to others.

Procedure To select any tool, click on the icon for that tool in the toolbox using the mouse. This will highlight the tool, indicating it has been selected. In addition to the default tools that appear in the toolbox when you start the program, most of the tools have alternates that appear as pop-up icons to the right of the toolbox. To access these, you press the mouse button on the tool in the toolbox until the pop-up icons appear, then drag to the tool you want to use, and release the mouse button. The alternate tools have functions that are closely related to the default tools from which they pop up. In most cases they can be accessed with a mouse-keystroke combination as well as from their pop-up icons.

POP-UP ICONS

When you choose a tool from a pop-up icon, it appears in the toolbox in place of the default tool with which it is associated. To reset a tool to its default, Shift-double-click that tool. To reset the whole toolbox to its defaults, Command-Shift-double-click any tool.

SHIFT-DOUBLE CK TOOL TO RESET TO DEFAULT
TO RESET WHOLE TOOLBOX

You can use the following shortcuts to activate many of the tools. For example, you can activate the Zoom-in tool from the keyboard using the Command key and the Spacebar (in combination with the mouse). When using the keyboard to change tools, hold down the key(s) *before* you press the mouse button.

- Holding down the Command key temporarily changes the current tool to whichever of the three selection tools currently appears in the toolbox, for selecting or moving objects on the page.
- Holding the Spacebar temporarily changes the current tool to the Hand tool for moving the page view in the window.
- Holding the Command key and the Spacebar temporarily changes the current tool to the Zoom-in tool for enlarging.

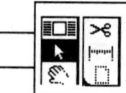

- Holding the Option key, the Command key, and the Spacebar temporarily changes the current tool to the Zoom-out tool for reducing.

You will find these keystroke shortcuts useful when you are performing an action with one tool (for example, the Pen tool), and need to use another tool (for example, the Selection tool) to modify the action. In such cases, you do not have to divert your attention away from the drawing area of your screen, access the toolbox, select a new tool, and complete your activity. You simply hold down the appropriate key(s).

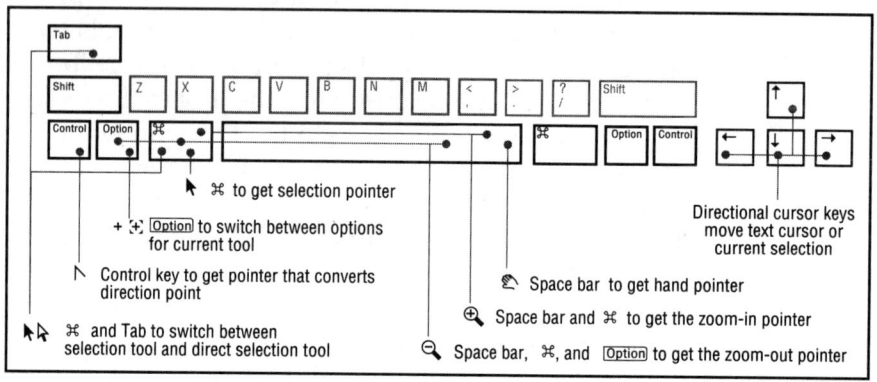

Keyboard shortcuts for the toolbox

The basic mouse operations used with the tools are *clicking* and *dragging*. The Spacebar, the Command key, the Shift key, the Control key, and the Option key all work interactively with the mouse. The Shift and Option keys are used to modify or constrain the action of mouse clicks, mouse drags, and the action of the Command key and the Spacebar.

- Pressing the Shift key after pressing the mouse button constrains the action of tools. For example, when you are drawing with the Pen tool, straight lines are constrained to 45-degree angles. When you are drawing with the Rectangle or the Oval tool, rectangles are constrained to squares, and ovals are constrained to perfect circles. Similarly, movements are constrained to 45-degree angles when you drag an object with the Selection tool.

| TOOLS

- When you move or transform an object, Option-clicking on the Selection tool, or Option-clicking on the artwork after selecting the Rotate tool, Scale tool, Reflect tool, or Shear tool results in a dialog box that lets you enter numeric values for the action of the tool. This is a useful alternative to moving or transforming objects visually. Each of the transformation tools (Rotate, Scale, Reflect, and Shear) has an alternate pop-up tool that produces a dialog box, but you can always transform objects numerically without choosing the alternate tool by using the Option-click shortcut.
- When you move or transform an object, Option-dragging produces a copy of the selected object. This is a useful alternative to the Copy and Paste commands.

PART I

Tools

The Selection Tools

Overview There are three selection tools: the Selection tool, the Direct-selection tool, and the Object-selection tool. You use the selection tools primarily to select objects for further manipulation or transformation. You also use the selection tools to move objects, and to adjust curves by dragging curve segments, anchor points, or direction lines. The Selection tool is the default tool, that is, the tool that is selected when Illustrator is first opened. It is also the most frequently used tool. In Illustrator, you must always select an object before you take action on it. Thus, you will probably use the selection tools more than any others.

Handwritten margin note:
(1) SELECT OBJECT.
(2) TAKE ACTION ON IT.

Procedure Choose the Selection tool by clicking the icon in the toolbox. When the Selection tool is active, the mouse pointer changes to a solid arrow.

Choose the Direct-selection tool by dragging to its pop-up icon in the toolbox and releasing the mouse button. When the Direct-selection tool is active, the pointer changes to a hollow arrow.

Choose the Object-selection tool by dragging to its pop-up icon in the toolbox and releasing the mouse button or by pressing the Option key when the Selection tool is selected. When the Object-selection tool is active, the pointer changes to a solid arrow with a small plus sign beside it.

Holding down the Command key temporarily accesses the current selection tool, that is, the selection tool that appears in the toolbox. When the Command key is pressed, you can toggle between the Selection and Direct-selection tools by pressing the Tab key. You cannot, however, toggle the Object-selection tool to one of the other selection tools using this shortcut.

Selecting Objects Objects that you create and manipulate in Illustrator include text objects, anchor points, line segments, direction lines, paths, and grouped objects. The two basic methods for selecting objects are to click on the object or to drag a selection marquee around the object.

TOOLS

 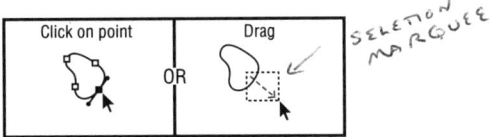

Two methods of selecting objects

Both of these methods are standard in many graphics applications and on the desktop of the Macintosh. The previous figure shows both methods of selecting objects. If two or more objects overlap, clicking will select the topmost one, and dragging the selection marquee around the objects selects both. (The selection marquee is a rectangle of dashed lines that appears when you drag the mouse onscreen without selecting any objects first.)

The selection tools differ only in the kinds of objects they select. Objects that can be selected with the Selection tool are anchor points, line segments, grouped objects, and text objects. Selecting an anchor point also selects any segments that are connected to it, whereas selecting a segment does not select any anchor points.

The Direct-selection tool behaves identically to the Selection tool except in the case of grouped objects and paths that contain text. Clicking or dragging the Selection tool over a grouped object selects the entire group; using the Direct-selection tool allows you to select individual anchor points and line segments from a grouped object. Similarly, clicking or dragging the Selection tool over a path that contains text selects both the path and the type; using the Direct-selection tool allows you to select anchor points and line segments from the path without selecting the type.

To select an entire path that is part of a grouped object, Option-click the path with the Direct-selection tool. Subsequent Option-clicks continue to add to the selection. If the grouped object consists of only one group, the second Option-click selects the entire group, but if the group is made up of objects that are also groups, Option-clicking adds those groups to the selection, one by one. This technique, called "up-selecting," is particularly useful when working with grouped objects, such as graphs, that contain many sub-groups. (See Modifying Graphs in Part III: Techniques.)

Pressing the Command key and the Tab key toggles between the Selection tool and the Direct-selection tool.

The Object-selection tool selects complete paths (anchor points and their connecting line segments) or text objects. Clicking or dragging the Object-selection tool over part of a path selects the entire path. Holding down the Option key while the Selection tool is active accesses the Object-selection tool.

 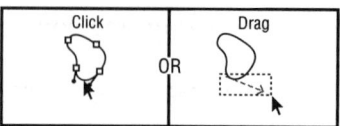

To select a line segment without selecting the anchor point, click anywhere on the segment or drag the selection marquee over the segment

 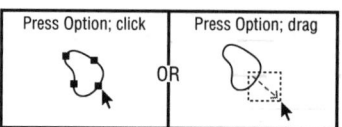

To select all of the anchor points and connecting line segments of an ungrouped path, Option-click anywhere on the path or Option-drag the selection marquee

To select an entire text object, use the Selection tool or the Object-selection tool to click on the baseline of the text, drag the selection marquee around the baseline of text, or, if the text has a path, click the path. If a text object contains multiple linked text blocks, use the Direct-selection tool to select a single text block by clicking or dragging a selection marquee around the baseline of the text.

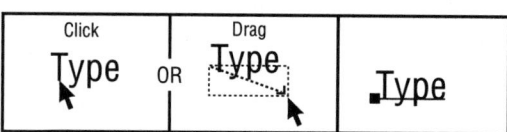

Two methods of selecting type

To extend a selection to include a second object (after one object is selected), Shift-click on the desired objects or hold down the Shift key and drag a selection marquee around the desired objects. The same action applies for deselecting individual objects in a group selection: You can select any number of objects, then Shift-click to deselect one or more.

| TOOLS |

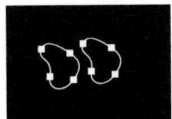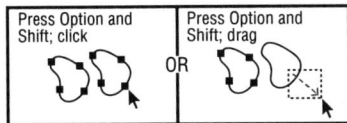

To select more than one object, hold down the Shift key before you select each object

Moving Objects   To move a selected object visually on the screen, drag it using the Selection tool. Shift-dragging constrains the movement to a multiple of 45-degree angles—that is, you will be able to move the object only along one of eight angles: 0°, 45°, 90°, 135°, 180°, 225°, 270°, and 315°. Option-dragging moves a copy of the selected object and leaves the original in place.

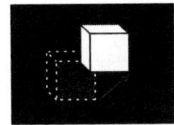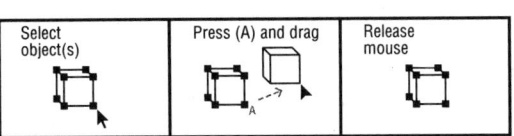

Moving objects

To move a selected object a specified distance, first select the object with the Selection tool, then Option-click the Selection tool icon in the toolbox. A Move dialog box appears, which allows you to specify the distance and direction of the move, whether to move pattern tiles, and whether to move the selected object or a copy of it.

The Distance field is already selected when you call up the Move dialog box. To change this distance, simply type, in the unit of measure shown (centimeters, inches, or points, as determined by the Preferences command), the new distance you wish to move the object.

Next, notice that the Direction defaults to the angle of the previous move. If you do not want the Direction to be the same as the previous one, click the button next to the direction you want—Horizontal, Vertical, or Angle. Directions of angled moves can be specified in degrees, with horizontal as 0° and angles measured counterclockwise for positive values, clockwise for negative values.

If you want to move pattern tiles, click in the Move pattern tiles box. A check box appears indicating this choice is selected. When you have specified all your choices for the move, click on either the OK button to move the selected object or the Copy button to move a copy of the selected object.

PART I

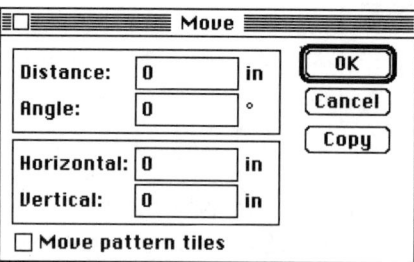

Option-click the Selection tool icon in the toolbox and in the Move dialog box enter the distance and angle you want selected objects to move

You can also move selected objects by pressing the arrow keys (available on most keyboards). The increment of movement per keystroke can be set in the Preferences dialog box. (See Preferences in Part II: Commands.)

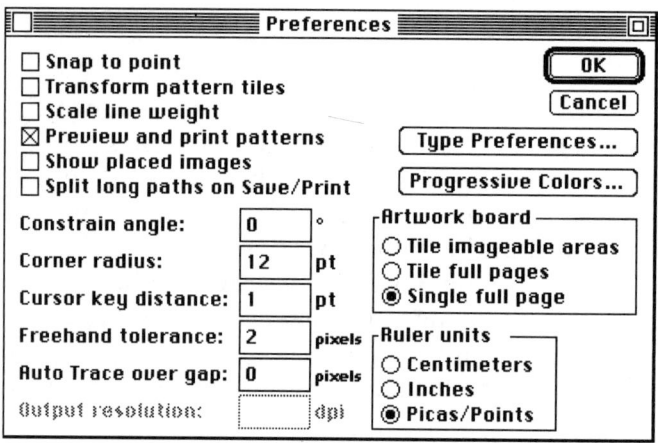

Cursor key distance in the Preferences dialog box determines the increments for movement with the arrow keys

Using the Option key to obtain the Object-selection tool while dragging a selection marquee is not the same as Shift-dragging or Option-dragging. To use the Option key with the marquee, you must hold down the key *before* pressing the mouse button. To Shift-drag or Option-drag, you must hold down the key *after* pressing the mouse button to select the object you want to drag.

TOOLS	

Tips Since the selection tools are used so frequently, always use the Command key to access the Selection pointer temporarily while using another tool. For example, draw a curve with the Pen tool, then hold down the Command key and use the Selection pointer to adjust it. To switch between the Selection tool and the Direct-selection tool, hold down the Command key and press the Tab key. The only time you need to click on a Selection tool icon in the toolbox is when you want to move an object a specified distance.

You can see the distance and angle of a move by first moving an object visually on the screen and then Option-clicking on the Selection tool to see the numeric values in the dialog box. This can be useful if you want to duplicate the same movement later. (See also Select All in Part II: Commands.)

The Zoom Tools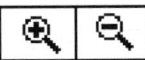

Overview Use the Zoom-in and Zoom-out tools to change the level of magnification at which you view your file. Illustrator provides nine levels of magnification, each increased or decreased by a factor of two. From actual size (100%), you can zoom in (magnify) to 200%, 400%, 800%, and 1600%, and zoom out (reduce) to 50%, 25%, 12.5%, and 6.25% of actual size.

Procedure Choose the Zoom-in tool by clicking its icon in the toolbox, or hold down the Command key and the Spacebar to select the Zoom-in tool temporarily if you have another tool already selected. The mouse pointer changes to a magnifying glass with a plus sign in the center. When you release the Command key and Spacebar, the previously selected tool will once again be selected.

Choose the Zoom-out tool by dragging to its pop-up icon in the toolbox and releasing the mouse button, or by pressing the Command-Option-Spacebar to select the Zoom-out tool temporarily if you have another tool already selected. The mouse pointer changes to a magnifying glass with a minus sign in the center. When you release the Command and Option keys and the Spacebar, the previously selected tool will once again be selected.

The following figure shows the various pointer shapes for the zoom tools: a plus sign enlarges the view, a minus sign reduces the view, and an empty Zoom icon indicates that you have enlarged or reduced to the limit.

⊕ ⊖ ◯

The appearances of the zoom tools: (1) A plus sign enlarges the view, (2) a minus sign reduces the view, (3) an empty Zoom icon indicates that you have enlarged (or reduced) to the limit

To zoom in to the center of the active window, double-click the Zoom-in tool icon in the Toolbox. To zoom out from the center of the active window, hold down the Option key and double-click the Zoom-in tool icon. Note that double-clicking does not select the Zoom-in tool, but leaves the currently selected tool in effect.

Tips   The Zoom-in tool is particularly useful when you need to magnify an area in order to see the anchor points for fine, detailed adjustment, or when you are working with several points or paths lying close together. The following figure illustrates the benefit of using the Zoom-in tool to magnify a section of your image for modification purposes.

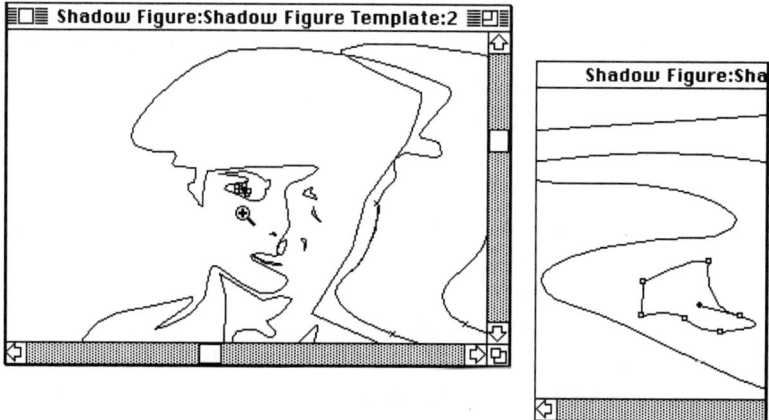

Reduced and close-up views of the same detail

| TOOLS | |

Always use the Command key and Spacebar to magnify a detail of your drawing; this method is much faster than clicking the icon in the toolbox.

The zoom tools remain active in Preview mode. The other tools that do so are the Page tool, the Measure tool, and the Hand tool.

The Hand Tool

Overview You can use the Hand tool as an alternative to the scroll bars. The Hand tool can move the image of your artwork in the active window vertically, horizontally, and diagonally. It moves the whole page, not the selected objects on the page. Think of the Hand tool as your own hand and the image in the active window as a piece of paper sitting on your desk. Just as you place your hand on top of the paper and move it across your desk, so the Hand tool moves the image across the screen. By using the Hand tool, you can scroll diagonally with one movement instead of having to click on two scroll bars to accomplish the same movement. You can also use the Hand tool to go quickly to the Actual Size or Fit In Window view, as described in the Procedure section that follows.

Procedure Choose the Hand tool by dragging to its pop-up icon in the toolbox beside the zoom tools and releasing the mouse button, or hold down the Spacebar when a different tool is selected to activate the Hand tool temporarily. When you release the Spacebar, the previously selected tool will once again be active. When the Hand tool is active, the mouse pointer changes to a hand. To scroll with the Hand tool, position the hand on the active window, hold down the mouse button, and drag in the direction you wish to scroll. The following figure demonstrates using the Hand tool to scroll diagonally across the active window.

PART I

Dragging the Hand tool to scroll diagonally on the screen

To change to Fit In Window view, double-click on the Hand tool icon in the toolbox as an alternative to using the Fit In Window command (see Fit In Window in Part II: Commands). To change to Actual Size, Option-double-click on the Hand tool icon in the toolbox as an alternative to using the Actual Size command (see Actual Size in Part II: Commands). To make use of either of these shortcuts, you must first select the Hand tool from its pop-up icon so that it appears in the toolbox. Note that double-clicking the Hand icon does not select the Hand tool, but leaves the currently selected tool still in effect.

The following figure summarizes the three ways of using the Hand tool to change views of your image in the active window.

Move view in window
Select tool (or press Space bar),
then drag

Fit in window
Double-Click
on toolbox icon

Actual Size view
Option Double-click
on toolbox icon

Three uses of the Hand tool icon in the toolbox

16

| TOOLS | T |

Tips Always use the Spacebar to access the Hand tool quickly while another tool is selected. The only time you need to click on the Hand tool icon in the toolbox is when you want to change to an Actual Size or Fit In Window view.

The Hand tool is one of the tools that remain active in Preview mode. The others are the Zoom tools, the Measure tool, and the Page tool.

The Type Tools

Overview Use the type tools to create text objects, into which you will type or import text, or to edit existing text. There are three type tools: the Type tool, the Area-type tool, and the Path-type tool. Use the Type tool to create text at an alignment point or to define a rectangle into which you type text. Use the Area-type tool to fill an existing path of any shape with text. The path may be open or closed. Use the Path-type tool to type text along a path.

Procedure Choose the Type tool by clicking the icon in the toolbox. The mouse pointer changes to an I-beam surrounded by a dotted box in the active window. Choose the Area-type tool by dragging to its pop-up icon in the toolbox and releasing the mouse button. The pointer changes to an I-beam surrounded by dotted parentheses in the active window. Choose the Path-type tool by dragging to its pop-up icon in the toolbox and releasing the mouse button. The pointer changes to an I-beam intersected by a dotted wavy line in the active window.

Creating Point Text Choose the Type tool and click the mouse to set an alignment point. As shown in the following figure, the crossbar on the I-beam sets the baseline and anchor point for the text. The text you type forms one continuous line unless you break it by inserting a Return character.

▪**Creating point text**—Click the Type tool to set an alignment point.

Point text

17

Creating Rectangular Text Choose the Type tool and drag to define a rectangular area. A blinking insertion point appears in the rectangle. Text typed into a rectangle wraps automatically to fit inside the rectangle. If there is too much text to fit inside the rectangle, a small plus sign appears at the end of the text. To display the overflow text, you can enlarge the rectangle using the Direct-selection tool or, using the same tool, duplicate the rectangle by Option-dragging. The overflow text automatically flows into the second rectangle, and the two rectangles form a single text object. Rectangles created with the Type tool are unpainted paths (their Fill and Stroke are both set to None), but you can assign them a Fill and Stroke using the Style command (see Style in Part II: Commands).

Rectangular text

Filling an Existing Path with Text Choose the Area-type tool and click on the path you want to fill with text. The path may be either open or closed. A blinking insertion point appears in the path. As with rectangular text, the text wraps to fit inside the path, and the presence of overflow text is indicated by a small plus sign at the end of the text. Clicking on a path with the Area-type tool changes its Paint attributes to a Fill and Stroke of None.

TOOLS

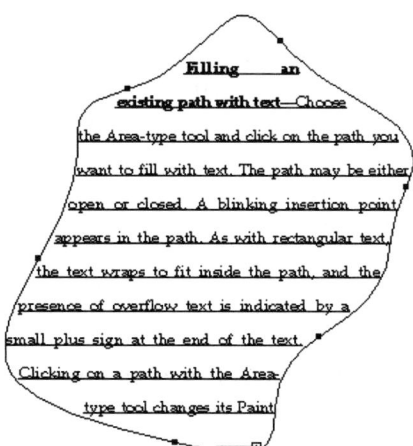

Area text

Creating Type along a Path   Choose the Path-type tool and click on the path along which you want to place the text. The path may be open or closed. A blinking insertion point appears on the path. The text you type follows the shape of the path. Clicking on a path with the Path-type tool changes its Paint attributes to a Fill and Stroke of None.

Path text

Selecting Text   To modify all the text in a text object, use the Selection tool to select the entire text object. To modify a single block in a text object, or to change a text path without changing the text itself, use the Direct-selection tool. To move type along a path, select the type with the Selection tool, then drag the I-beam that appears at the start of the text. Drag the I-beam across the path to flip the text across the path.

PART I

Use any of the type tools to select part of the text in a text object. When you move any of the type tools over existing text, the pointer changes to an I-beam. Illustrator follows standard Macintosh text-editing conventions. Click the I-beam to create an insertion point at which you can add text by typing; delete text using the Delete key. Drag the I-beam to select a range of characters. Double-click to select a complete word and triple-click to select a complete paragraph. You can change any of the Paint or Type attributes of text selected using the type tools without affecting the rest of the text in the text object.

Tips   To quickly incorporate formatted text in a columnar layout into your artwork, first type and format the text using a word-processing application. Then drag the Type tool to create a text rectangle and use the Import Text command from the File menu to import the text into the rectangle. Most of the text's formatting is retained. To accommodate overflow text, duplicate the text rectangle by Option-dragging it with the Direct-selection tool.

To flow text through several paths, use the Area-type tool to click on the first path, then choose the Import Text command. Use the Object-selection tool to select the text-filled path and the other paths into which the text should flow, then use the Link command from the Type menu. The text flows into the paths according to the paths' stacking order, from back to front. The text flows into the backmost path first and the frontmost path last.

The Freehand Tool

Overview   Use the Freehand tool to draw a continuous line of any shape freehand—that is, without clicking and dragging each anchor point (as required when using the Pen tool).

Procedure   Choose the Freehand tool by clicking the icon in the toolbox or by holding down the Control key when the Pen tool is active. The mouse pointer changes to an x in the active window. Hold down

TOOLS	

the mouse button and begin drawing your object by dragging the mouse along the path you wish to draw.

Dragging quickly results in fewer anchor points in a given distance than dragging slowly does. You can also force more or fewer anchor points per distance by adjusting the tolerance level through the Preferences dialog box (see Preferences in Part II: Commands). A low tolerance value results in more anchor points per given distance than does a high tolerance value. The following figure shows the effects of different tolerance settings.

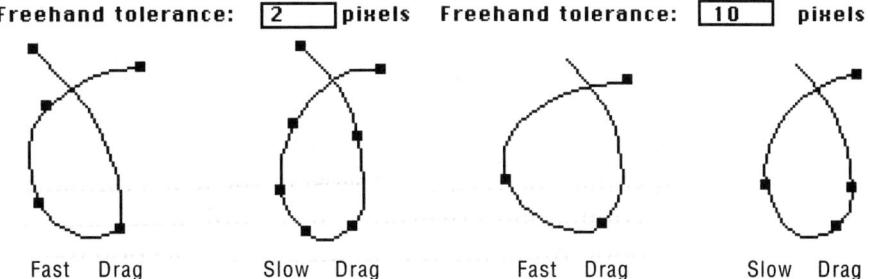

Set tolerance in the Preferences dialog box to control the number of anchor points created by the Freehand tool: (1) Line drawn with a tolerance value of 2 pixels; (2) Line drawn with a tolerance value of 10 pixels

After you have drawn a path with the Freehand tool, you can adjust the line segments and anchor points as described under the Pen tool and set Stroke and Fill patterns as described under the Style (Paint Menu) command in Part II. You can also erase anchor points while you are drawing by holding down the Command key and backing up along the line you have just traced with the Freehand tool.

 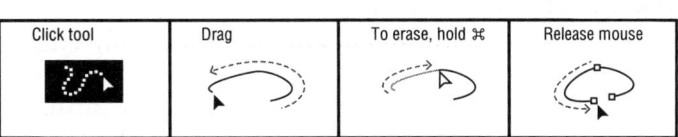

Using the Freehand tool

21

PART I

Tips Use a high tolerance setting (in the Preferences dialog box) and drag the Freehand tool quickly unless you need a lot of anchor points for fine adjustments; note that anchor points increase the amount of disk space required by an illustration. You can always add anchor points with the Scissors tool if you need more (see The Scissors Tool).

You can change the Freehand tool to the Pen tool without returning to the tool palette: Hold down the Control key (or the Z key on the Macintosh Plus), and the Freehand tool will change to the Pen tool.

The Autotrace Tool

Overview You use the Autotrace tool to trace automatically the path around any solid object that is part of a template. (See Templates in Part III: Techniques.) This is faster and easier than tracing a template with the Freehand tool or the Pen tool. It works best if the template is composed of distinct areas of solid black or solid outlines with curved edges. The Autotrace tool always creates rounded joins and is therefore not used to trace objects with pointed corners and straight lines.

Procedure Choose the Autotrace tool by dragging to its pop-up icon beside the Freehand tool in the toolbox and releasing the mouse button. The mouse pointer changes to an x. Position the x pointer and click on the edge of a solid object in the template layer to trace a path around that object. You can adjust the sensitivity of the Autotrace tool in the Preferences dialog box (see Preferences in Part II: Commands). With the Autotrace gap distance set at 0 in the Preferences dialog box, the Autotrace will read every pixel in the template. If the gap distance is set at 1, the Autotrace jumps across one-pixel gaps and connects them. If it is set at 2, the Autotrace jumps across two-pixel gaps and connects them. This can be useful if your template is very sketchy.

TOOLS

Path drawn with the Autotrace tool

Once you have drawn a path with the Autotrace tool, you can adjust the line segments and anchor points as described under the Pen tool, and set Stroke and Fill patterns as described under the Style (Paint Menu) command.

To trace only part of a shape, click on the Autotrace tool and position the x on the edge of the template at the point where you wish the tracing to begin. Instead of clicking, drag the cursor to the second point where you wish the tracing to end, then release the mouse button. Only the distance between those two points is traced.

Tracing part of a shape

To trace hollow shapes, [...] the shape first. Then [...] shape will always be [...] set the hollow shape [...] Dimensional Effects i[...]

Warning   Do not use the Autot[...] lines or rectangles, si[...] Use the Pen or Rectan[...] shapes.

Tip   As a rule, use the Au[...] curved edges. Use t[...] tremely ragged or irr[...]

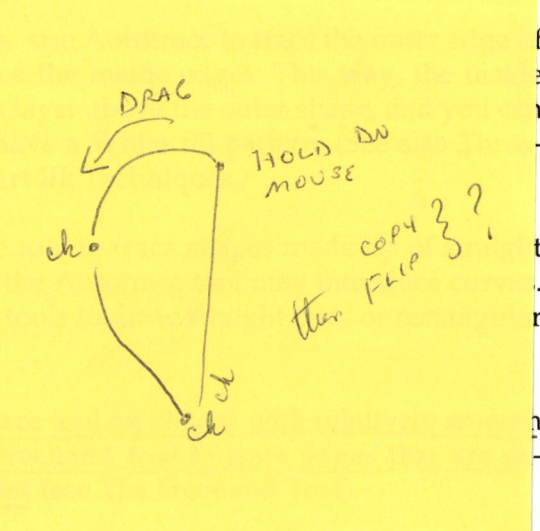

PART I

The Pen Tool

Overview   You will use the Pen tool more than any other tool to create paths. A path is any line or shape drawn in Illustrator. Paths may be composed of both curved and straight line segments and may be open (straight or curved lines) or closed (shapes).

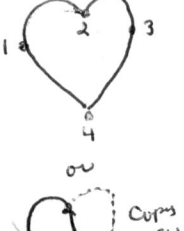

Procedure   Choose the Pen tool by clicking the icon in the toolbox. The mouse pointer changes to an x in the active window. To use the Pen tool, position the x pointer on the screen and click the mouse button. This positions an anchor point on the screen. Before releasing the mouse button, drag the x pointer to set a direction line for the anchor. As you drag the x pointer around the screen while holding down the mouse, the direction line for the anchor point changes. When you release the mouse button, the anchor point and direction lines are set and the pointer changes to a +, ready to position the second anchor point along the path. Reposition the pointer and repeat for each new anchor point.

   The direction lines do not print. They are tangent to the line of the curve and determine in which direction and how deep the curve will be drawn.

   Drawing a Straight Line   Click the mouse button once to position the first anchor point. Do not drag the mouse yet. The mouse pointer changes to a +, indicating that the next point you click with the mouse will create another anchor point on the current path. Click again to set the anchor point for the other end of the straight line. A straight line automatically appears on the screen, connecting the two anchor points. Holding the Shift key before clicking on the second point constrains the line to 45-degree angles. The following figure shows how the steps combine to result in a straight line.

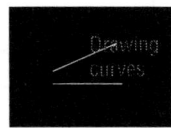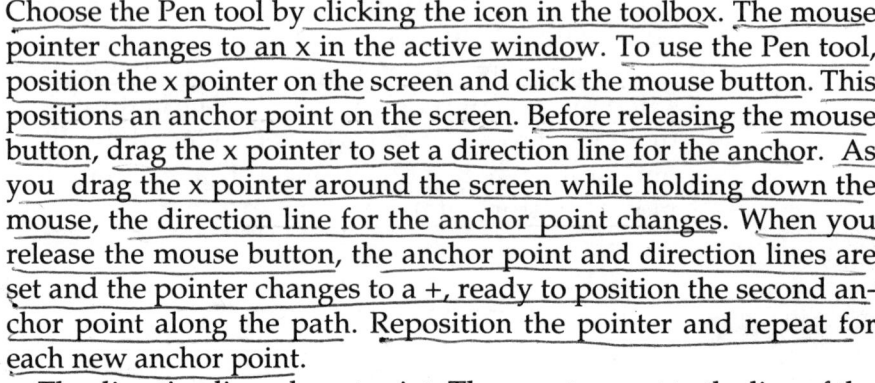

Drawing straight lines

24

TOOLS

[Handwritten margin note: HOLD DOWN MOUSE TO CR 1ST. PT. — DRAG TO CR. DIRECTION LINE, RELEASE MOUSE]

[Handwritten margin note: CR 2ND pt = Complete curve]

Drawing a Curve Hold down the mouse button to position the first anchor point, drag to create a direction line, then release the mouse button. The mouse pointer changes to a +, indicating that the next point you click or drag with the mouse will create another anchor point on the current path. If you click the second anchor point, you complete a curve (the curved line automatically appears on the screen). You then have the option of continuing the current path with either a straight line (by clicking the third point) or with another curve (by dragging the third point). If you drag the second anchor point, you can continue drawing a smooth curved line (by clicking or dragging the third point). Repeat the process to continue the path. The following figure illustrates the drawing of a curved line.

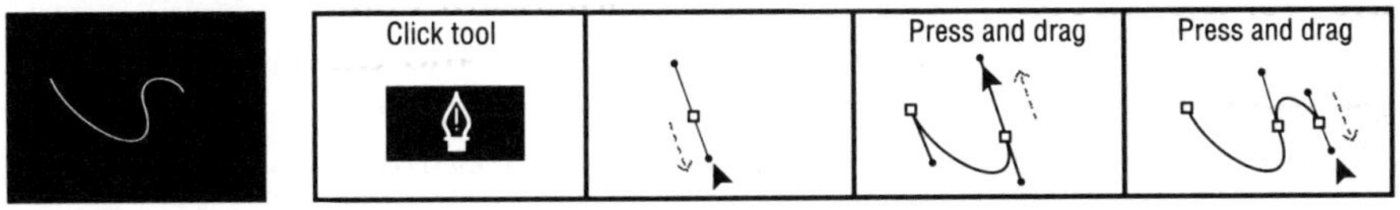

Drawing curved lines

It will require practice with the Pen tool to learn where anchor points are best placed and how to drag direction lines. The following suggestions should help you understand the principles of drawing curves in Illustrator.

- Direction lines are always tangent to the curves they create. In dragging a direction line after positioning an anchor point, drag in a direction that is tangent to the curve you intend to draw. Drag the direction line a distance that is about one third of the length of the curve between the current and the next anchor points.

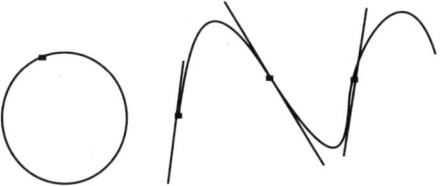

A tangent is a straight line that touches a curve at only one point

25

PART I

- Anchor points along a curved path are best placed where the direction of the curve changes. They are usually not required in the middle of continuous curves, such as the peak of a hill or the bottom of a valley. You can think of the anchor points as the places along a winding mountain road where you would turn the wheels of the car from pointing right to pointing left, or vice versa. Remember that when you are driving around the hump of a curve you are holding the wheels in one direction, and an anchor point is not required. By following this guide, you can create curves that are easy to control and that can be edited with a minimum number of anchor points—two goals for efficiency and economy of disk space.

Anchor points placed where the direction of the wheels would change in driving around curves in a road

The goal is to build paths as efficiently as possible using the minimum number of anchor points. While the first rule for dragging direction lines is useful, the second rule governing the placement of anchor points is of primary importance. It is easier to edit paths by moving direction lines than to do so by adding and deleting anchor points.

The Option key lets you create corner points along a curve—points where the curve changes direction abruptly, not gradually. To create a corner point, first click to set the anchor point and drag to set the direction line. Then hold down the Option key, click on the anchor point you have just set, and drag a new direction line.

 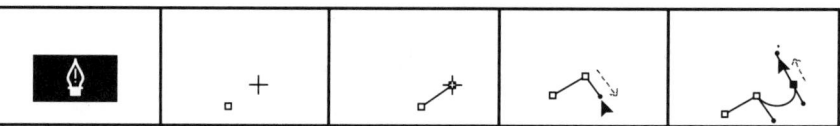

Creating corner points

TOOLS

Use combinations of the techniques that have been described to create paths composed of curved and straight line segments.

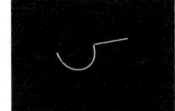

Click tool	Press and drag	Press and drag	Press Option and click	Release Option; click

Drawing paths composed of curved lines and straight lines

Closing a Path   To close a path and thereby create a solid shape, click the final anchor point position on top of the first anchor point of the path. The pointer changes from a + to an x, indicating that the Pen tool is available to start a new path.

Completing an Open Path   To complete an open path (that is, end one path without closing it), click the Pen tool icon in the toolbox or hold down the Command key to change the pointer to the Selection tool and then click anywhere on the page. The pointer changes from a + to an x, indicating that the Pen tool is available to start a new path.

Editing a Path   To edit a path, use the Selection tool to move an anchor point, drag a curved line segment, or adjust direction lines. The following figure shows a path edited in each of these ways.

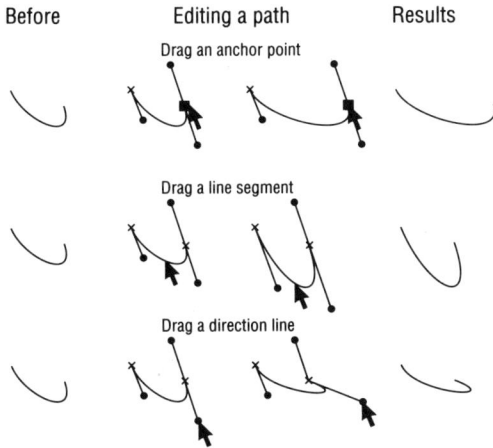

Three methods of editing a path

Warning If you forget to click the Pen tool icon in the toolbox to start a new path after completing an open path, you will end up with a line joining the last anchor point in the previous path to the first anchor point on your new path. If this happens, simply press Delete once to remove the new anchor point. Then click the Pen tool icon, or hold down the Command key to change the pointer to the Selection tool and click anywhere on the page to start a new path.

Tips You will find that using the Command key shortcut to switch to the Selection tool makes it easier to adjust curves while you draw. This way you don't need to end the path by going to the toolbox to select the Selection tool. You can resume adding points to the same path after adjusting part of the path.

To draw a straight line of an exact length, create one anchor point, then Option-click on the Selection tool to get the Move dialog box. Enter the desired length of the line in the Distance field and click Copy to make a copy. Select both anchor points and use the Join command to draw a line connecting the two points (see Join in Part II: Commands).

Use the Scissors tool to open a closed path or to split an open path into two paths. (See The Scissors Tool.) Use the Add-anchor-point Tool to add anchor points along an already-drawn line segment. (See The Add-anchor-point Tool.)

The Rectangle Tools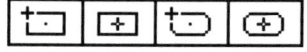

Overview You use the rectangle tools to create rectangular objects or squares. The rectangle tools produce objects composed of two grouped paths: a rectangular path, consisting of four straight-line segments joined at the corners, and a single point in the center of the rectangle, which you can use to align the rectangle relative to other centered objects (text or graphics). There are four rectangle tools: the Rectangle tool, the Centered-rectangle tool, the Rounded-rectangle tool, and the Centered-rounded-rectangle tool. The Centered-rectangle and Centered-rounded-rectangle tools draw rectangles from center to edge rather than from corner to corner, and the Rounded-rectangle and Centered-rounded-rectangle tools create rectangles with rounded corners of the radius specified in the Preferences dialog box. (See Preferences in Part II: Commands for more details.)

Procedure   You can draw a rectangle visually on the screen or create one with dimensions and rounded corners as specified numerically in a Rectangle dialog box.

Three ways to use the rectangle tools: (1) drag diagonally to draw a rectangle from corner to corner; (2) hold down the Option key and drag diagonally to create a rectangle from center to edge; (3) hold down the Shift key and drag diagonally to create a perfect square

Drawing a Rectangle Visually on the Screen   Choose the Rectangle tool by clicking the icon in the toolbox. The mouse pointer changes to a + in the active window. Press the mouse button to position a corner of the rectangle, then drag diagonally and release the mouse to complete the rectangle. To construct rectangles from center to edge (rather than from corner to corner), choose the Centered-rectangle tool by dragging to its pop-up icon in the toolbox and releasing the mouse button or press the Option key while the Rectangle tool is active. To constrain a rectangle to a perfect square, press the Shift key while you drag the mouse (Shift-drag) diagonally. To construct rectangles with rounded corners, use the Rounded-rectangle or Centered-rounded-rectangle tool. The default corner radius for the Rounded-rectangle and Centered-rounded-rectangle tools is set in the Preferences dialog box (see Preferences in Part II: Commands).

Drawing a Rectangle with Numerically Specified Dimensions Choose any of the rectangle tools, then click once in the active window. The Rectangle dialog box appears. Use the dialog box to enter specific dimensions for a rectangle, including width, height, and corner radius. The point at which you clicked on the screen defines the upper left corner of the rectangle if the Rectangle or Rounded-rectangle is selected, or the center point of the rectangle if the Centered-rectangle or Centered-rounded-rectangle tool is selected.

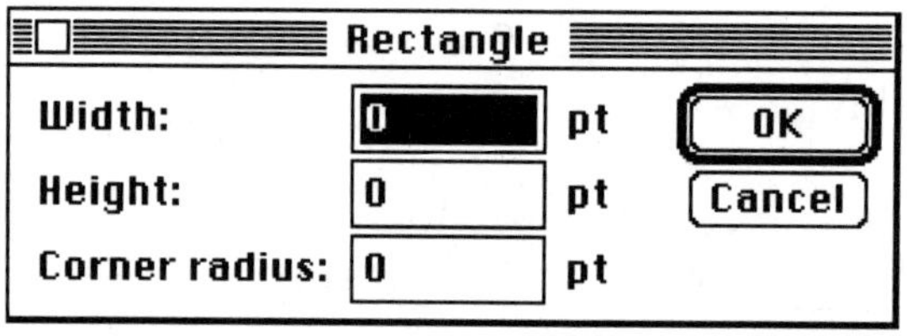

The Rectangle dialog box

The default corner radius for the Rectangle and Centered-rectangle tools is 0 points. The default corner radius for the Rounded-rectangle and Centered-rounded-rectangle tools is 12 points. (You can change the default radius using the Preferences command.) As you increase the value (up to a maximum of 1296 points), the corner radius becomes more curved, approaching an oval shape as shown in the following figure. The corner radius cannot exceed half the length of the short sides of the rectangle. If you enter a larger value, Illustrator will draw the largest oval that can fit into the rectangle. Setting the corner radius to 0 points creates rectangles with square corners. Points are the default unit of measurement (1point = $\frac{1}{72}$ of an inch). To use inches or centimeters, you can change the unit of measurement under Ruler units in the Preferences dialog box. (See Preferences in Part II: Commands.)

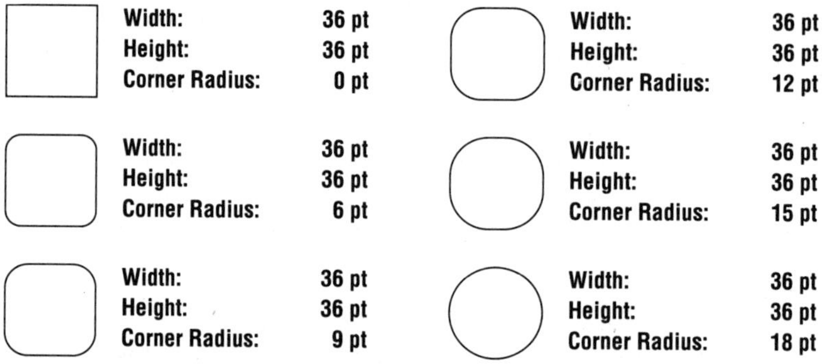

Examples of rounded corners

Tip A rectangle is grouped as one object when it is first drawn. You can modify the grouped rectangle using the Scale, Rotate, Reflect, and Shear tools, but to move individual anchor points you must first

TOOLS

ungroup the rectangle (see the Group and Ungroup commands in Part II), or use the Direct-selection tool to select only those parts of the rectangle that you want to move.

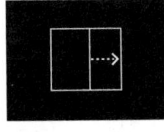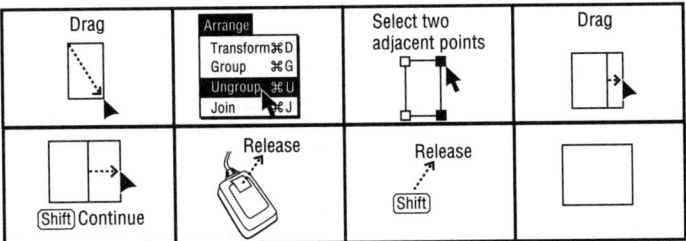

Ungroup to modify a rectangle, or use the Direct-selection tool

The Oval Tools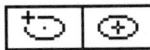

Overview You use the oval tools to create elliptical objects or circles. The oval tools produce an object composed of two grouped paths: an elliptical path, consisting of four curved segments joined by anchor points every 90°, and a single point in the center of the ellipse, which you can use to align the object with respect to other centered objects (text or graphics). There are two oval tools, the Oval tool and the Centered-oval tool. The Centered-oval tool draws ellipses from center to edge rather than from edge to edge.

Procedure With the Oval tool, you can draw ellipses visually on the screen or create an ellipse with dimensions specified numerically in the Oval dialog box.

Drawing an Oval on the Screen Choose the Oval tool by clicking the icon in the toolbox. The mouse pointer changes to a + in the active window. To create an ellipse, you define the opposite corners of the imaginary rectangle that contains the ellipse. Click the mouse button to define one corner of the bounding rectangle, then drag and release the mouse button at the diagonally opposite corner. To construct ellipses from center to edge (rather than from edge to edge), choose the Centered-oval tool by dragging to its pop-up icon in the toolbox and releasing the mouse button or press the Option key while the Oval tool is active. To constrain ellipses to perfect circles, press Shift while you drag the mouse (Shift-drag) in the desired direction. In both cases, the farther you drag from the starting point, the larger the object becomes. These techniques are shown in the following figure.

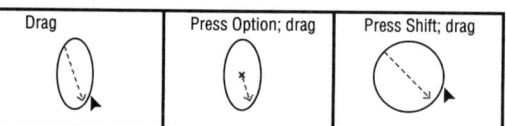

Three ways to use the oval tools: (1) drag diagonally to draw an ellipse from edge to edge; (2) hold down the Option key and drag diagonally to create an ellipse from center to edge; (3) hold down the Shift key and drag diagonally to create a perfect circle

Drawing an Ellipse with Numerically Specified Dimensions
Click on the Oval tool icon in the toolbox, then click once in the active window. The Oval dialog box appears, which you use to enter specific dimensions (width and height) in points. (You can change the unit of measure shown in the dialog box with the Preferences command; see Preferences in Part II). The oval width and height must be between 0 and 1296 points. As with the Rectangle tool, the point at which you clicked the tool on the screen defines either a corner of the imaginary bounding rectangle (if the Oval tool is selected) or the center of the ellipse (if the Centered-oval tool is selected).

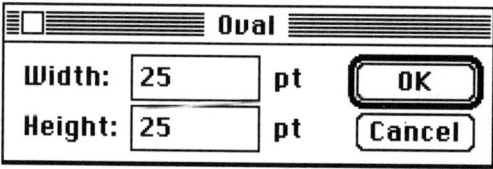

The Oval dialog box

Tip   An oval is a grouped object when it is first drawn. You can modify the grouped oval using the Scale, Rotate, Reflect, and Shear tools, but to move individual anchor points you must first ungroup the

| TOOLS | |

oval (see the Group and Ungroup commands in Part II) or use the Direct-selection tool to select only those parts of the oval that you want to move.

The Blend Tool

Overview Use the Blend tool to transform one object into another object in a series of steps. You create the starting object and the resulting object using Illustrator's tools. The intermediate objects are created automatically during the transformation process.

Procedure Create two objects. One object represents the beginning of the transformation series, and the second object represents the resulting object after the transformation series is completed. Select one or more anchor points on each object. These will serve as corresponding reference points during the transformation. Next, click the Blend tool in the toolbox. This changes the mouse pointer to a cross-hair pointer. Click the cross-hair pointer on one point of each of the two objects: these points will be the primary points of correspondence throughout the transformation. When you click a point on the second object, the Blend dialog box appears as shown in the following figure. You can enter a number from 1 to 1296 to determine how many intermediate objects will be created by the blending process.

The Blend dialog box

The first object you click after you select the Blend tool will fall on the bottom layer of the blended series of objects; the second object will fall on the top layer.

PART I

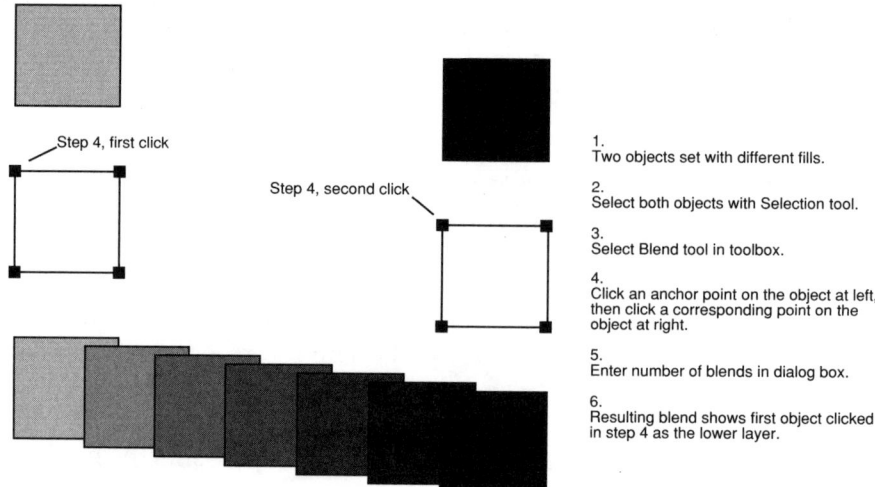

1. Two objects set with different fills.

2. Select both objects with Selection tool.

3. Select Blend tool in toolbox.

4. Click an anchor point on the object at left, then click a corresponding point on the object at right.

5. Enter number of blends in dialog box.

6. Resulting blend shows first object clicked in step 4 as the lower layer.

Sequence of layers when leftmost rectangle was clicked first and rightmost rectangle was clicked second

You can use the Blend tool for a variety of effects: to create a series of gradual changes of color or pattern, to create a series of gradual changes from one shape to another, or to create different views of the same shape using the Scale, Rotate, Reflect, or Shear tools.

Both the starting object and the resulting object must be either closed or open paths; you cannot blend a closed path with an open path. (See The Pen Tool for definitions of open and closed paths.) The following figures illustrate three examples of blending.

 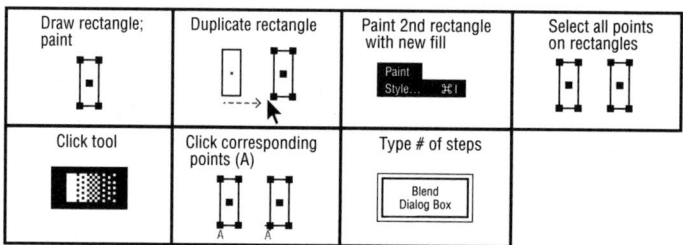

Blending to create gradual changes in color or shading

34

TOOLS

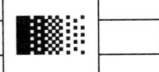

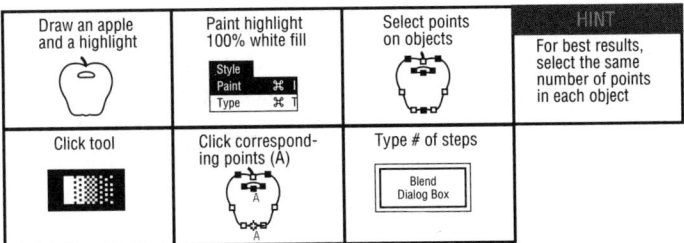

Blending to create a three-dimensional appearance

Example of shapes changed by using the Blend tool

Before using the Blend tool, select the points of the two objects in pairs; that is, hold down the Shift key, then click the Selection tool on a point on the first object, then click the Selection tool on the corresponding point on the second object. You can select more than one pair of points. Generally speaking, you select only one pair if the two objects and all blended results have the same shape. Select more than one pair of points if the two objects have very different shapes, or if you want the blended results to assume new shapes. Different sequences of pairs produce different results.

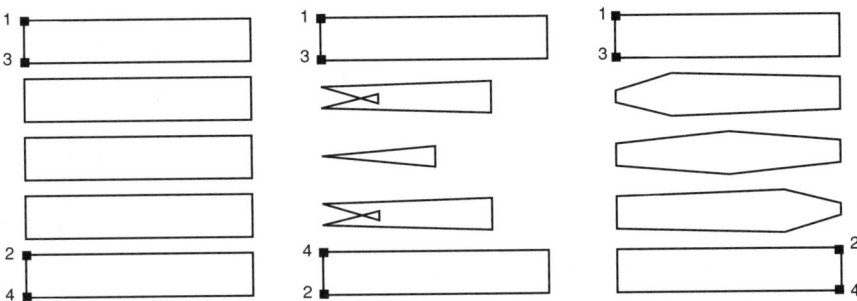

Selecting different pairs of anchor points produces different effects

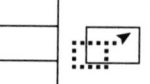

Tip When you are using a 300-dpi laser printer, 25 blends are usually adequate for creating a gradual transition from white to black. On a 600-dpi printer, 45 blends are usually adequate. On a 1270-dpi phototypesetter, you need approximately 200 blends; on a 2540-dpi phototypesetter, use at least 448 blends. Using too few blends may create "banding"; that is, the colors may not transition smoothly.

The Scale Tools

Overview You use the scale tools to change the size of selected objects. Scaling an object stretches or compresses it horizontally, vertically, or both, relative to some fixed point you choose. There are two scale tools: the Scale tool and the Scale-dialog tool. Use the Scale tool to scale objects visually on the screen. To scale objects numerically, use the Scale-dialog tool or press the Option key when you click to set the origin for the scaling transformation. The scale tools are one of four kinds of transformation tools; the others are the rotate and reflect tools and the Shear tool. The Option key works consistently with each: Option-clicking to set the origin of transformation always brings up a dialog box, allowing you to set transformation parameters numerically.

Procedure First select the object(s) to be scaled. Then choose the Scale tool by clicking the icon in the toolbox. The mouse pointer changes to a + in the active window. You can scale objects visually on the screen or by an amount specified in the Scale dialog box.

Scaling Objects Visually on the Screen Click to set a point of origin for the scaling transformation. The pointer changes to an arrowhead. Position the pointer away from the point of origin and drag away from the origin to enlarge the object or towards the origin to reduce the object. Shift-dragging the arrowhead constrains the direction of dragging to horizontal, vertical, or a 45° angle, resulting in horizontal, vertical, or proportional scaling respectively. Option-dragging the arrowhead leaves the original object unchanged and produces an enlarged or reduced scaled duplicate. Shift-Option-dragging produces a constrained duplicate.

| TOOLS | 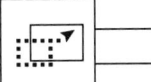 |

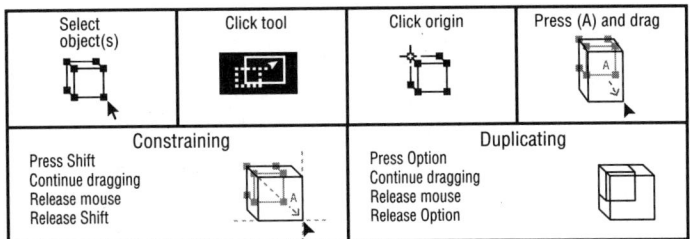

Scaling objects visually on the screen: (1) click the Selection tool anywhere on the path, then (2) select the Scale tool and click to establish an origin point, and (3) drag to scale the object relative to the origin. Use the Shift key to constrain scaling; use the Option key to produce a duplicate

Scaling Objects by a Specified Percentage   To scale by a specified amount, use the Scale-dialog tool or hold down the Option key when you click to set a point of origin for the scaling transformation. The Scale dialog box appears as shown in the following figure; it allows you to specify Scale parameters, which include Uniform scale, Non-uniform scale, and Scale pattern tiles (see the Style and Pattern commands under the Paint menu in Part II: Commands). The Scale dialog box also allows you to make a copy of the scaled object by clicking on Copy. If you select uniform scaling (that is, scaling equally in the x and y directions), you can also scale line weights.

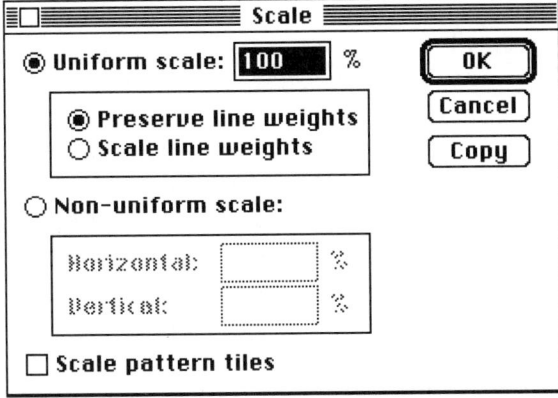

Option-click the origin point to enter scaling amounts through the Scale dialog box

37

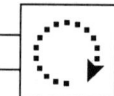

PART I

You can create a set of concentric shapes by selecting a path, then using the Scale tool. Click at the center of the shape to set the origin of the transformation, then Option-drag to produce a transformed copy. Press Command-D (to select Transform Again from the Arrange menu) to produce a series of objects scaled to the same proportion. Draw the outer edge first and produce progressively smaller duplicates layered on top of the first object (see Transform Again in Part II: Commands).

Tip *See also*: The Blend tool, which can be used to create a series of concentric shapes, and the Print command, which can be used to scale whole illustrations during printing.

The Rotate Tools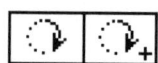

Overview Use the rotate tools to rotate selected objects relative to a fixed point. There are two rotate tools, the Rotate tool and the Rotate-dialog tool.

Procedure First select the object(s) to be rotated, then choose the Rotate tool by clicking the icon in the toolbox. The mouse pointer changes to a + in the active window. You can rotate objects visually on the screen or by an amount specified in the Rotate dialog box.

Rotating Visually on the Screen Click to set a point of origin for the rotation. This point functions like an anchor when you rotate the object. When you click the mouse, the pointer changes to an arrowhead. To make the object rotate, position the pointer away from the point of origin, hold down the mouse button, and drag in the direction of the desired rotation. Release the mouse button when you have rotated as much as you want.

TOOLS

 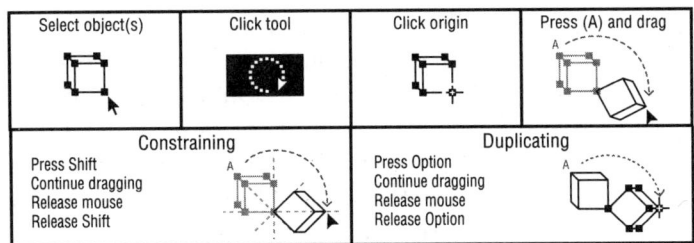

Rotating objects visually on the screen: (1) click the Selection tool anywhere on the path, then (2) select the Rotate tool and click to establish an origin point, and (3) drag to rotate the object relative to the origin. Use the Shift key to constrain rotation; use the Option key to produce a duplicate

Shift-dragging the arrowhead (pressing the Shift key as you drag the mouse) constrains the rotation to multiples of 45-degree angles. Option-dragging the arrowhead (pressing Option when you release the mouse) leaves the original object unchanged and produces a rotated duplicate.

Rotating by a Specified Amount Choose the Rotate-dialog tool by dragging to its pop-up icon in the toolbox and releasing the mouse button or hold down the Option key when you click to set a point of origin for the rotation transformation. The Rotate dialog box appears, as shown in the following figure, allowing you to specify the angle of rotation (in degrees) and whether or not to rotate pattern tiles if the object is filled with a custom pattern (see Style (Paint Menu) and Pattern in Part II: Commands). You can also make a copy of the rotated object by clicking the Copy button before you click the OK button. When parameters are set as you wish, click on OK. Angles are measured counterclockwise, with zero at three o'clock. You can rotate objects in a clockwise direction by entering a negative number.

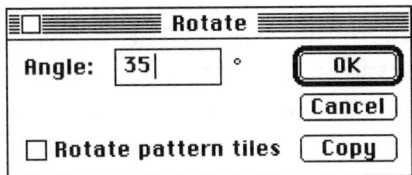

Option-click the origin point to enter the angle of rotation through the Rotate dialog box

PART I

Tip To create a radially symmetrical object, such as a flower, draw a single petal, then use the Rotate tool or the Rotate-dialog tool and the Transform Again command from the Arrange menu to produce rotated copies. This reproduces the original petal and is complete when the rotated copies form a flower. For best results, Option-click the origin point to get the Rotate dialog box and enter the number of degrees yielded by the following formula:

(number of degrees) = 360° / (number of symmetrical elements)

This procedure is shown in the following figure. See Radial Symmetry: Method 1 and Method 2 in Part III for other examples using the Rotate tool.

 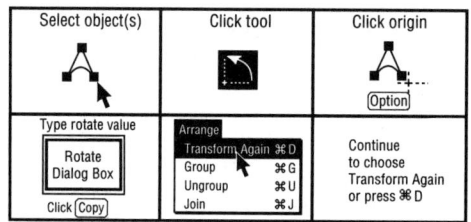

Radially symmetrical objects can be created with the Rotate tool or the Rotate-dialog tool and the Transform Again command

The Reflect Tools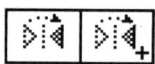

Overview You use the reflect tools to transform an object into a mirror image of itself. There are two reflect tools: the Reflect tool and the Reflect-dialog tool.

Procedure First select the object(s) to be transformed, then choose the Reflect tool by clicking the icon in the toolbox. The mouse pointer changes to a + in the active window. You can reflect objects across an axis that you set visually on the screen or at an angle specified in the Reflect dialog box.

TOOLS	

Reflecting a Mirror Image Visually on the Screen   Select the object, choose the Reflect tool, and click the + pointer at some point on the object to set a point on the axis of reflection. The pointer changes to an arrowhead. Position the pointer away from the point of origin and click to define a second point on the axis of reflection, then drag to pivot the object around the axis if needed.

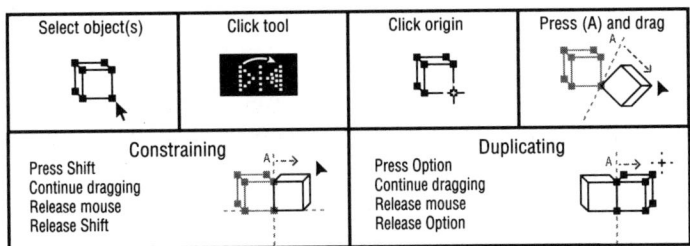

Reflecting objects visually on the screen (1) click the Selection tool anywhere on the path, then (2) select the Reflect tool and click to establish point on the axis of reflection; (3) click to establish a second point and thereby establish the axis of reflection; (4) drag to pivot the object around the axis. Use the shift key to constrain the reflection axis; use the Option key to produce a duplicate

Shift-dragging the arrowhead (pressing Shift and dragging the mouse) constrains the reflection to multiples of 45-degree angles. Option-clicking the arrowhead (pressing Option before releasing the mouse) leaves the original object unchanged and produces a reflected copy.

Reflecting by a Specified Amount   Choose the Reflect-dialog tool by dragging its pop-up icon in the toolbox and releasing the mouse button or by holding down the Option key when you click to set a point of origin for the reflection transformation. The Reflect dialog box appears, allowing you to specify which axis to reflect across: horizontal, vertical, or angled. You can make a copy of the object, reflected, by clicking on the Copy button prior to clicking on OK.

The axis for reflection is specified by angles measured counterclockwise, with zero at three o'clock. You can reflect over an axis in a clockwise direction from three o'clock by entering a negative number.

 PART I

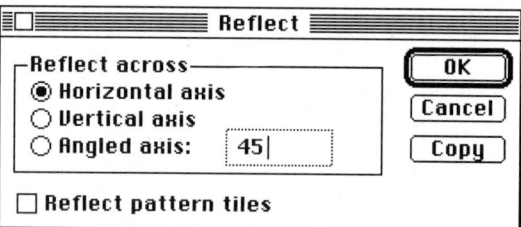

Option-click the origin point to enter the angle of reflection through the Reflect dialog box

Warning   The Reflect tool is one of the most difficult tools to control at first. The further you move away from the origin point to drag, the more incrementally, and therefore more slowly, the reflection will occur.

Tip   To avoid unwanted effects, always group the object, then make a copy by holding down the option key as you use the Reflect tool. If the copy is correct, delete the original. If the effect is not correct, you can delete the copy and try again.

The Shear Tools

Overview   You can use the shear tools to change the angle between the axes of selected objects. (Normally the *x* and *y* axes are set at 90-degree angles.) Shearing is easy to picture if you think of it as describing the action of the blades of scissors; see the following figure. (The shear tools are unrelated to the Scissors tool, however.) There are two shear tools: the Shear tool and the Shear-dialog tool.

In shearing, the change of the angle between the axes is similar to the movement of the blades on scissores

42

| TOOLS | |

Procedure   First select the object(s) to be sheared, then choose the Shear tool by clicking the icon in the toolbox. The mouse pointer changes to a + in the active window. You can shear objects visually on the screen or at an angle specified in the Shear dialog box.

Shearing Visually on the Screen Select the object to shear, select the Shear tool, and click on the object to set a point of origin for the shear axis. When you release the mouse, the pointer changes to an arrowhead. Position the pointer away from the point of origin and drag. The direction in which you drag defines the axis of shear: if you drag left or right you change the angle of the vertical axis; if you drag up or down you change the angle of the horizontal axis. The distance you drag defines the angle of shear.

Shift-dragging the arrowhead constrains the axis of shear to multiples of 45-degree angles. Option-dragging the arrowhead leaves the original object unchanged and produces a sheared copy.

In the following figure the top boxes demonstrate the result of shearing an object visually, the lower left illustration shows how Shift-dragging limits shearing to 45-degree increments, and the lower right illustration shows how to create a sheared duplicate copy, leaving the original in place, using Option-drag.

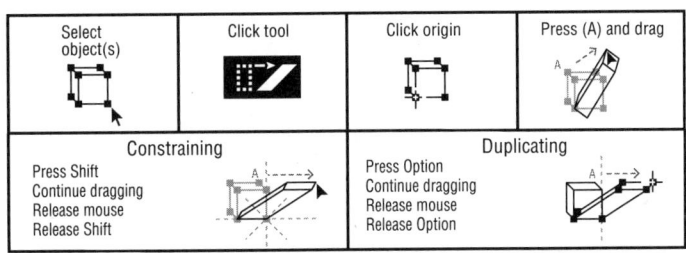

Shearing objects visually on the screen: (1) click the Selection tool anywhere on the path, then (2) select the Shear tool and click to establish an origin point, then (3) drag horizontally to change the angle of the y axis, or vertically to change the angle of the x axis. Use the Shift key to constrain shearing to 45-degree increments; use the Option key to create sheared copy

Shearing by a Specified Amount Select the object, then choose the Reflect-dialog tool by dragging to its pop-up icon in the toolbox

PART I

and releasing the mouse button, or hold down the Option key when you click to set a point of origin for the shearing transformation. The Shear dialog box appears, allowing you to specify the angle of shear, the axis to shear along, and whether or not to shear pattern tiles (see Style (Paint Menu) and also Patterns in the Commands section). You can also specify that a copy of the sheared object be made by clicking the Copy button before clicking OK. The figure below shows the Shear dialog box.

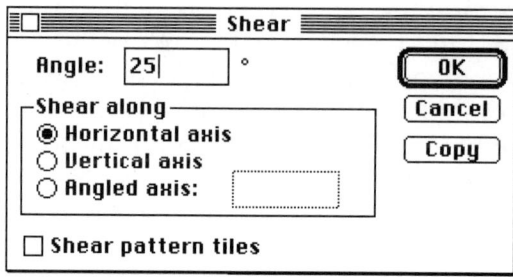

Option-click the origin point to enter the angle of shear through the Shear dialog box

The Scissors Tool

Overview   You use the Scissors tool to break a path into two or more separate objects. Splitting a closed path produces one open path. Splitting an open path produces two open paths. (See The Pen Tool for definitions of open and closed paths.)

Procedure   Choose the Scissors tool by clicking the icon in the toolbox. The mouse pointer changes to a + in the active window. Click on the path at the point where you want to split the path. You can split a path anywhere except at the endpoints of an open path. The Scissors tool splits the path, producing two new endpoints which are selected, as shown in the top part of the following figure.

TOOLS

 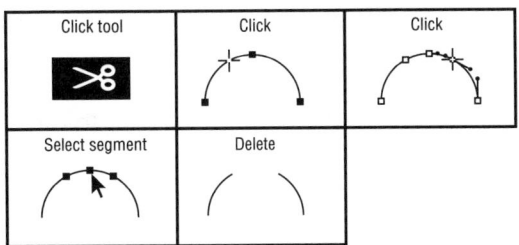

First click the Selection tool anywhere on a path, then select the Scissors tool and click on a line segment to cut the line (and create two endpoints)

Tip After splitting a path, you can use the Selection tool to separate the new endpoints of the two paths. Click the Selection tool in any open space in the drawing window to deselect all objects. Click on the location of the two new endpoints. This selects the frontmost of the two endpoints, which you can then drag to separate the ends of the path(s).

The Add-anchor-point Tool

Overview You use the Add-anchor-point tool to add a new anchor point to an existing path.

Procedure Choose the Add-anchor-point tool by dragging to its pop-up icon next to the Scissors tool in the toolbox and releasing the mouse button, or hold down the Option key when the Scissors tool is active. The mouse pointer changes to a + in the active window. Click on a path at the point where you want to add a new anchor point. The Add-anchor-point tool adds a new anchor point, which is selected, to the path at the point at which you clicked.

 This is different from the operation of the Scissors tool. The Scissors tool creates two new anchor points, one on top of the other, and splits the path. The Add-anchor-point tool adds only one new anchor point and does not split the path.

45

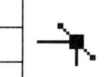

PART I

The Delete-anchor-point Tool

Overview You can use the Delete-anchor-point tool to delete an anchor point from an existing path.

Procedure First click anywhere on the path from which you wish to delete the anchor point, then choose the Delete-anchor-point tool by dragging to its pop-up icon next to the Scissors tool in the toolbox and releasing the mouse button. The mouse pointer changes to an + in the active window. Click on the anchor point you wish to delete. The anchor point is deleted and the remaining adjacent anchor points are joined by a new line segment.

Tip If you want to delete an anchor point and its adjoining line segments, for example to redraw a section of a path, do not use the Delete-anchor-point tool. Instead, use the Selection tool or the Direct-selection tool to select the anchor point, then press the Delete key. This removes the anchor point and the adjacent line segments, leaving the adjacent anchor points selected.

The Convert-direction-point Tool

Overview You use the Convert-direction-point tool to convert an anchor point from a smooth point to a corner point or vice versa.

Procedure First select the anchor point you wish to convert, then choose the Convert-direction-point tool by dragging to its pop-up icon next to the Scissors tool in the toolbox and releasing the mouse button; alternatively you can hold down the Control key when any selection tool is active. The mouse pointer changes to a + in the active window. To convert a smooth point to a corner point, simply click the point you wish to convert. To convert a corner point to a smooth point, place the pointer over the anchor point, then drag to create a direction point.

| TOOLS |

Tip The quickest way to access the Convert-direction-point tool is by using the Control-key shortcut when a selection tool is active. If you are using a tool other than a selection tool, first hold down the Command key to access the selection tool, then, with the Command key still pressed, hold down the Control key to access the Convert-direction-point tool. When you release the keys, your previous tool selection will still be in effect.

The Measure Tool

Overview You can use the Measure tool to measure the distance and angle relative to the x axis between any two locations on the page.

Procedure Select the Measure tool, then click on two points. The points do not have to be anchor points. The Measure dialog box, shown in the following figure, displays the distance and angle between the two points you have clicked.

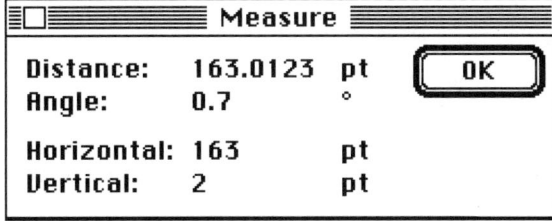

The Measure dialog box

Tips To ensure that the distance being measured is a straight horizontal or vertical line between two points, and not slightly angled, hold the Shift key before clicking the second measuring point. This provides for accurate width or height of an object without an accidental angled move of the mouse.

The Measure tool is one of the tools that remain active in Preview mode. The others are the zoom tools, the Page tool, and the Hand tool.

PART I

The Page Tool

Overview   You use the Page tool to control the tiling of an Illustrator file onto printed pages. The Illustrator drawing area is a square measuring 18 by 18 inches. When you print a file, Illustrator tiles, or subdivides, it into pages that match the paper size used in your printer. In other words, the Page tool lets you specify where the pages break.

Procedure   Choose the Page tool by clicking the icon in the toolbox. The mouse pointer changes to a + in the active window. When you hold down the mouse button a dotted rectangle appears, marking the area that can be printed on a single $8\frac{1}{2}$-by-11-inch page. The mouse is positioned at the lower left corner of the page. Use the mouse to drag the rectangle to define where you wish the pages to break, as shown in the following figure.

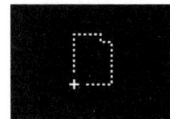 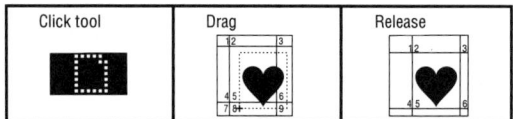

Drag the dotted rectangle to set page breaks

Tips   The Page tool is easiest to use in the Fit In Window view (see Fit In Window in Part II: Commands). Illustrator displays page numbers at the lower left corner of each page boundary on the screen.

The Page tool is one of the tools that remain active in Preview mode. The others are the zoom tools, the Measure tool, and the Hand tool.

The Graph Tools

Overview   You use the graph tools to create graphs from numeric data. There are six graph tools: the Grouped-column graph tool, the Stacked-column graph tool, the Line graph tool, the Pie graph tool, the Area graph tool, and the Scatter graph tool. They differ only in the kind of graph each creates. The default graph tool is the Grouped-column graph tool.

| TOOLS | |

Procedure   Choose the graph tool corresponding to the kind of graph you wish to create, either by clicking the icon in the toolbox or by dragging to the pop-up icon and releasing the mouse button. The mouse pointer changes to a + in the active window.

Creating a Graph Visually   Drag to define a rectangular area that has the dimensions you desire for the graph. Hold down the Option key to draw the rectangle from center to edge, rather than from corner to corner. (This is identical to the procedure for using the Rectangle Tools.) An empty graph of the shape and dimensions you defined appears, and the Graph Data window opens.

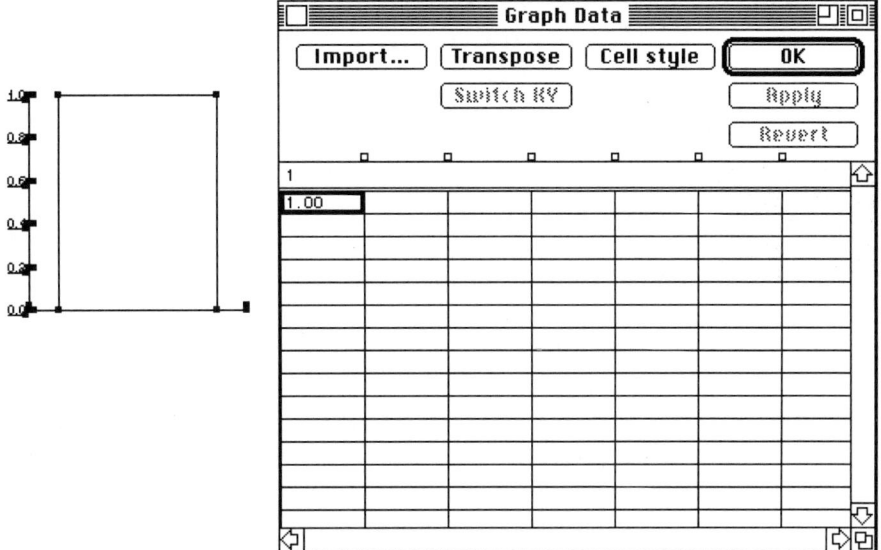

An empty graph with the Graph Data window

Creating a Graph with Numerically Specified Dimensions Click one of the graph tools in the drawing window at the upper left corner of the area in which you want to create the graph, or hold down the Option key and click the center of the area in which you want to create the graph. The Graph dialog box appears, containing fields in which you enter the desired measurements for the graph's width and height. The measurements are specified using the measurement system specified in the Preferences dialog box. (See Preferences in Part II: Commands). When you click OK to close the Graph dialog box, a graph with the dimensions you defined appears, and the Graph Data window opens.

Entering Data The Graph Data window, unlike most dialog boxes, is a true window with a close box and title bar. You can move it around the screen and leave it open as you continue to work on your graph. The lower part of the Graph Data window contains an area similar to a spreadsheet where you enter or import the data you wish to graph.

The data entry area contains *cells* arranged in rows and columns. You enter each label or value in a separate cell. Labels are words or numbers used to describe a row or column—normally, you enter these in the first row or column. To use numbers as labels, you must put them in quotes, otherwise Illustrator will interpret them as values.

You can type data directly into the data entry window, you can paste it from another Graph Data window or from a spreadsheet application, or you can import it from a disk file by clicking the Import button in the Graph Data window. Imported data must be in Tab-delimited text-only format. You can specify the number of decimal places used in each cell and the width of the columns in the Graph Data window by clicking the Cell style button and entering the appropriate values in the dialog box that appears. Note that the column width value has no effect on the width of the columns in the graph itself, only in the Graph Data window.

Once you have entered the data, you can click OK to close the window and apply the data to your graph. If you click Apply, the data is applied to the graph and the Graph Data window remains open. (See Graph Data in Part II: Commands.)

Editing Graphs Graphs are created as grouped objects. If you ungroup a graph, you will no longer be able to update it with new data. Instead of ungrouping to modify individual elements in a graph, select them using the Direct-selection tool. (See Graph Style, Graph Data, Use Column Design, and Use Marker Design in Part II: Commands.)

TOOLS

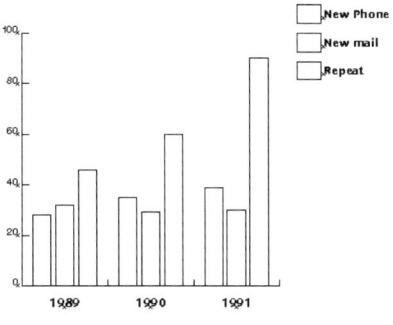
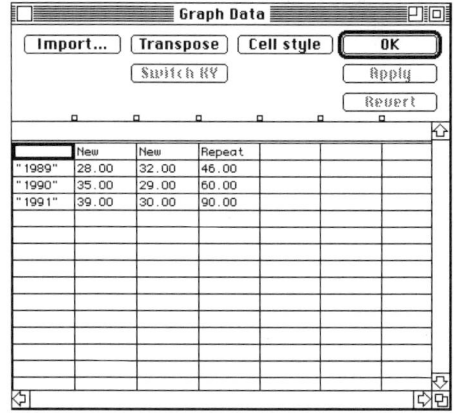

A grouped-column graph and the associated Graph Data window

Tips Each graph type is suited to illustrate particular types of data. For a given set of data, one graph type is usually more appropriate than the others. Grouped column graphs are best for comparing one item to another or for comparing several items over time. Stacked column graphs are best for comparing a group of variables over time or for showing the relationship of parts to the whole. Line graphs show the trend of one or more items over time. The y axis represents values while the x axis represents time. Pie graphs show percentages of a total. Area graphs, like line graphs, show fluctuations over time, but also emphasize totals. Scatter graphs are unique in that each axis measures a value. Data points are plotted as paired sets of coordinates along the x and y axes. If you are unsure which kind of graph best illustrates your data, experiment with the different graph types.

Each graph that you create has its own Graph Data window but you can quickly create a series of graphs based on the same data by pasting the data from one Graph Data window to another. First, select all the data in the Graph Data window associated with your existing graph and choose Copy. Then choose a different graph tool and create a new graph. Finally, select the upper left cell in the new Graph Data window, choose Paste, and click Apply in the Graph Data window. The new graph is updated to reflect the data you paste. You can repeat this procedure to create as many different kinds of graph as you wish. You can also use the Graph Style command to change a graph, as described in Part II.

Part II: Commands

Introduction to Commands

Choosing a Command

In Part II, you will find a description of how to choose commands and make dialog box entries. Part II first gives an overview of the menu titles, followed by an alphabetical listing of all the commands in Adobe Illustrator. Adobe Illustrator, like all applications that run on a Macintosh, displays a menu bar at the top of the screen, listing the names of the menus of available commands. Commands are displayed below each menu title. To select a command, position the mouse pointer over the menu title, hold down the mouse button, drag down the menu until the desired item is highlighted, then release the mouse button.

Some commands can be selected using keyboard shortcuts instead of the mouse. The shortcuts are listed on the menus next to the commands that have shortcuts. A ⌘ symbol represents the Command key, an up arrow symbol (⇧) indicates the Shift key, and a ⌥ symbol represents the Option key.

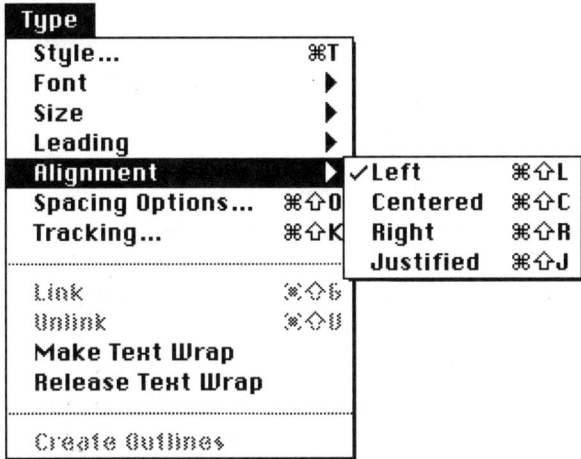

Type menu (with Alignment command submenu displayed) shows keyboard shortcuts for nine commands

Some of the command names displayed on the menus are followed by an ellipsis (...). A dialog box will be displayed whenever you use one of these commands, offering the user the opportunity to select from various options, enter information required by the command, or cancel the command. Note that commands that are not followed by an ellipsis have an immediate result that cannot be canceled unless the Undo command is available.

The Font, Size, Leading, and Alignment commands displayed on the Type menu are followed by a right-pointing triangle. When you hold the mouse button down on one of these commands, a hierarchical submenu appears beside the menu command. To select a command from the submenu, drag across to the submenu, then drag down the submenu until the desired item is highlighted and release the mouse button.

Dialog Box Entries

Commands followed by an ellipsis on the menu list result in the display of a dialog box on the screen. A dialog box is a window displayed on the screen, and most dialog boxes can be moved around on the screen by dragging the title bar, just as any other window can be moved. A dialog box may contain any or all of the following:

- Warnings or messages.
- Boxes for typing text or numbers.
- Scrolling lists of fonts or file names.
- Pop-out menus that let you choose from a list of alternatives.
- Check boxes that let you choose one or more options from a list.
- Radio buttons, small circular buttons that are used to select one option from a list of several mutually exclusive choices.
- Larger rectangular buttons that close the dialog box, offering options such as OK and Cancel, or that open additional dialog boxes.

Choose a command that is followed by an ellipsis on the menu list. When the dialog box appears, make selections or text entries as appropriate, then click on one of the rectangular buttons to close the dialog box. Some of the general procedures that apply to all dialog boxes are described here. Specific dialog box entries are described in detail under the specific commands that display dialog boxes, in the alphabetical listing that follows this section.

Warnings or Messages If the dialog box displays only the text of a warning or message, you have the option of clicking OK (to indicate that you have read the message) or Cancel (to indicate that you have read the warning and you wish to cancel the current command).

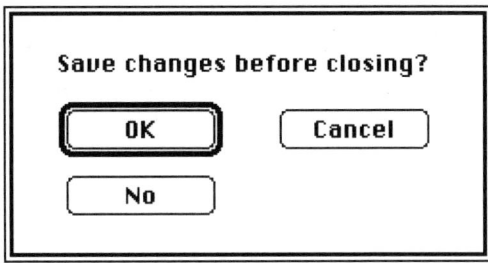

Dialog box with a warning or message

Text Boxes If there are any text boxes for typing text or numbers in the dialog box, the cursor will normally be positioned in the first such box when the dialog box opens. You can move the cursor from one text box to another by clicking on the text label that describes the entry, using the mouse to position the pointer inside the text box and clicking to position the cursor, or by pressing the Tab key. You can select text inside a text box by clicking on the text label that describes the entry to select all of the text, using the mouse to drag the cursor over the text, double-clicking to select a word, or tabbing into the text box to select all of the text.

Scrolling Lists Lists of fonts or file names are often displayed in a small window within the dialog box, with scroll bars on the right for moving up or down the list. You select from a scrolling list by using the scroll bar (if necessary) to find the name you wish to select, then clicking on the name to highlight it. In some cases, you can jump ahead in a long alphabetical list by typing the first letter of the name you wish to choose.

Introduction   PART II

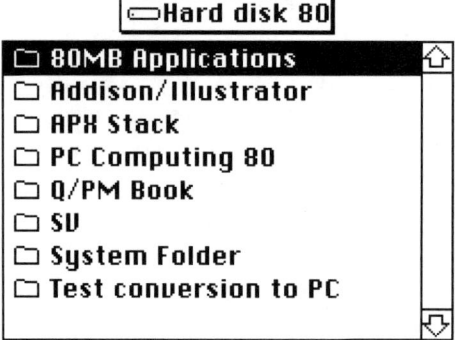

Scrolling list of files from the New, Open, or Place dialog box

Pop-out Menus   Some text boxes are framed by a drop-shadow, indicating that you can choose from a list of alternatives by holding the mouse button as you click on the text box to display the pop-out menu, then drag the mouse to make your selection.

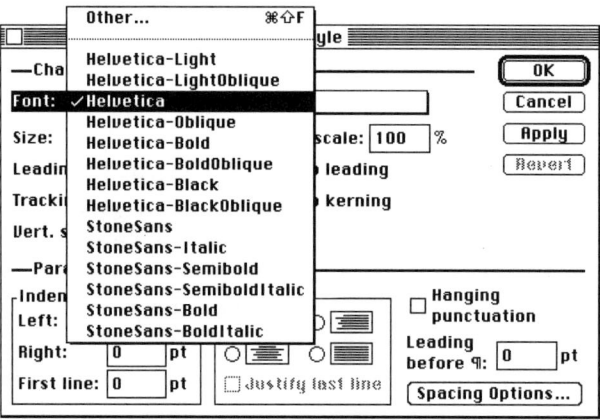

Font pop-out menu in Type Style dialog box

Check Boxes   You can choose one or more options from a list that displays check boxes. Options that are selected show an x inside the box. An empty check box indicates that the option is not selected. Check boxes are toggles: clicking on an empty box selects the option, clicking on a box with an x deselects the option. You can also select or deselect these options by clicking on the text label that describes the entry.

Printer Effects:
☒ Font Substitution?
☒ Text Smoothing?
☒ Graphics Smoothing?
☒ Faster Bitmap Printing?

Check boxes from the Page Setup dialog box

Radio Buttons Small circular buttons are used to select one option from a list of several mutually exclusive choices. The current selection is indicated by a dark circle inside the button. You can change the selection by clicking on another button in the list or by clicking anywhere on the text label that describes that option.

Paper: ⦿ US Letter ○ A4 Letter
○ US Legal ○ B5 Letter

Radio buttons from the Print dialog box

Rectangular Buttons Larger rectangular buttons are used to close the dialog box, offering options such as OK and Cancel, or to open additional dialog boxes. Often, one rectangular button is framed in a double-rule border, indicating that pressing the Return key will have the same effect as clicking on that button.

[Eject]
[Drive]

[Open]
[Cancel]

Control buttons from the Open dialog box

Introduction   PART II

Menus

Apple Menu

As in other Macintosh applications, the Apple menu contains all of the Macintosh desk accessories that you have installed in your system folder, along with a command specific to Illustrator called About Adobe Illustrator®. The accompanying figure shows the pull-down Apple menu.

The alphabetical listing later in Part II contains descriptions of the About Adobe Illustrator® command and other Apple menu desk accessories that are especially useful with Illustrator, including the Control Panel (for setting up color display on a Mac II) and the Chooser. If you use MultiFinder, the Macintosh system software that allows you to switch between several active applications, the titles of the active applications also appear under the Apple menu. You can switch to an application by choosing it from the Apple menu. (See About Adobe Illustrator®, Chooser, Control Panel, and Application Titles Running under MultiFinder.)

You can add desk accessories to the Apple menu using the Font/DA Mover application program that is supplied by Apple on the Macintosh system disk, or the desk accessory's installation program. You can also add fonts to the System using the Font/DA Mover application. Refer to your Macintosh user manual for more information on how to do this.

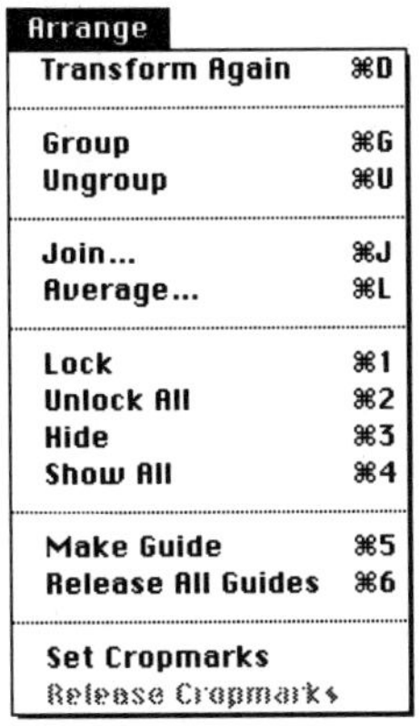

Arrange Menu

Arrange	
Transform Again	⌘D
Group	⌘G
Ungroup	⌘U
Join...	⌘J
Average...	⌘L
Lock	⌘1
Unlock All	⌘2
Hide	⌘3
Show All	⌘4
Make Guide	⌘5
Release All Guides	⌘6
Set Cropmarks	
Release Cropmarks	

The Arrange menu, shown in the accompanying figure, has commands that affect the arrangement of an object or objects. Commands in the Arrange menu allow you to repeat a transformation, group and ungroup objects, join endpoints, average anchor points, lock, unlock, hide and show objects, convert paths to guides and vice versa, and include crop marks in your illustration.

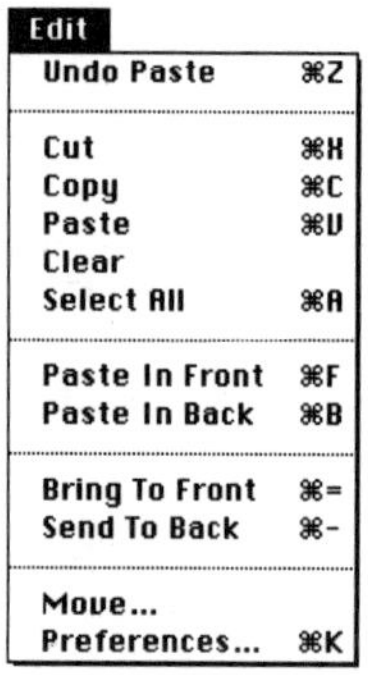

| Introduction | PART II |

```
┌─────────────────────┐
│ Edit                │
├─────────────────────┤
│ Undo Paste      ⌘Z  │
├─────────────────────┤
│ Cut             ⌘X  │
│ Copy            ⌘C  │
│ Paste           ⌘V  │
│ Clear               │
│ Select All      ⌘A  │
├─────────────────────┤
│ Paste In Front  ⌘F  │
│ Paste In Back   ⌘B  │
├─────────────────────┤
│ Bring To Front  ⌘=  │
│ Send To Back    ⌘-  │
├─────────────────────┤
│ Move...             │
│ Preferences...  ⌘K  │
└─────────────────────┘
```

Edit Menu

The Edit menu, shown in the accompanying figure, contains commands for general editing of your Illustrator work, including undoing or redoing your last operation, managing the Macintosh Clipboard (a storage area in the computer's memory from which the contents can be retrieved using the Paste command) by cutting or copying to it and pasting from it, selecting all the objects in a file, deleting selected objects, pasting objects in front or in back of other objects, moving objects, and assigning preferences.

Although different applications have different menu commands, and hence different keyboard shortcuts, the Command-key equivalents for Undo, Cut, Copy, and Paste are constant throughout all Macintosh applications. Knowledge and use of these keyboard shortcuts are basic to Macintosh literacy—if you learn only four Command-key menu equivalents, they should be Undo, Cut, Copy, and Paste. These Command-key menu equivalents use the four keys located closest to the left-hand Command key: Command-Z is Undo, Command-X is Cut, Command-C is Copy, and Command-V is Paste.

File Menu

The File menu, shown in the accompanying figure, has commands that apply to entire Illustrator files. When you start an Illustrator session, the File menu is likely to be the first menu you access. You use File menu commands to open new or existing Illustrator files, to import text or graphics into your illustration, to close and save Illustrator files you are working on, to prepare files for printing and to print Illustrator artwork, and to quit an Illustrator session.

Graph Menu

The Graph menu, shown in the accompanying figure, contains commands for working with graphs. You use the Graph menu to choose a graph style; to enter or modify graph data; to define a design for use in graphs; and to use a design for graph columns or data markers.

Introduction

PART II

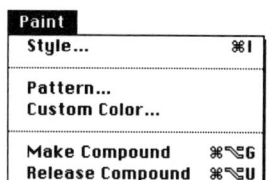

Paint Menu

The Paint menu, shown in the accompanying figure, affects the way the elements of your illustration are painted. This menu has commands to set paint attributes when filling or stroking paths or type. The Paint menu also provides commands for defining custom colors and patterns, and for creating compound objects.

Type Menu

The Type menu, shown in the accompanying figure, contains all the Illustrator text formatting commands. You use Type menu commands to set the font, font size, leading, and alignment; to adjust word and letter spacing; to set tracking and kerning; to link and unlink text objects; to make text wrap around objects; and to convert type into editable paths.

View Menu

The View menu, shown in the accompanying figure, affects the way your artwork is displayed on the screen. This menu contains commands to create multiple views of your file and to control what is displayed in the active window. You can preview the image as it will appear when printed, preview only the currently selected object or objects, view the artwork and template together, view only the artwork, or view only the template. The View menu also contains commands to fit an entire file into a window or to display the file in its actual size and commands that allow you to show or hide the rulers and unpainted objects. (See also The Zoom Tool in Part I for methods of changing magnifications of artwork.)

Window Menu

Because you can open more than one Illustrator file at a time and open more than one window on a single file, the Window menu, shown in the accompanying figure, provides commands that open new windows or change the active window from one open window to another. The window that is active will have a check mark next to its name in the Window menu.

If your drawing is complex, you can open several windows containing different views of the same document. The Window menu provides an easy way to switch from one view to another. (See New Window.)

Commands

About Adobe Illustrator®...

Overview   Choosing About Adobe Illustrator® from the Apple menu displays a dialog box that shows the version of Illustrator you're using, the authors of Illustrator, a copyright notice, and the amount of free memory available (in bytes and as a percentage of total memory). As your artwork becomes larger, the free memory will decrease.

The About Adobe Illustrator® dialog box

Procedure   Choose About Adobe Illustrator® from the Apple menu after starting Adobe Illustrator by double-clicking the program icon on the desktop.

Warning   Illustrator will open on a machine with 1 Mb of memory, but you will not be able to produce complex artwork because of memory limitations. Illustrator prefers 2 Mb of RAM to function efficiently.

Actual Size

Overview The Actual Size command displays the file in its actual size in the active window. The file is centered in the active window and scaled so that one screen pixel represents one point (approximately $\frac{1}{72}$ of an inch). The keyboard shortcut is Command-H.

Procedure To view the illustration in actual size, choose Actual Size from the View menu, press Command-H, or Option-double-click on the Hand tool icon (if visible) in the toolbox. Actual size is shown in the first view in the accompanying figure.

 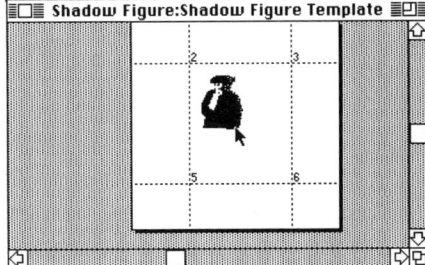

Artwork in Actual Size and Fit In Window views

Tip Use the Zoom tool to make artwork larger than actual size when working on fine details in your drawing.

Alignment

Overview The Alignment command offers four alignment options for selected text: Left, Centered, Right, and Justified. Alignment options apply to text on a paragraph-by-paragraph basis. The keyboard shortcuts are Command-Shift-L for Left, Command-Shift-C for Centered, Command-Shift-R for Right, and Command-Shift-J for Justified.

| This is an example of text aligned left | This is an example of text aligned centered | This is an example of text aligned right | This is an example of justified text |

Text aligned left, centered, right, and justified

Procedure First select the text you want to align. To select a complete text object, use the Selection tool. To select a single paragraph, click the Text tool to make an insertion point anywhere in the paragraph or drag to make a selection anywhere in the paragraph. To select several paragraphs, drag the Text tool to select them. To apply the alignment option to the selected text, choose Alignment from the Type menu, then drag across to the submenu and choose the desired option, or use one of the keyboard shortcuts: Command-Shift-L for Left, Command-Shift-C for Centered, Command-Shift-R for Right, and Command-Shift-J for Justified.

Tip To apply alignment and other paragraph-level formatting options such as indents, it is not necessary to select the entire paragraph or paragraphs to which you wish to apply the format. Selecting any part of the paragraph, or placing an insertion point in the case of a single paragraph, is all that is required.

Application Titles Running under MultiFinder

Overview MultiFinder allows you to use multiple software applications simultaneously. When you are running MultiFinder, a list of all open applications appears below the list of desk accessories under the Apple menu. Choosing an application from the Apple menu makes it the active application, displays that application's menu bar, and makes its most recently active window visible.

Procedure Choose an application that has already been started under MultiFinder and that is displayed under the Apple menu.

You can run Adobe Illustrator with other applications. For example, you can concurrently run MacPaint to create or edit bitmaps (see Glossary) as templates for Illustrator artwork; you can use

MacDraw to create or edit PICT files (see *PICT format* in the Glossary) as templates for Illustrator artwork, and you can run a page composition application (such as PageMaker or QuarkXPress) to place Illustrator artwork with text and graphics from other sources on a final page layout. Under MultiFinder, you need not quit one application to start another.

Warnings   For maximum efficiency, you should have at least 1 Mb of memory for each application open under MultiFinder. Otherwise you may not be able to open more than one application at a time.

You cannot open the same document with more than one application at a time. For example, if you try to place an Illustrator document in a page composition application without first closing the document in Illustrator, you will get a message informing you that the file is busy.

Artwork & Template

Overview   The Artwork & Template command displays both the Illustrator artwork and your template in the active window. You can use a template to trace over objects, and you can use bitmapped or PICT files as templates. The template appears on screen when you use this command, but it will not print. The keyboard shortcut is Command-E.

Procedure   Choose Artwork & Template from the View menu or press Command-E. The template is displayed if you are linked to this Illustrator file. (See also Open and New for methods of loading or changing templates.)

Artwork Only

Overview   The Artwork Only command displays only the Illustrator artwork in the active window. The keyboard shortcut is Command-W.

| Average | PART II |

An illustration shown in Artwork Only view

Procedure   Choose Artwork Only from the View menu or press Command-W when you wish to see your artwork without the template.

Average...

Overview   The Average command moves two or more selected anchor points to the average position of the selected points along the axis you specify: the horizontal axis, vertical axis, or both axes. You can average points and text objects. The keyboard shortcut is Command-L.

Procedure   Select two or more anchor points or objects with the Selection tool, then choose Average from the Arrange menu or press Command-L. If you don't properly select two or more anchor points, you will get an alert message asking you to "please select two or more points to average." (See The Selection Tools for methods of selecting points and objects.) The Average dialog box, shown in the next figure, appears, offering the options of averaging along the horizontal axis, the vertical axis, or both (the default setting). If you average points along both axes, they move to the same location—that is, halfway between their original positions. If you average along one axis only, each point moves to the halfway point along that axis.

COMMANDS — Average

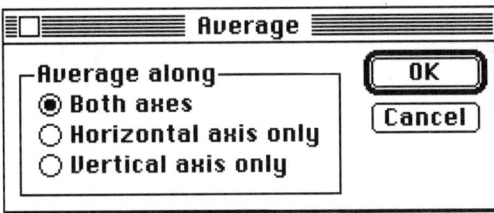

The Average dialog box

The following figure shows the effect of averaging two anchor points along both the horizontal and vertical axes.

Two anchor points, before and after using the Average command

Tips   Averaging two or more anchor points enables you to maintain a curved path while bringing two points together before using the Join command (see Join). Otherwise the Join command creates a straight line between the two points. Remember that averaging does not join anchor points. If you wish to join the points, you must use the Join command after averaging. First, select the endpoints you wish to average with a selection tool. Choose Average from the Arrange menu, or press Command-L. Then choose Join from the Arrange menu, or press Command-J. The following figure illustrates how this is done.

Connect two endpoints

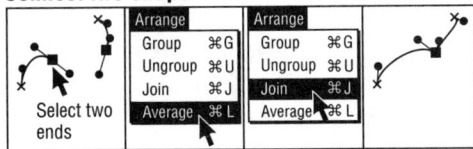

Connecting endpoints

Bring To Front — PART II

The Average command is also useful for aligning blocks of text along a horizontal or vertical axis, as shown in the following figure.

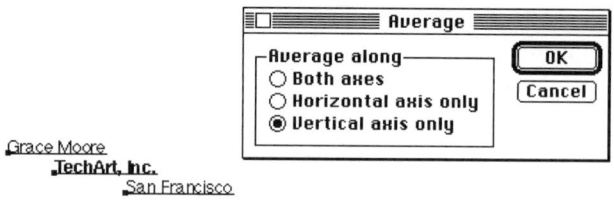

Text blocks before and after averaging along a vertical axis

Bring To Front

Overview The Bring To Front command moves selected objects to the top layer in the artwork. The keyboard shortcut is Command-= (equal sign).

Procedure Select the object or objects you wish to move to the front layer and choose Bring To Front from the Edit menu or press Command-=. If a selection itself is composed of more than one layer, the layers retain their relative positions.

If you want to resequence the layering of an object, start by selecting the layer you want to become the bottom layer. Choose Bring To Front from the Edit menu, then select each layer in the order you want it to appear, from the bottom up, and use Bring To Front until the desired layer is on top.

Warning Illustrator is normally very reliable in maintaining the order of layers when rearranging objects or groups of objects. However, if you have a complex illustration and use these commands frequently on groups of objects, you might find that you have inadvertently sequenced some objects improperly. Always check your artwork carefully by using the preview commands or by printing the illustration after rearranging layers.

| COMMANDS | Clear |

Chooser

Overview   Since the AppleTalk network lets you connect up to thirty devices on a single network, you can have more than one printer available to any Macintosh. The AppleShare network also allows more than one file server to be accessed. The Chooser lets you select which printer you will use to print your artwork or which file server you wish to access.

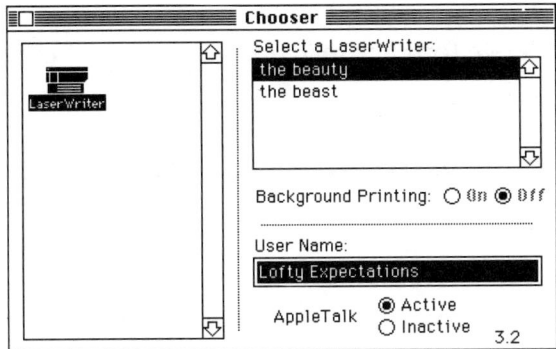

The Chooser dialog box

Procedure   Select Chooser from the Apple menu. Click on a printer driver icon or the AppleShare icon. A list of all available devices will appear. Then click on the appropriate device name. Click the close box when you are done.

Warning   The dialog box displays only those devices for which the power switch is on. If the full list of printers on your network is not displayed, it may be due to a loose cable connection between your machine and the printer.

Clear

Overview   The Clear command deletes all selected objects from the artwork. This command is the equivalent of pressing the Delete (or Backspace) key. Cleared objects are not stored in the Clipboard.

| Control Panel | PART II |

Procedure Select the object or objects to be cleared using any of the techniques described under The Selection Tools in Part I. Then choose Clear from the Edit menu or press the Delete (or Backspace) key.

Warning Since objects deleted with the Clear command or the Delete (or Backspace) key are not copied to the Clipboard (a storage area in the computer's memory from which the contents can be retrieved using the Paste command), you must use the Undo command immediately if you wish to reverse the command and retrieve the objects (see Undo/Redo).

Tip Using the Delete (or Backspace) key is the most efficient method of clearing objects.

Close

Overview The Close command closes the active Illustrator window. You can also close the active window by clicking the window's close box.

Procedure Choose Close from the File menu or click the close box in the upper left corner of the active window. If you have more than one window open on the same file, this action simply closes the active window. If you have only one window open on the file, this action closes the window and closes the file.

    If you made any changes to the Illustrator file since you last saved it, Illustrator displays a dialog box asking whether you want to save your changes whenever you use the Close command. If you click OK and the current window is named Untitled art, Illustrator displays the Save As dialog box so you can assign the file a name (see Save As).

Control Panel

Overview Choosing Control Panel from the Apple menu displays the Control Panel, which is standard with Macintosh System software version 4.1 or later. Icons in the main portion of the General Control Panel provide access to different system functions. Using the Control Panel, you can change some of the configuration settings of your Macintosh, including the desktop pattern, the blinking rate of the text insertion point, the blinking rate of pull-down menus, the system time, the system date, the date format (a 12-hour or 24-hour clock), the speaker volume, the amount of RAM cache in use, and whether the RAM cache is on or off.

The icons in the left column represent different parts of your Macintosh System configuration. Three of these are of particular interest to Illustrator users: the General Control Panel, the Monitors Control Panel (for setting color display on the Macintosh II), and the ATM icon (for activating Adobe Type Manager).

Procedure   Choose Control Panel from the Apple menu. The Control Panel appears, as shown in the following figure. When you have made the desired adjustments, click the close box to close the window.

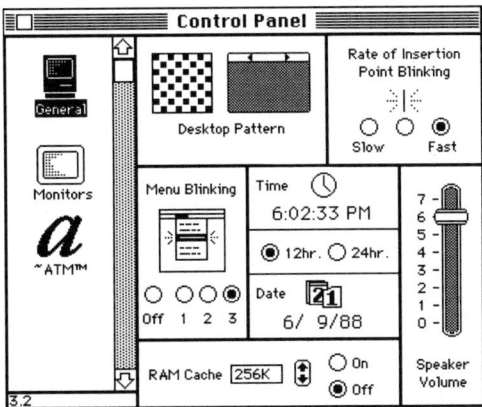

The General Control Panel

Click the General icon in the Control Panel to gain access to the RAM cache controls. If you are running Illustrator on a Macintosh equipped with 1Mb of RAM, you should turn the RAM cache off. If you have larger amounts of RAM available and are running under MultiFinder, you may wish to use the RAM cache; although Illustrator will not benefit from it, other applications may.

| Control Panel | PART II |

If you are using a Macintosh II equipped with a color monitor and you wish to use Illustrator's color preview features, you can set the monitor to either 16 or 256 colors, depending on how much memory you have installed on your video card. To do this, click the Monitors icon in the left column of the Control Panel and make the appropriate selections by scrolling through the Colors scroll box and then clicking on the desired number of colors, as shown in the following figure.

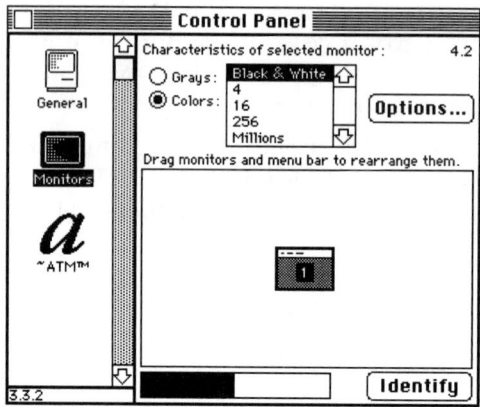

The Monitors Control Panel

You need to install and activate ATM (Adobe Type Manager version 2.0), which comes with Adobe Illustrator 3, in order to use the Create Outlines command. To install ATM you simply copy the ATM program icons into the System Folder as described in the ATM installation instructions that come with the Illustrator package. To activate ATM (or turn it off, to save memory and let the system run a little faster) you click the ATM icon in the scrolling window on the left of the Control Panel window and make selections in the dialog box.

Tip   If you do not need to display color, you can have quicker screen response and save memory by selecting two colors and changing to black-and-white mode.

Copy

Overview The Copy command copies the selected objects to the Clipboard (a "storage area" in the computer's memory from which the contents can be retrieved using the Paste command), leaving the objects in place as artwork and replacing whatever was previously in the Clipboard. The keyboard shortcut is Command-C.

Procedure Select the object or objects to be copied, then choose Copy from the Edit menu, or press Command-C.

You can copy an Illustrator file into a PICT format which can then be pasted into Microsoft Word, PowerPoint, and some other (but not all) Macintosh applications that cannot handle PostScript formats. To do this, hold down the Option key and choose Copy from the Edit menu or press Option-Command-C. This action copies not only the PostScript information in the Illustrator file, but the screen bitmap as well, making it possible to paste the artwork into the other applications that support bitmapped or PICT formats. (See *bitmap* in the Glossary.)

Warning The Copy command in conjunction with the Option key will work as described only if adequate memory is available.

Tips The Copy command is most useful when you want to store selected objects in the Clipboard for repeated use (over a short period), when you need to paste the copies between layers (not onto the top layer), and when you need to copy selected elements from one document to another.

Otherwise, copy objects by holding the Option key as you move an object with a selection tool or when you use any of the transformation tools (the Scale, Rotate, Reflect, and Shear tools). This is a more efficient method of copying objects when you want to align the copies or when you want to combine the copy procedure with a movement or a transformation before using the Transform Again command (from the Arrange menu) to repeat the procedures. (See The Selection Tools, The Scale Tool, The Rotate Tool, The Reflect Tool, and The Shear Tool in Part I for methods of copying selections without storing them in the Clipboard.)

| Create Outlines | PART II |

The Copy command does not delete objects from the artwork; to delete objects use the Cut or Clear command or the Delete (or Backspace) key (see Cut and Clear).

As does the Cut command, the Copy command replaces the contents of the Clipboard.

Create Outlines

Overview The Create Outlines command converts an entire selected text object into editable path outlines which you can then manipulate by moving anchor points and direction points, just as you would any other path. The Create Outlines command retains all the formatting and paint attributes of the selected type. However, once a text object has been converted to outlines, it becomes a set of graphic objects rather than text, so it can no longer be edited or formatted using type tools or commands.

Procedure Select the text object you wish to convert using the Selection tool, then choose Create Outlines from the Type menu. Each character in the text object is then converted into a compound path. (See Make Compound.)

Warnings Adobe Type Manager software 2.0, which is included in the Adobe Illustrator package, must be installed in your system to use the Create Outlines command. If you do not have ATM version 2.0 or later, the Create Outlines command in the Type menu is grayed, indicating that it is not available.

In addition, the Type 1 outline fonts (printer fonts) must be available in your System Folder for the text you wish to convert to outlines, including the printer fonts that might also be installed in your printer—such as the PostScript fonts that come built in to the Apple LaserWriter series.

Tip You can only convert an entire text object to outlines. If you want to convert a single character, such as a drop cap, create a separate text object containing only that character.

Custom Color...

Overview   The Custom Color command displays the Custom Color dialog box and lists the custom colors you have created and stored, or the Pantone colors included on the Illustrator disks (if you have opened that document). It also lets you create new custom colors or change existing custom colors.

Procedure   Choose Custom Color from the Paint menu. You do not have to select any objects to customize a color. The Custom Color dialog box appears, as shown in the following figure, allowing you either to create your own custom colors by naming a new color and then entering the percentages of cyan, magenta, yellow, and black, or to select an existing color and adjust the percentage mix of colors.

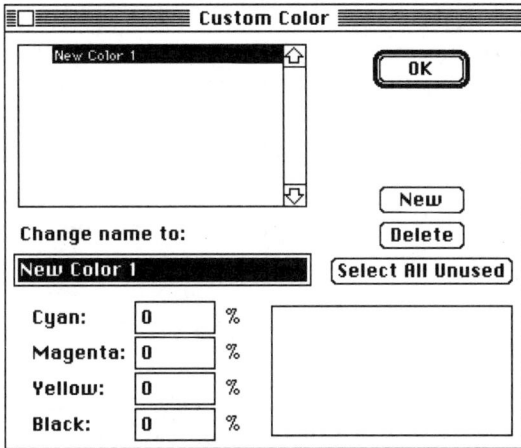

The Custom Color dialog box

To create a new custom color, click New and type a name in the text box below Change name to: (or you can use Illustrator's default naming convention, New Color 1). Type percentage values for Cyan, Magenta, Yellow, and Black. You can see the resulting color mix in the lower right corner of the dialog box if you have a color monitor, but the best way to ensure a precise color match is to use

Custom Color — PART II

the percentages from a process color swatchbook (available in art supply stores). By clicking New, you can continue to add more custom colors.

To edit an existing color, click on the name of the color in the list at the top left of the dialog box, then change the percentage values and/or the name of the color. Changes made to an existing color will be reflected in the artwork wherever that color has been used.

To create a new color based on an existing color, first click on the existing color name and make a note of the percentage values. Then click New, type a name for the new color, and enter percentage values that vary from those you noted for the existing color.

Click Delete to remove the selected name (and color) from the list. Objects that were filled with that color will revert to the default fill pattern (100 percent black).

Click Select All Unused to select the names of all colors that are not currently used in the artwork. You can delete these colors to save memory and storage space.

The names of newly created colors appear in the Paint Style dialog box when you select its Custom Color button.

You can print custom colors for spot color (see Appendix B).

You can use one of the Pantone color files as a basis for creating custom colors by opening the file along with your artwork. However, you should avoid modifying the Pantone color file itself: Always close the Pantone color file without saving any changes.

Warning   If you select an existing color and change the name and percentage values, the effect is to delete the previous color from the list and replace it with the new entry. Any objects that used the original color take on the new color. If you don't want this to happen, follow the procedure outlined above for creating a new color based on an existing color.

Tips   If you want to create your own library of custom colors, save them all in a file created for this purpose. You can make any color available for use in a new file by simply opening the file that contains the desired color.

If you want a set of custom colors to be available automatically whenever you use Illustrator, create an Illustrator file containing all the custom colors you want, then name it Adobe Illustrator Startup, and place it in the folder containing the Illustrator application. (If you keep the application on the desktop, place the Adobe Illustrator Startup file in your startup disk's disk window.) You can also include patterns, fonts, and graph designs in the Adobe Illustrator Startup document. These elements will automatically be available whenever you use Illustrator.

Cut

Overview The Cut command deletes the selected object or objects from the Illustrator artwork and stores it in the Clipboard (a storage area in the computer's memory), replacing whatever was previously in the Clipboard. The cut object can be pasted back into the current file or another Illustrator file using the Paste command. The keyboard shortcut is Command-X.

Procedure Select the object or objects you wish to cut, then choose Cut from the Edit menu or press Command-X. To view the contents of the Clipboard, select Show Clipboard from the Window menu. (See also Show/Hide Clipboard in this section and Window Menu earlier in Part II.)

Tips Use the Cut command whenever you wish to remove selected objects from the artwork and temporarily store them in the Clipboard. If you want to remove objects from the artwork but do not want to lose the contents of the Clipboard, select one of these alternatives to the Cut command:

- Press the Delete (or Backspace) key, or choose the Clear command from the Edit menu. This action removes the selected objects from the artwork but it does not store them in the Clipboard. (See also Clear.)
- Before using the Cut command, move the contents of the Clipboard back to the artwork by choosing Paste (see Paste).
- Drag the selected objects off to the side of the illustration for storage; they will remain part of the artwork until you delete them.

Define Graph Design | PART II

Define Graph Design...

Overview   The Define Graph Design command displays the Define Graph Design dialog box, which allows you to create a new graph design or delete, paste, or change the name of an existing graph design. The scrolling list displays all existing graph designs. The keyboard shortcut is Command-Shift-Option-G.

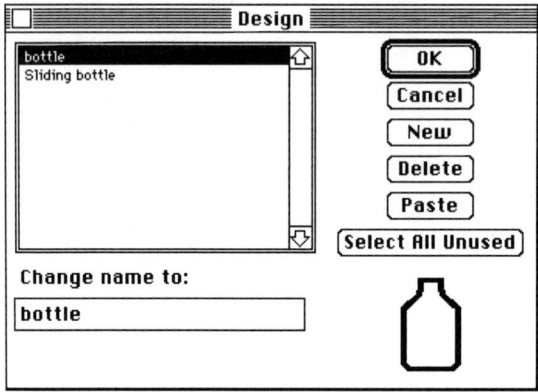

The Define Graph Design dialog box

Procedure   Draw a graph design shape or design and color it. Using the Rectangle tool, draw a rectangle around your art defining the "tiling element." Select the rectangle and use the Send To Back command to position it behind the design. Select both the design and the rectangle. Then choose Define Graph Design from the Graph menu. The Define Graph Design dialog box appears, as shown in the preceding figure. Click New to display the selected graph design in the bottom right area of the dialog box and name the graph design by entering the name in the text box. When you close this dialog box, the graph design will then be available in the Use Column Design and Use Marker Design dialog boxes.

COMMANDS   **Define Graph Design**

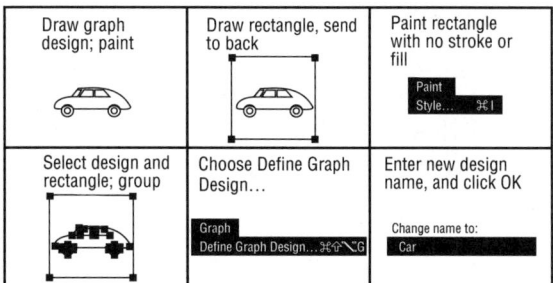

Procedure for creating a graph design

    To create a sliding graph design, you must add a horizontal guide to indicate where the design will be stretched or compressed.
    Follow the procedure for creating a graph design until you have the design in front of the rectangle, then use the Pen tool to draw a horizontal line at the point where you want the design to be stretched or compressed. Select all parts of the design including the horizontal line, then choose Group from the Arrange menu or press Command-G.
    Use the Direct-selection tool to select only the horizontal line, then choose Make Guide from the Arrange menu or press Command-5.
    Use the Selection tool (not the Direct-selection tool) to select the entire design, then choose Define Graph Design and follow the procedure for naming a new graph design.

    Click New to store the graph design under a new name.
    Click Delete to remove the selected name (and graph design) from the list. Graphs that used that graph design will revert to the default graph design.
    Click Select All Unused to select the names of all graph designs that are not currently used in the artwork. You can delete these graph designs to save memory and storage space.
    Click Paste to paste a copy of the graph design on the page if you want to edit the design, then close the dialog box, edit the design artwork, select it, and choose Define Graph Design again to store the changed design under the same name or a new name.

| Fit In Window | PART II |

If you save the changed design using the same name, Illustrator offers you two options: Redefine and Recreate changes the graph design definition and recreates graphs using the design so that they use the changed design, while Redefine Only updates the graph design for future use, but leaves existing graphs that use the design unchanged.

Click OK to close the dialog box and record the changes, or click Cancel to close the dialog box without recording any changes.

Tips If you frequently use custom graph designs, save them in a file created for this purpose. Opening the file will make your previously created graph designs available in other open Illustrator files.

If you want a set of graph designs to be available automatically whenever you use Illustrator, create an Illustrator file containing all the graph designs you want, then name it Adobe Illustrator Startup, and place it in the folder containing the Illustrator application. (If you keep the application on the desktop, place the Adobe Illustrator Startup file in your startup disk's disk window.) You can also include patterns, colors, and fonts in the Adobe Illustrator Startup document. These elements will automatically be available whenever you use Illustrator.

Fit In Window

Overview The Fit In Window command displays the entire 18-by-18-inch working area, centered, in the active window. The keyboard shortcut is Command-M.

Procedure Choose Fit In Window from the View menu, or press Command-M, or double-click on the Hand tool icon in the toolbox, to fit the entire illustration into the active window. The effect of this command is shown in the accompanying figure.

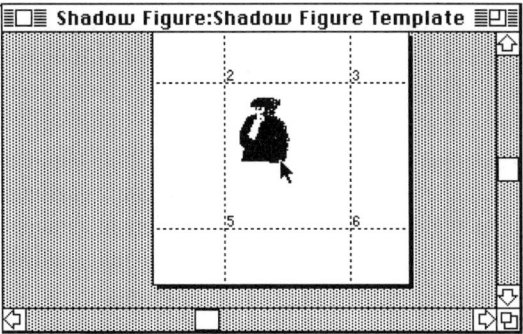

Artwork in Fit In Window view

Tips Use this command to preview your artwork periodically to find stray objects and to ensure that the artwork falls squarely within the page boundaries (indicated on the screen by dotted lines).

To go to Fit In Window, you can double-click on the Hand tool icon in the toolbox. Note that this does not select the Hand tool, but leaves the currently selected tool in effect.

Font

Overview The Font command gives access to the Font submenu, from which you can choose a font. In its default state, the Font submenu contains only two commands, Helvetica (the default font) and Other. Choosing Other from the menu or using the keyboard shortcut, Command-Shift-F, opens the Font dialog box, allowing you to choose a different font. Fonts that you have used in the current session are added to the font menu. Unlike most Macintosh applications, Illustrator lists only PostScript fonts, and it lists them by their PostScript names (for example, Helvetica-Bold rather than BHelvetica Bold). System fonts like Chicago, Geneva, and Monaco, for which no PostScript font exists, do not appear in either the Font menu or the Font dialog box.

Procedure Choose this command to change the font for selected text or to choose a font for a new text object. If the font you wish to use appears on the submenu, you can choose it directly. If you want to use a font that is installed in your system, but does not appear on the submenu, choose Other, or press Command-Shift-F. The Font dialog box appears, listing all the currently installed PostScript fonts, with the font family name in the list on the left and the different weights and styles for that family in the list on the right.

Choose the font family from the list on the left and the individual font from the list on the right, then click OK to confirm your selection and close the Font dialog box. The font you chose appears on the Font submenu until you quit the Illustrator application.

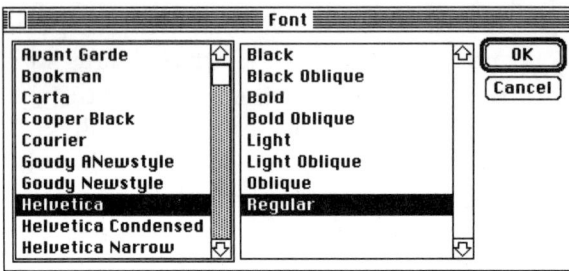

The Font dialog box

Tips

Use the Command-Shift-F shortcut when the font is the only type attribute you want to change. If you want to change several type attributes, use the Style command instead. (See Style (Type Menu).)

You can customize your Font menu by creating an Illustrator file containing text that uses the fonts you want to appear on the menu. You can make any font available on the submenu by simply opening the file that contains the desired font.

If you want a set of fonts to be available on the submenu automatically whenever you use Illustrator, create an Illustrator file containing all the fonts you want, then name it Adobe Illustrator Startup and place it in the folder containing the Illustrator application. (If you keep the application on the desktop, place the Adobe Illustrator Startup file in your startup disk's disk window.) You can also include patterns, colors, and graph designs in the Adobe Illustrator Startup document. These elements will automatically be available whenever you use Illustrator.

| COMMANDS | Graph Data |

Graph Data...

Overview The Graph Data command opens the Graph Data window, where you enter or import the data you wish to graph. (This is the same window that appears when you create a graph using the Graph tool.) This command is dimmed unless a graph is selected. Use the Graph Data command to open the Graph Data window for an existing graph. You can then modify the data and update the graph to reflect the changes you have made. The keyboard shortcut is Command-Shift-Option-D.

Procedure Use the Selection tool to select the graph for which you want to change the data, then choose Graph Data from the Graph menu, or press Command-Shift-Option-D. The Graph Data window for that graph opens.

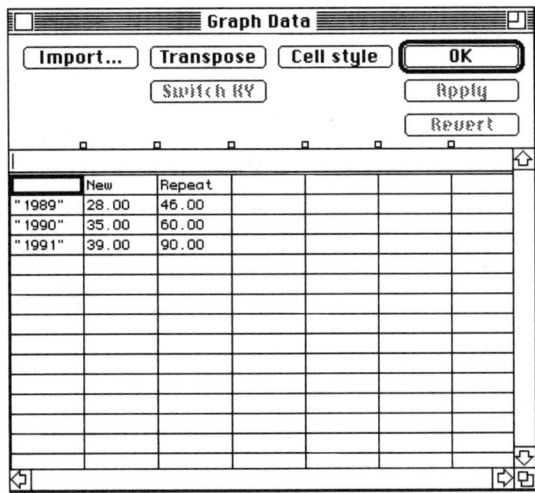

The Graph Data window

Entering Data The lower part of the window is a data entry area similar to a spreadsheet. The data entry area contains *cells* arranged in rows and columns. You enter each label or value in a separate cell. *Labels* are words or numbers used to describe a row or column—normally, you enter these in the first row and column. To use

87

numbers as labels you must put them in quotes, otherwise Illustrator will interpret them as values. If you want a label to have multiple lines, use the vertical line character (|) to indicate line breaks. You can move from cell to cell using the mouse, the Tab and Return keys, or the Arrow keys. Tab moves the current selection one cell to the right, and Return moves it one cell down.

You enter *data series* in the worksheet columns and *categories* in the rows. Labels entered at the top of columns label a data series, and are known as *legends*. Different data series are depicted in graphs by using a different fill for each—the legends appear as a key to the different fills. Categories appear as labels on the *x* axis in column, line, and area graphs. Pie graphs have only one category. Scatter graphs are unique in that they plot data points as paired sets of coordinates along the *x* and *y* axes, with both axes measuring values. Scatter graphs also lack categories.

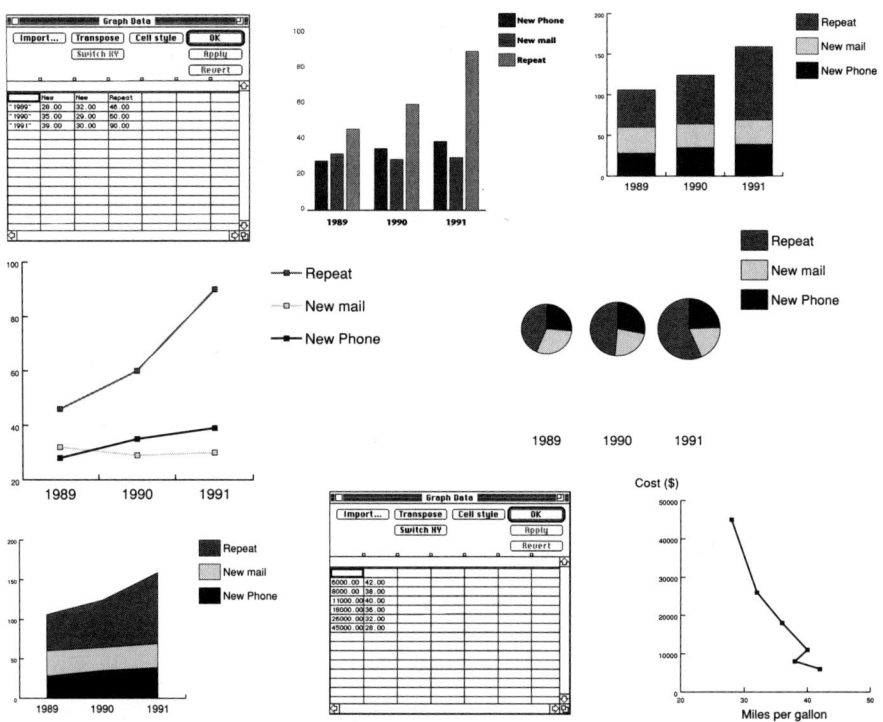

Examples of data and the resulting graphs, one for each graph type

You can type data directly into the data entry window, you can paste it from another Graph Data window or from a spreadsheet application, or you can import it from a disk file by clicking the Import button in the Graph Data window. Imported data must be in Tab-delimited text-only format.

The upper part of the Graph Data window contains seven control buttons: Import, Transpose, Cell Style, Switch XY, OK, Apply, and Revert. A description of each follows.

Import... Clicking this button presents an Open dialog box, containing a list of all files on the current disk or in the current folder. Click the name of the file you want to import, then click Open or double-click the file name. The data is imported and entered into the worksheet in the Graph Data window. Note that, although the file list shows all files, the only files that can be successfully imported into the Graph Data window are those in Tab-delimited text-only format. (This is the format used by most databases and spreadsheets when you choose Save As Text. In the case of spreadsheets, each column is separated by a tab and each row is separated by a carriage return.)

Transpose If you accidentally enter graph data backwards (in rows instead of columns or vice versa) you can use the Transpose button to convert your columns to rows and rows to columns.

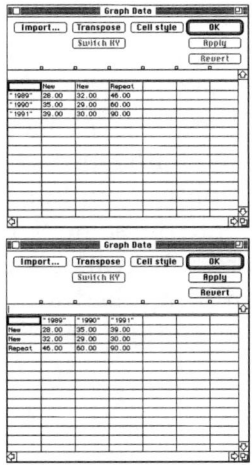
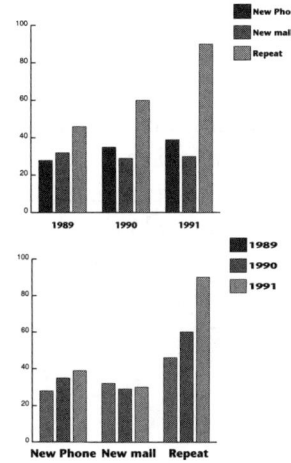

Grouped column graph and data before and after transposing

Cell Style You can specify the number of decimal places (from 0 to 10) used in each cell and the width of the columns (from 3 to 20) in the Graph Data window by clicking the Cell Style button and entering the appropriate values in the dialog box that appears. Note that the column width value has no effect on the width of columns in the graph itself, only in the Graph Data window.

Switch XY This option is available only for scatter graphs. It transposes the x and y axes.

OK Clicking this button closes the window and applies the data to your graph.

Apply Clicking this button applies the data to the graph so you can see the changes on the screen but leaves the Graph Data window open. (You might need to move the Graph Data window in order to see the changed graph.)

Revert Clicking this button returns your data to the state it was in when you last applied it to your graph. If you change your data without applying it to the graph, close the Graph Data window by clicking its close box; a message appears asking if you want to apply the changes to the graph. (See also The Graph Tools in Part I.)

Graph Style...

Overview The Graph Style command opens the Graph Style dialog box. Use this command to change an existing graph from one type to another or to customize the options associated with a particular graph type. All graph types except the area graph have options. Grouped column and stacked column graphs share the same options, as do line and scatter graphs. Some options are only available when the entire graph is selected, while others can be applied to parts of graphs. The keyboard shortcut is Command-Shift-Option-S.

| COMMANDS | Graph Style |

Procedure   Select a graph using the Selection tool, then choose Graph Style from the Graph menu, or press Command-Shift-Option-S. The Graph Style dialog box appears, containing four sets of options.

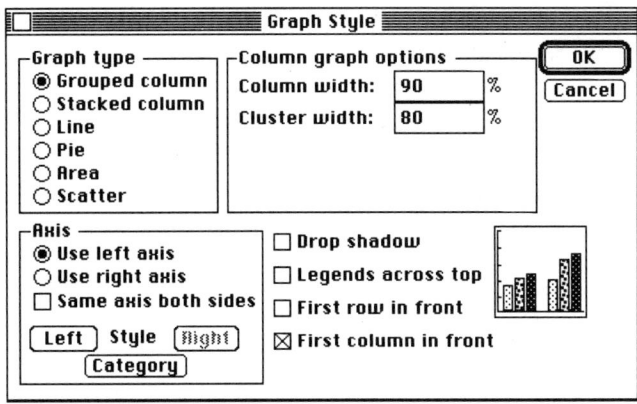

The Graph Style dialog box

Graph Type   The Graph type area at the upper left of the dialog box has six radio buttons, allowing you to choose among different types of graphs. The choices are: grouped column, stacked column, line, pie, area, or scatter.

A detail of the Graph Style dialog box—detail: Graph type

Axis   The Axis options at the lower left of the dialog box control the axis attributes of your graph. You can specify whether to display the *y* axis on the left side, on the right side, or on both sides of the graph. The default is Use Left Axis. The Same Axis Both Sides option is dimmed unless the entire graph is selected. If you select the Same Axis Both Sides option, you can select either Use Left Axis or Use Right Axis. However, if you have manually set axis attributes for an axis, you should select that axis if you want those attributes to be used. Pie graphs have no axis, so these options are dimmed when a pie chart is selected.

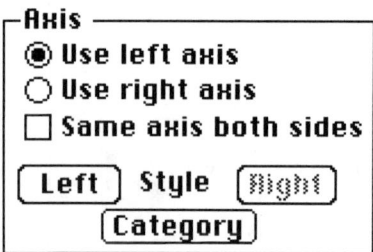

A detail of the Graph Style dialog box showing the Axis options

The Left, Right, and Category buttons open the Graph Axis Style dialog box, where you can specify tick mark options for each axis. (Tick marks are lines placed perpendicular to the axes to mark the units of measurement or the divisions between categories.) You must select the entire graph to use these options.

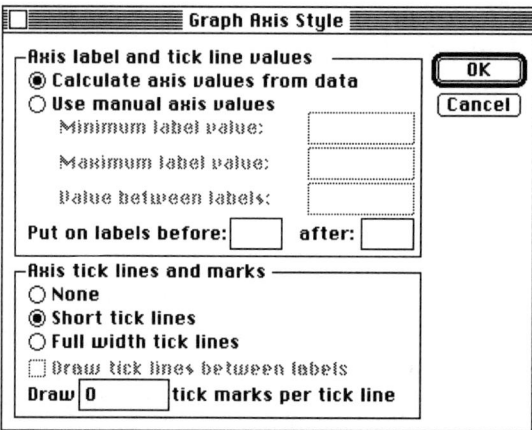

The Graph Axis Style dialog box

The Axis label and tick line values options apply only to axes that show values. In all types except for pie and scatter graphs this is the y, or vertical, axis. In a scatter graph, both axes measure values, and the Category button is relabeled to read Bottom.

Calculate Axis Values from Data   The default option automatically assigns tick marks and value labels to the axis.

Use Manual Axis Values   Lets you specify a minimum and maximum label value and the value between labels. If you do not want any labels to appear on the axis, enter zero in the Value Between Labels field.

Put On Labels Before/After   Lets you add information to value labels. For example, you may want to add a dollar sign before dollar values or percentage or degree signs after values that reflect these measurements.

The Axis tick lines and marks options apply to all axes. You can specify no tick marks, short tick marks, or full width tick marks that stretch the full width of the graph. Tick lines are placed at value labels. You can also specify a number of intermediate tick marks, which are then spaced evenly between the tick lines, according to the number of tick marks per tick line you specify. The Draw tick lines between labels option applies only to the category, or x, axis. It is dimmed when a value axis is selected.

A third set of four options is at the lower right of the dialog box. The Drop Shadow option places a drop shadow behind the graph elements. This option is more effective with column and pie charts than with line graphs. The Legends Across Top option places the legends in a horizontal row across the top of the graph, rather than as a vertical list at the right. This option is only available when the entire graph is selected. The two remaining options in the set, First Column in Front and First Row in Front, apply mainly to grouped column graphs when the columns overlap one another. First Column in Front, the default option, places the first column of data in the worksheet as the frontmost object in the graph. (For area graphs, you must select this option, otherwise some data may not be displayed.) The First Row in Front option places the first row of data in the worksheet frontmost in the graph.

The remaining set of options varies according to the type of graph. There are no additional options for area graphs. The options for the other graph types are described here.

Grouped-Column and Stacked-Column Graphs For grouped-column and stacked-column graphs, the options are Column width and Cluster width. Both are expressed as percentages. A cluster is a group of columns corresponding to a row in the worksheet. The default values are 90 percent for column width and 80 percent for cluster width. This leaves space between both the columns and the clusters. Setting the values to 100 percent makes both the columns and the cluster fit flush against each other. Values above 100 percent make the columns overlap. For stacked-column graphs, set the cluster width to 100 percent and use only the column width option to adjust the width of the columns. The entire graph must be selected to use these options.

Line and Scatter Graphs The options for line and scatter graphs are Mark data points, Connect data points, Fill lines, and Edge-to-edge lines. Mark data points places square markers at each data point. Connect data points draws lines that connect the data points and makes the Fill lines option available. This option creates a line of a width that you specify and fills it with the appropriate fill for the data series. Edge-to-edge lines extends the lines beyond the first and last data points to the full width of the graph. This option is not available for scatter graphs.

Pie Graphs The pie graph options are Standard Legends, Legends in Wedges, and No Legends. The Standard Legends option places the worksheet column labels outside the graph. The Legends in Wedges option places the label for each worksheet column in the corresponding wedge of the pie. The No Legends option omits the labels entirely.

Group

Overview — The Group command combines selected objects into a group. Objects that are grouped can be selected with a single click of the Selection tool, making this command especially useful in maintaining control of multiple layers and selections in a complex drawing. The keyboard shortcut is Command-G.

Procedure — Select an ungrouped path, or any group of objects, using any of the techniques described in The Selection Tools in Part I, and choose Group from the Arrange Menu or press Command-G. If you select some but not all of the anchor points in a path, this command adds the entire path to the group.

A group itself can be composed of subgroups. Select a set of elements and group them, then select additional elements, including the grouped set, and group again. You need to invoke the Ungroup command twice to ungroup both sets in this instance (see Ungroup).

You can modify grouped paths using any of the transformation tools (Scale, Rotate, Reflect, and Shear) or the Style commands from the Paint or Type menus. To modify grouped paths by moving individual line segments, anchor points, or direction lines, you must use the Direct-selection tool. Rectangles and ovals drawn with the Rectangle or Oval tool are automatically grouped when you draw them.

Tips — Clicking on objects with the Selection tool tells you whether objects are grouped or ungrouped. If all anchor points are selected (that is, they all display as black rather than white squares), the elements are grouped. When you click on an ungrouped object, only the line or anchor points touched by the Selection tool are selected.

You can transform and move grouped objects as a whole, but grouped objects retain their individual paint and type attributes as set or determined via the Style command in the Paint and Type menus, respectively (see Style commands). If you choose the Style command from the Paint menu and a group of objects with different paint attributes is selected, the Paint Style dialog box (invoked by the Style command under the Paint menu) will display only those selections that are common to all elements in the group. If you make no entries in the Paint Style dialog box, all elements of the group retain their different attributes. If you change the paint or type attributes for a group, all the objects in the group will be changed to the new attributes. (See Tip under Select All for grouping objects that share the same attributes. See also the Style commands under the Paint and Type menus.)

Hide

Overview The Hide command hides all selected objects from view in both Artwork and Preview modes and in the printed artwork. The keyboard shortcut is Command-3.

Procedure Select an object or objects with a selection tool and choose Hide from the Arrange menu or press Command-3. Hidden objects do not display in Preview mode, nor do they appear on printed versions. You can redisplay all hidden objects by choosing the Show All command (Command-4) (see Show All).

Holding down the Option key while choosing Hide from the Arrange menu hides all unselected objects.

Warning You lose the Hide attribute when you quit or save the document.

Tips This command is extremely useful for complex drawings. You can hide parts of the illustration, making the artwork less complex and reducing the time it takes Illustrator to refresh the screen in Preview mode. You can also hide parts of drawings as you complete them, leaving only incomplete objects visible on the screen. (See also Lock. See other Hide commands listed with the Show/Hide prefix.)

Hide Clipboard, Rulers, Toolbox, or Unpainted Objects (see Show/Hide)

Import Text...

Overview The Import Text command imports text from disk files in Microsoft Word 4.0, MacWrite 2.0, WriteNow 2.0, RTF (Rich Text Format), and plain text formats. This command appears on the menu only when a text insertion point is active—otherwise the command is Place Art.

Procedure Choose one of the Text tools and position the text insertion point on the page, then choose Import Text from the File menu. Illustrator displays the Import Text dialog box, which lists all text files in a supported format on the selected disk, as shown in the following figure.

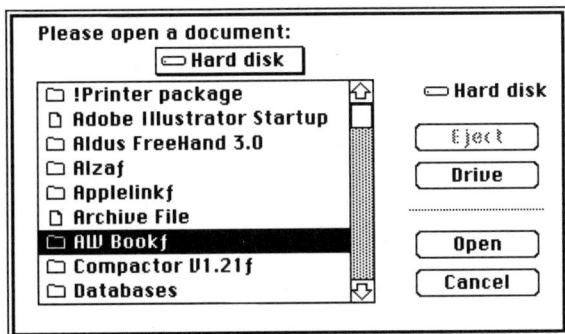

The Import Text dialog box

To select a file, scroll through the file list to locate the desired file name, click on the name, and then click the Open button, or double-click on the file name. The Drive button and Eject button operate as described under the Open command. The text from the file you select appears at the insertion point. If you import the text as point text, each paragraph will appear on a single line. If you import the text into a rectangular or irregular text area, it will word-wrap to fit the text area. If you import text at an insertion point created with the Path-type tool, only the first paragraph of the text will appear.

Imported text retains most of the formatting applied in the original document. If you import text from any application except Microsoft Word and the text contains fonts that are not installed in your system, a message appears informing you that the text will print inaccurately. If you import text from a Microsoft Word document containing fonts that are not installed in your system, those fonts are changed to Helvetica. You can change the font to one that is installed in your system by using the Font or Style commands from the Type menu.

Join...

Overview The Join command connects two endpoints with a straight line segment or, if the two points you wish to join are on top of one another, replaces them with one point. In the latter case, the Join dialog box, shown in the following figure, allows you to choose a smooth point or a corner point. The keyboard shortcut is Command-J.

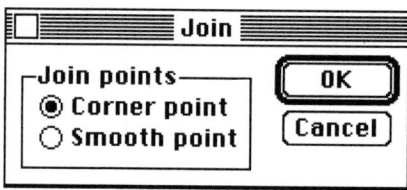

The Join dialog box

Procedure Select two ungrouped endpoints with the Selection tool and choose Join from the Arrange menu or press Command-J. You must have only two endpoints selected when you use this command, and the endpoints must not belong to a grouped object.

If you select two points that are not already touching, the Join command creates a straight line that connects the two points. When the endpoints are joined, both endpoints and the straight line segment between them become selected.

Two endpoints, before and after using the Join command

If you select two points that are already within two pixels of each other (or the Snap to point setting in the Preferences dialog box is two pixels), using the Join command results in the Join dialog box, which allows you to determine whether the joined point will be a corner or smooth.

To join two points that have been averaged, use the Join command immediately after using the Average command (see Average).

To join two points that result when the Scissors tool is used on a line segment, use the Join command immediately after the Scissors tool (see The Scissors Tool in Part I). This is one way of adding a new anchor point to a path. A more direct method is to use the Add-anchor-point tool. (See The Add-anchor-point Tool in Part I.)

Tip   Some paths may appear closed until you try to use a command that requires that the path be closed. If you make this mistake, you will get an alert box with a message that the path is open. To find the endpoints along what looks like a closed path, scroll along the path in maximum magnification (see The Zoom Tool). Anchor points that fall along the closed path display as white boxes when you select any part of the path, or as black boxes when you select the anchor points themselves. Endpoints, on the other hand, display as small x's rather than boxes. (See The Pen Tool for descriptions of how to create open or closed paths.)

Leading

Overview   The Leading command gives access to the Leading submenu, from which you can specify the leading—the vertical space between baselines—of selected text. Leading is measured in points. If a line of type contains characters with different leading specifications, the

Link | PART II

line uses the largest leading value. The Leading submenu offers a choice of eleven preset leading values, plus Auto leading, which sets the leading at 120 percent of the font size, and the Other command, which lets you specify leading values that do not appear on the submenu. The keyboard shortcut for the Other command is Command-Shift-S.

Procedure Choose the Leading command to change the leading for selected text. If the leading value you wish to use appears on the submenu, you can choose it directly. If you want Illustrator to apply auto leading, choose Auto. If you want to use a different value, choose Other, or press Command-Shift-S. The Font Size dialog box appears, showing the current settings for both font size and leading. You can enter values in points for both font size and leading in the Font Size dialog box, to an accuracy of one one-hundredth of a point.

Tip If you want to change only the leading and/or font size of selected text, use the Command-Shift-S keyboard shortcut to open the Font Size dialog box. You can also increase leading by holding down the Option key while pressing the down arrow key or decrease leading by holding down the Option key while pressing the up arrow key. The leading changes by the increment specified in the Type Preferences dialog box using the Preferences command. (See the Preferences command in this section.) To change other attributes in addition to the size or leading, use the Type Style command, or press Command-T, instead (see Style (Type Menu)).

Link

Overview This command links a text object with another path or paths, which are automatically converted to text paths. The linked objects become a single text object. The keyboard shortcut is Command-Shift-G.

| COMMANDS | Lock |

Procedure   Select the text object and the path or paths you want to link, then choose Link from the Type menu or press Command-Shift-G. If the original text object contains overflow text, that text flows into the linked path or paths in the order in which they were created. It is not necessary to change the linked paths to text paths—the Link command automatically does this. You can change the order before linking by using the Send To Back and Bring To Front or Paste In Front and Paste In Back commands—the frontmost object is always last in the flow.

If you want to change the flow order after linking the objects, you must unlink them again. However, you can replace one of the linked paths with a different one without unlinking. To do so, use the Direct-selection tool to select the path you want to remove and choose Clear from the Edit menu. The path disappears, and the text it contained flows into the remaining path. If there is too much text to fit, a plus sign appears at the lower right corner of the path. Then create or select the path into which you want the text to flow, extend the selection to include the text object, and choose Link once more.

Tip   If you are working with text in columns, you can quickly produce a series of linked columns with identical dimensions, without using the Link command. Create the first column by dragging a rectangle with the Type tool and type or import the text. To create additional linked columns, select the text rectangle by Option-clicking with the Direct-selection tool, then Option-drag to create an exact duplicate. Any overflow text flows into the duplicate rectangle.

Lock

Overview   The Lock command locks selected objects so you cannot select, move, or modify them until you unlock them. This command protects parts of your illustration from accidental changes. The keyboard shortcut is Command-1.

Procedure   Select an object or objects and choose Lock from the Arrange menu or press Command-1. Locked objects remain locked until you use the Unlock command. The locked attribute is stored with the document when you close it and remains with the document when it is reopened until the Unlock command is used.

Tips Use this command when you create complex artwork. Locked objects can be seen but not selected, thus enabling you to work easily with adjacent objects without affecting the locked objects. See Tip under Select All for locking all elements except the group you are currently working on.

The Lock command is especially useful when working with grid systems. (See also Grid: Methods 1– 4 in Part III.)

Make Compound

Overview This command combines multiple selected paths into a single compound object. The keyboard shortcut is Command-Option-G. The most common use of compound objects is to create a hole in an object so that you can see through it. When the paths making up a compound object overlap, a hole appears where they overlap. When you create a compound path, all of the objects in the compound path take on the paint attributes of the backmost object in the compound path. Compound paths behave like grouped objects. To select part of a compound path, you must use the Direct-selection tool. If you copy part of a compound path by Option-dragging with the Direct-selection tool, the copy is also part of the compound path. The editable paths created by the Create Outlines command on the Type menu are also compound paths.

You can select two or more existing compound paths and combine them into a single compound path. You can use the Blend tool to create a blend between two components of a compound path, but you cannot create a blend between one entire compound path and another. You can also use compound paths as masking objects, although you may encounter problems when printing if you make the masking object overly complex.

Procedure To create a compound path, first make sure that the objects you want to see through are in front of the background object. Then, select all of the objects you want to include in the compound path and choose Make Compound from the Paint menu or press Command-Option-G.

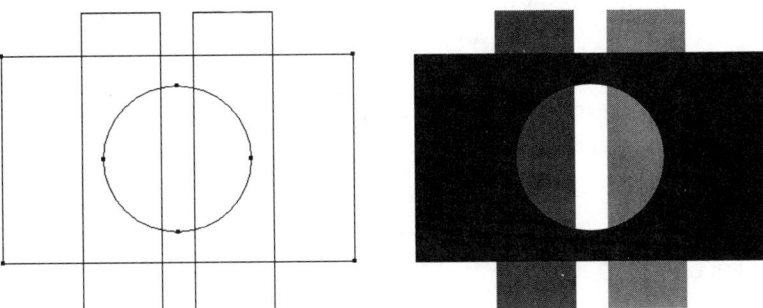

Artwork Only view (left) shows path selected before choosing Make Compound to create the see-through object shown in Preview mode (right)

Tips When you are learning to create compound paths, open a second window on your artwork and use it to preview the compound path.

You can use a group of type outlines created with the Create Outlines command (that is, a word or a phrase) as a masking object. To do so, select all the letters you want to use as a masking object, then choose Make Compound from the Paint menu. Finally, choose Style from the Paint menu, and click the Mask option. See Mask under Style (Paint Menu) for more information on using masking objects. See Masking a Mask and Holes in Solid Objects in Part IV.

Make Guide

Overview The Make Guide command converts a selected object or objects into guide objects. The keyboard shortcut is Command-5. Guide objects appear as dotted lines in the artwork window, but they neither preview nor print. If the Snap to point option is turned on in the Preferences dialog box, objects will snap to the guide object whenever they are within two pixels of the guide object.

Procedure Select the objects you want to convert, then choose Make Guide from the Arrange menu or press Command-5. The selected objects become a guide object and appear as dotted lines in the artwork view.

Make Text Wrap — PART II

To select a guide object, hold down the Shift and Control keys while clicking the object with a selection tool. To convert a guide object back into a path, hold down the Shift and Control keys while double-clicking the object with a selection tool. To delete a guide object, first convert it back to a path or paths, then press Delete.

Tip — Guide objects are particularly useful for setting up perspective grids. (See Grid: Method 2 in Part III.)

Make Text Wrap

Overview — The Make Text Wrap command makes type in an area wrap around another path or paths. It is used primarily to run text around a graphic object. You can make one or more text objects wrap around a path. The path around which you want the text to wrap must be in front of the text object.

Procedure — Select the text object or objects that you want to wrap and the graphic object around which you want them to wrap, using the Selection tool, then choose Make Text Wrap from the Type menu. The text then wraps around the graphic object, and the text object and the graphic object around which the text wraps are grouped.

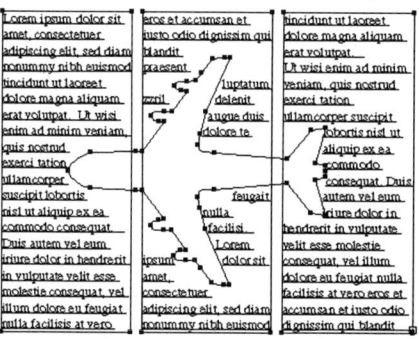 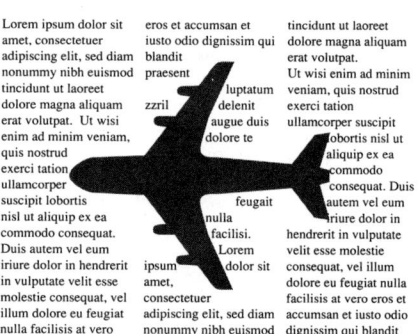

Text wrapped around a graphic

| COMMANDS | Move |

Tip You can control text wrapping precisely by creating an unstroked, unfilled path that you place over the graphic object around which you want the text to wrap. Adjust the text wrap by adjusting the unpainted object to achieve the desired text wrap.

Move...

Overview Use this command to move a selected object or objects a specified distance. The Move command provides an alternate means of opening the Move dialog box. The other method is to Option-click the Selection tool icon in the toolbox. The Move dialog box allows you to specify the distance and direction of the move, whether to move pattern tiles, and whether to move the selected object or a copy of it.

Procedure Select the object or objects you want to move using a selection tool, then choose Move from the Edit menu. The Move dialog box appears. To move an object horizontally or vertically, enter the desired distance in the Horizontal or Vertical field. The unit of measurement used is that specified in the Preferences dialog box. (See Preferences.) Positive numbers move the object toward the right and top of the page; negative numbers move the object toward the left and bottom of the page.

To move an object diagonally, you can specify either horizontal and vertical distances or a distance and an angle for the move. Angles are calculated in degrees from the x (horizontal) axis: positive angles specify a counterclockwise move, and negative angles specify a clockwise move. If you enter horizontal and vertical distances, the diagonal distance and angle are automatically displayed in the other fields. Conversely, if you enter a diagonal distance and angle, Illustrator calculates and displays the horizontal and vertical distances. When you have entered the desired values, click OK to close the dialog box and complete the move.

To create an offset copy of the selected object rather than moving the object itself, click Copy instead of OK. The dialog box closes, and a copy of the selected object appears offset from the original at the distance you specified.

New | PART II

Warning   The distance and direction specified in the Move dialog box are relative to the *x* and *y* axes, which are normally, but not necessarily, parallel to the edges of the window. The value entered in the Constrain angle field in the Preferences dialog box determines the orientation of the *x* and *y* axes. If the axes are rotated, moves are made relative to the rotated axes.

Tips   You can create step-and-repeat designs rapidly using the Move and Transform Again commands. Create the repeating element of your design using any of Illustrator's tools, then select the element, move a copy the desired distance using the Move command, and produce subsequent copies by choosing Transform Again from the Arrange menu or pressing Command-D.

When you use the Measure tool to measure a distance, the Move dialog box is automatically updated to reflect the distance and angle you just measured. To move an object a measured distance without recording the measurements, you can measure the distance with the Measure tool, then choose Move and click OK.

New ...

Overview   The New command creates a new Illustrator artwork file. The keyboard shortcut is Command-N. You have the option of opening a template—a bitmapped or PICT file that you can trace or use as a background. Template elements do not print out as part of the Illustrator artwork.

Procedure   Choose New from the File menu or press Command-N. Illustrator displays a dialog box, shown in the figure on the facing page, listing all of the bit-mapped and PICT files available on the disk (see *bitmap* and *PICT format* in the Glossary).

| COMMANDS | New |

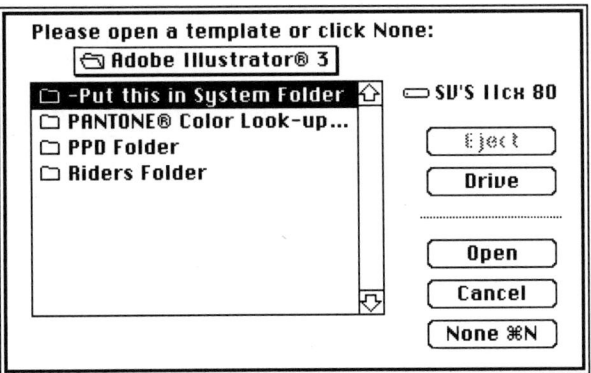

The New dialog box

You can select one of these bitmapped or PICT files as a template file and use it as the background from which to trace new artwork. If you do not want to use a template, click the None button. If you click the None button, Illustrator presents you with an untitled, blank page. You can cancel the entire command by clicking the Cancel button or by using the keyboard shortcut, Command-(period).

To open a new document without a template, press Command-Option-N. Illustrator opens a new untitled document without displaying a dialog box.

Tips   As with other Macintosh applications, Illustrator opens a file and assigns it the name Untitled art in the title bar. You can change the name of the file by choosing Save or Save As from the File menu. You can also name the file when you close it by clicking the file's close box or by choosing Close from the File menu. If you close the file using either of these methods and you have unsaved work on the screen, Illustrator displays an alert box asking if you want to save changes. If you click the Yes button, Illustrator displays the Save As dialog box (see Save As).

| New Window | PART II |

New Window

Overview   The New Window command creates a duplicate window of the active file. The original window and its duplicate are linked, so that changes to artwork in one window are duplicated in the second window. You can view one window in Preview mode and the other in Artwork mode and zoom in one window independently of the other.

Procedure   Choose New Window from the Window menu. The duplicate window appears slightly offset from the original window. The newly created view becomes the active window, which you can move, resize, or close just like any Macintosh window.

When two or more views of the same file are on the desktop, Illustrator assigns each a number that appears in the window's title bar: Untitled art:1, Untitled art:2, and so on. When you close a window from a set of multiple views, Illustrator renumbers the remaining windows accordingly.

You can work in full views or overlapping views, and you can change the active window by choosing from the Window menu.

Artwork and Preview   Work in two views of the same illustration, one in Artwork Only (or Artwork & Template) view and one in Preview. This way, you can see the results of changes in real time as you work in the Artwork view on the wireframe image. Working in this way is especially good for making the final touches on artwork.

Preview and Artwork views

Actual Size and Close-up   Work in two different magnifications: an actual size (or smaller) view of the entire artwork and an enlarged view of the detail on which you are working. This allows you to see extended sections of long paths in the smaller view and to pinpoint anchor points easily in the enlarged view.

Two magnifications of wireframe artwork

The reduced view can be in either Artwork or Preview mode.

Artwork and Paint Palette   View the artwork of the illustration in one window and a palette of Paint settings in another window.

Artwork and Control Area   View the artwork of the illustration in one window and a control area of group selection icons or repeatedly used elements in another window. (See Control Panel in Part III for a specific application of this methodology.)

Multiple Illustrations   You can view two or more illustrations at once. This is useful when you want to compare images, overlay images, or copy elements from one document to another.

Warning   Working with windows open in the Preview mode may slow down the system if the illustration is complex, because the Preview mode constantly refreshes the screen. It may not be practical to work this way for long periods on complex drawings.

| Open | PART II |

Tip You can have several windows open on your screen at once (depending on the size of the files and the amount of memory available). You compound the possibilities by having three or more windows open at once.

Open...

Overview The Open command opens an existing Illustrator file or a template file. The keyboard shortcut is Command-O. The number of files you can have open simultaneously is limited by available RAM. You can switch between windows by selecting one of the open windows listed under the Window menu.

Procedure Choose Open from the File menu or press Command-O. Illustrator displays the Open dialog box, as shown in the following figure, listing all Illustrator files and template files on the selected disk.

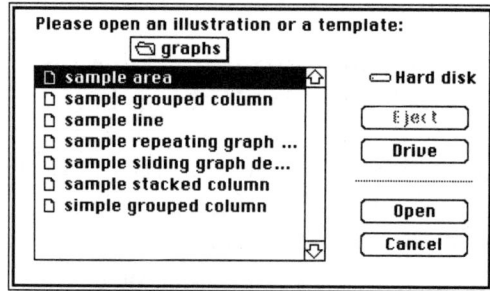

The Open dialog box

To select a file, scroll through the file list to locate your desired file, click its name, and then click the Open button, or double-click on the file name. Click the Drive button to view the list of files from another disk. Click the Eject button to change disks. To work on an existing Illustrator file, select the file. Illustrator opens a new window displaying both the artwork and its template, if there is one. The window's title bar has a name in the form *Artwork:template*, where *Artwork* is the name of the Illustrator file and *template* is the name of the template file.

To create a new Illustrator file based on an existing template file, select the template file from the Open dialog box. Illustrator opens a new window with the name *Untitled art:template* in the title bar, where *template* is the template file name. You can change the Illustrator file name from *Untitled art* to something more meaningful when you save the Illustrator file.

Tips From the desktop, double-click the icon of an Illustrator document to bring up the file immediately at startup time.

You can force Illustrator to prompt you for a template file whenever you open an existing Illustrator artwork file by holding down the Option key when you choose Open from the File menu. By using the Option key in this way, you can work on existing artwork without being forced to continue using the template that you may have traced originally. In addition, you can open a different template and add a second traced drawing to existing artwork.

Page Setup...

Overview The Page Setup command controls the page settings that determine how an artwork file will be printed. The Page Setup command lets you select the paper size, the reduction or enlargement percentage, the page orientation (tall or wide), and special printer effects, such as font substitution, smoothing, and faster bitmap printing. This command affects the printing of each page for the file in the active window.

Procedure Choose Page Setup from the File menu. Illustrator displays the Page Setup dialog box, which is specific to the printer driver you select with the Chooser from the Apple menu (see Chooser). The next figure shows the Page Setup dialog box for the LaserWriter printer driver, used by most PostScript laser printers.

Page Setup — PART II

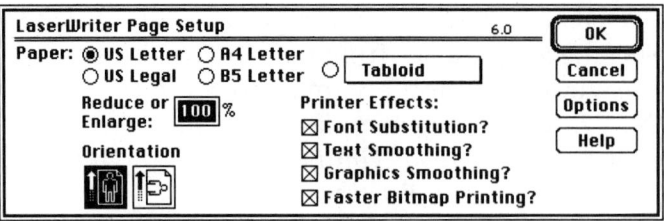

The Page Setup dialog box for the LaserWriter printer driver, used by most PostScript laser printers

Set the Paper setting to match the paper tray loaded in the printer. Select this setting by clicking on the desired option. The Orientation setting lets you choose whether your artwork will be printed vertically (tall) or horizontally (wide) on the page. The Reduce or Enlarge setting lets you specify a percentage reduction or enlargement. You can print enlarged drawings in pieces on several pages. The Printer Effects options—Font Substitution, Text Smoothing, Graphics Smoothing, and Faster Bitmap Printing—have no effect on Illustrator files. You can leave them all checked, which are their default settings.

The Options button, when clicked, displays a second dialog box, the Options dialog box, shown in the following figure. This dialog box lets you flip the image vertically or horizontally, invert (reverse) the image, align bitmap printing more precisely by way of a 4 percent reduction, use an unlimited number of downloadable fonts in a document (Adobe Systems recommends that you avoid using this option when printing Illustrator documents), or use a larger print area than normal (which will reduce the allowable number of downloadable fonts). The print area option has no effect on Illustrator files.

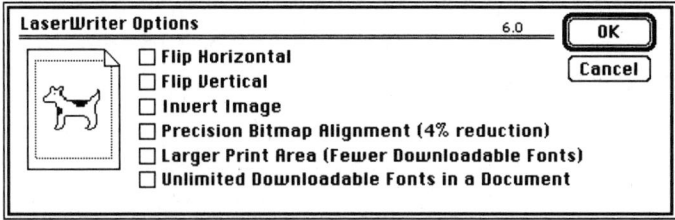

The Options dialog box

You can also choose Help from the Page Setup dialog box. Click on the Help button to get details on how Page Setup options affect printing.

Paste

Overview The Paste command pastes the contents of the Clipboard to the center of the active window, on top of all the other objects. The keyboard shortcut is Command-V.

Procedure After storing the desired objects in the Clipboard using the Copy or Cut command, choose Paste from the Edit menu or press Command-V. The pasted objects appear in the center of the screen and become the currently selected objects. All other objects are deselected.

Warning All pasted objects are selected when they appear on the screen. It's a good idea to use the Undo, Cut, Send To Back, Bring To Front, or Group command immediately, or move the pasted selections into position immediately, before clicking elsewhere and deselecting an ungrouped selection of pasted objects.

You cannot paste graphics from other applications into Illustrator. You can, however, paste text, provided that you first create an insertion point with one of the text tools.

Tip Pasting objects from the Clipboard does not remove them from the Clipboard. (See also Paste In Front and Paste In Back.)

Paste In Back

Overview The Paste In Back command pastes artwork from the Clipboard in back of all currently selected objects. The keyboard shortcut is Command-B.

Paste In Front — PART II

Procedure   Select an object or objects with a selection tool. Use the Cut or Copy command to store the object or objects you select in the Clipboard. Then select the objects in back of which you wish to paste the Clipboard objects, and choose Paste In Back from the Edit menu or press Command-B. If you have not selected any objects, the pasted objects become the backmost objects in the artwork, at the same location on the page from which they were cut or copied. The pasted objects become the currently selected objects and all other objects are deselected.

Warning   You cannot paste graphics from other applications into Illustrator. You can, however, paste text, provided that you first create an insertion point with one of the text tools.

Tips   This command is especially useful for pasting objects between other objects, as an alternative to the Paste In Front command (see Paste In Front).

If you simply want to move selected objects to the bottom layer, which is frequently required for masking or patterning, it is more efficient to use the Send To Back command than the Cut and Paste In Back commands.

Paste In Front

Overview   The Paste In Front command pastes artwork objects from the Clipboard in front of all currently selected objects. The keyboard shortcut is Command-F.

Procedure   Select an object or objects with a selection tool. Use the Cut or Copy command to store the object or objects you select in the Clipboard. Then select the objects in front of which you wish to paste the Clipboard objects, and choose Paste In Front from the Edit menu or press Command-F. If you have not selected any objects, the pasted objects become the frontmost objects in the artwork, at the same location on the page from which they were cut or copied. The pasted objects become the currently selected objects and all other objects are deselected.

| COMMANDS | Pattern |

Tips This command is especially useful for pasting objects between other objects. If you want to paste in front of all objects in your artwork—not in front of selected objects only—you can use the Paste command. Another difference between Paste and Paste In Front is that Paste brings the objects to the center of the window, whereas Paste In Front positions the objects over their last location.

If you want simply to move selected objects to the top of the artwork, it is more efficient to use the Bring To Front command than the Cut and Paste In Front commands.

Pattern...

Overview The Pattern command displays the Pattern dialog box, which allows you to create a new pattern or delete, paste, or change the name of an existing pattern. The scrolling list displays all existing patterns.

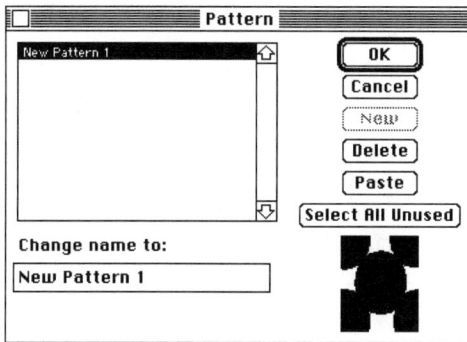

The Pattern dialog box

Procedure Draw a pattern shape or design and color it. Using the Rectangle tool, draw a rectangle around your art defining the tiling element. The rectangle need not completely surround the design. Select the rectangle and use the Send To Back command to position it behind the design. Select both the design and the rectangle. Then choose Pattern from the Paint menu. The Pattern dialog box appears, as shown in the preceding figure. Click New to display the selected

Pattern — PART II

pattern in the bottom right area of the dialog box and name the pattern by entering the name in the text box. When you close this dialog box, the pattern will then be available in the Paint dialog box.

Procedure for creating a pattern

Click Paste to paste a copy of the original tiling element artwork on the page if you want to edit the pattern, then close the dialog box, edit the pattern artwork, select it, and choose Pattern again to store the changed pattern under the same name or a new name.

Click Delete to remove the selected name (and pattern) from the list. Objects that were filled with that pattern will revert to the default fill pattern (100 percent black).

Click Select All Unused to select the names of all patterns that are not currently used in the artwork. You can delete these patterns to save memory and storage space.

Click OK to close the dialog box and record the changes, or click Cancel to close the dialog box without recording any changes.

You can apply patterns listed in this dialog box to selected objects by clicking the Pattern button in the Paint Style dialog box (see Style Paint Menu).

Tips

If you frequently use custom patterns, save them in a file created for this purpose. Opening the file will make your previously created patterns available, allowing you to use them in other Illustrator files. You can make any pattern available for use in a new file by simply opening the file that contains the desired pattern.

If you want a set of patterns to be available automatically whenever you use Illustrator, create an Illustrator file containing all the patterns you want, then name it Adobe Illustrator Startup, and place it in the folder containing the Illustrator application. (If you keep the application on the desktop, place the Adobe Illustrator Startup file in your startup disk's disk window.) You can also include custom colors, fonts, and graph designs in the Adobe Illustrator Startup document. These elements will automatically be available whenever you use Illustrator. (See Patterns: Methods 1–3 in Part III. See Japan Fan and Kimono in Part IV for use of patterns.)

Place Art...

Overview The Place Art command imports an Encapsulated PostScript (EPS) file. Scans, as well as files from Freehand, Cricket Draw, PageMaker, Pixel Paint, and other applications, may be saved in EPS format.

Procedure Choose Place Art from the File menu. Illustrator displays the Place Art dialog box, which lists all EPS files on the selected disk, as shown in the following figure.

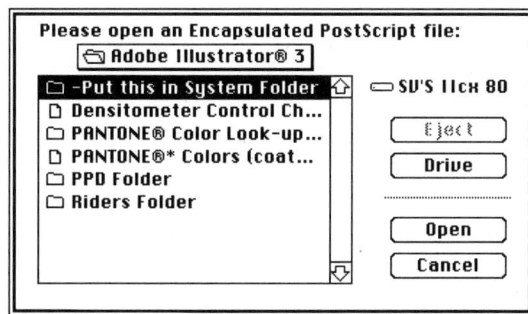

The Place Art dialog box

To select a file, scroll through the file list to locate the desired file name, click on the name, and then click the Open button, or double-click on the file name. The Drive button and Eject button operate as described earlier under Open. You can manipulate EPS files imported using the Place Art command as single objects with any of Illustrator's transformation tools (Scale, Rotate, Reflect, or Shear), but you cannot change the strokes of lines or of fill patterns or otherwise make detailed edits to the EPS graphic.

You can control how EPS images display in Artwork mode using the Show placed images option in the Preferences dialog box. When this option is turned off, EPS images display as a box with an x in the center in Artwork Only and Artwork & Template modes, but they Preview correctly. When Show placed images is turned on, a preview image appears inside the box. (See Preferences.)

Warning Illustrator will need to refer to the original EPS files whenever you open or print the document, unless you check the Include placed images option in the Save As dialog box. (See Save As.) Placed images cannot be edited in detail, so it's usually a good idea to keep a copy of the original EPS file in the same folder with your artwork.

Tip Files imported by the Place Art command can be masked, but they cannot be made into patterns.

Preferences...

Overview The Preferences command lets you change settings that affect how various commands and tools in Illustrator work. The keyboard shortcut is Command-K.

The Preferences dialog box

| COMMANDS | Preferences |

Procedure   Choose Preferences from the Edit menu or press Command-K. Illustrator displays the Preferences dialog box, shown in the figure on the facing page, which lets you set the preferences described in the following paragraphs by either clicking the appropriate checkbox or button or typing in desired values.

Snap to Point   This turns the Snap to point feature on or off. The normal default setting of Snap to point is on. Snap to point causes two points to snap together when they are within two pixels of each other and moves objects in two-pixel increments. With Snap to point off, you can move objects one pixel at a time. Snap to point is very useful for aligning objects, but you can turn this feature off when you are positioning objects very close to each other but do not want them to touch.

Transform Pattern Tiles   When turned on, this causes patterns within objects to be changed along with the path of the object when any transformation tool is used. (Transformation tools include the Scale, Rotate, Reflect, and Shear tools.) Otherwise, with Transform pattern tiles off (the default setting), only the path is transformed, not the pattern. (See description of Transform option under Style (Paint Menu).)

Scale Line Weight   When turned on, this causes line weights to be scaled when you are scaling an object by dragging the Scale tool. Otherwise, only the path is scaled, and the line weights retain their original value.

Preview and Print Patterns   This setting controls how patterns are viewed and printed. The default setting for Preview and print patterns is on, which allows you to view and print patterns fully. When Preview and print patterns is set off, the screen refreshes faster because you have instructed Illustrator not to preview the patterns, which take more time to draw. Also, when the setting is off, the illustrations print drafts without patterns, which will print faster than if printing with patterns.

Show Placed Images This setting controls how placed Encapsulated PostScript (EPS) images appear in artwork mode. When this setting is turned off, placed EPS images appear as boxes in the Artwork Only and Artwork & Template views. When the setting is turned on, a preview image of the placed artwork appears inside the box, provided that the EPS file contains a preview image. If the EPS file does not contain a preview image, this setting has no effect. The image will print correctly, but it appears as a box in Artwork Only view, and is invisible in Preview view.

Split Long Paths on Save/Print Turn this option on only if you experience problems printing a document containing long, complicated paths. The default setting for this option is off. If you use this option, you must enter a value for your printer's output resolution in the Output resolution field (described shortly). When this option is turned on, Illustrator checks the path length each time you save or print an image. If the path length exceeds the capabilities of your printer's memory, Illustrator breaks the path into pieces. Note that splitting paths changes your artwork. Once the paths have been split, you must either work with the separate shapes or rejoin the paths manually. For this reason, you should always keep a copy of your original artwork if you plan to use the Split long paths option. When you save the document, make sure you save a copy with the Split long paths option turned off.

Constrain Angle When set to zero degrees (default setting), this constrains all objects to the normal horizontal and vertical positioning. However, by changing this value, you can rotate the x and y axes of the artwork so that objects will draw at the angle specified. The x and y axes remain at right angles to one another, but are no longer vertical and horizontal. All transformation, constraining, and moving operations are performed relative to the x and y axes—if these are rotated from the vertical and horizontal, the operations will be translated by the same angle.

Corner Radius When set to zero points (the default), this results in rectangles with square corners. Adding points to this setting changes the square corners to curved corners. Corner radius values must be between 0 and 1296 points, but cannot exceed half the length of the short sides of the rectangle. If you enter a larger value, Illustrator will draw the largest oval that can fit into the rectangle. (See The Rectangle Tool in Part I for examples of different corner radius settings.)

Cursor Key Distance This determines the distance a selected object or group of objects will move when you press one of the arrow keys. You can enter a value from 1 to 1296 points (or decimal equivalents in other units of measure).

Freehand Tolerance This sensitizes the mouse movement and determines the number of anchor points that will be created when you use the Freehand tool to draw an object. When you enter a higher number, fewer anchor points occur along a path and the mouse becomes less sensitive. When the tolerance is set higher, using the Autotrace tool also yields fewer anchor points (see The Autotrace Tool in Part I). When you enter a lower value, more anchor points occur along a path because the mouse becomes more sensitive to movement. You can set the tolerance from one to ten pixels. If you set tolerance beyond this range, an alert box appears. (See The Freehand Tool for examples of different tolerance settings.)

Autotrace Over Gap This determines the number of pixels Illustrator reads when the Autotrace tool is in use. With Autotrace over gap set at zero (the default setting), the Autotrace tool will read every pixel in the template. With the setting at 2, Autotrace will jump across two-pixel gaps and connect the pixels on either side of the gap, which is useful if your template is very sketchy. With the setting at 1, Autotrace connects across one-pixel gaps.

Output Resolution This option is dimmed unless the Split long paths option is checked. When Split long paths is checked, you must enter a value for your printer's resolution in the output resolution field. Illustrator uses this value to determine how to split paths.

Type Preferences Clicking this button opens the Type Preferences dialog box, shown in the following figure. In the Type Preferences dialog box, you can choose the unit of measurement used for paragraph indents and vertical shifting. The default unit is picas and points, but you can also choose inches or centimeters. The units you select do not affect the units for font size, leading, or leading before paragraphs, which are always measured in points. You can also set the increments by which font size, leading, vertical shift, and tracking/kerning change when you use keyboard shortcuts. The default values are 2 points for size and leading, 2 points for vertical shift, and 0.02 ems for tracking and kerning.

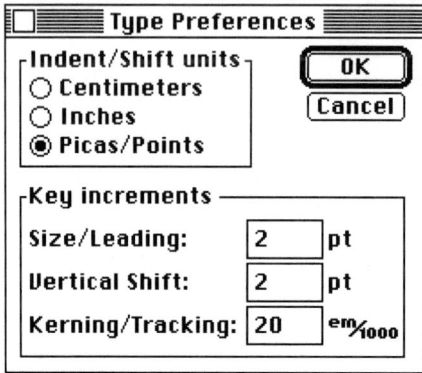

The Type Preferences dialog box

Progressive Colors Clicking this button brings up the Progressive Colors selection box, shown in the next figure. When you use this option with a sample progressive color bar provided by Adobe or your printer, you can adjust your monitor and screen colors for current lighting situations. This allows you to customize your monitor without mechanically altering internal settings. Double-clicking on a color swatch in the Progressive Colors box yields the Apple Color Picker, which allows you to choose from a palette of more than sixteen million colors.

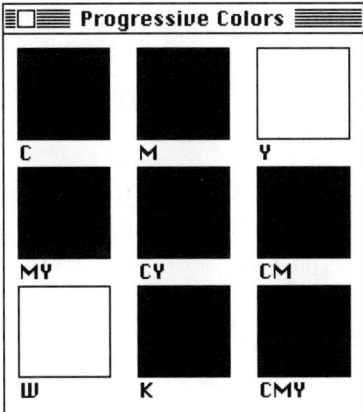

The Progressive Colors selection box

Artwork Board   This option determines how page breaks are displayed on the screen. The document work area is 18 inches (1296 points) square. The page breaks display the area that will fit on the paper size you select in the Page Setup dialog box. The default option is Single Full Page, which displays a single page centered in the work area. Tile Full Pages lets you display more than one page at a time, such as a two-page spread. To use this option, you need to position the pages with the Page tool. The page frame is only displayed if the entire page frame can fit into the work area. Tile Imageable Areas tiles the whole work area onto pages of the size specified in the Page Setup dialog box. You can move the pages using the Page tool. Page numbers appear on the pages for your reference, but they do not print.

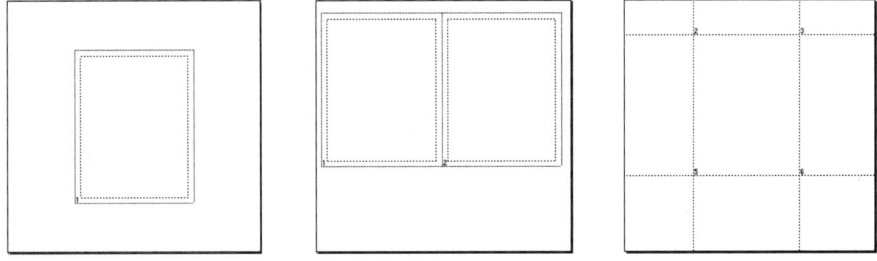

Single Full Page selected; Tile Full Pages selected; Tile imageable areas selected

Preview Illustration | PART II

Ruler Units These options, displayed in a box in the lower right portion of the dialog box, determine the units of measure displayed on the ruler. You can select Centimeters, Inches, or Picas/Points (the default).

Warning Preference settings cannot be reversed with the Undo command. They are stored as part of the Illustrator application settings and are *not* stored differently for each document. Before changing these values, make a note of the original settings in case you wish to revert. (Preference settings do not affect the artwork.)

Preview Illustration

Overview The Preview Illustration command displays a preview image of the artwork in the active window. The keyboard shortcut is Command-Y. A preview image is an approximation on the screen of how the artwork will look when it is printed.

An illustration shown in two different views: Artwork Only and Preview

Procedure Choose Preview Illustration from the View menu or press Command-Y to check the printed appearance of your artwork. The second view in the preceding figure shows a previewed illustration.

You cannot make changes to the artwork in Preview mode, but you can have multiple windows open with different views of a file. One window can show the image in Artwork Only mode, and the

| COMMANDS | Preview Selection |

other window can show the image in Preview mode. The window containing the preview image is updated whenever you make changes to the artwork (see also New Window).

You can use the Hand tool, zoom tools, Measure tool, and Page tool in the Preview mode but you cannot change the artwork.

Warning Working with a Preview window open may slow down processing as you work.

Tips You will use this command so frequently that you should learn to use the keyboard shortcut, Command-Y.

If you wish to stop the page from previewing after you have invoked the Preview Illustration command, but before the screen has finished redrawing in Preview, press Command-(period).

Preview Selection

Overview The Preview Selection command is identical to the Preview Illustration command except that it displays a preview image of only the currently selected object or objects in the active window. The keyboard shortcut is Command-Option-Y.

Procedure Select the object or objects you want to preview using any of the selection tools, then choose Preview Selection from the View menu or press Command-Option-Y to check the printed appearance of the currently selected object or objects.

As with the Preview Illustration command, you cannot make changes to the artwork in Preview mode, but you can have multiple windows open with different views of a file.

Tips Previewing only the current selection is faster than previewing the whole illustration. Use the Preview Selection command to check the printed appearance of individual components or details in your artwork.

Print...

Overview The Print command prints the artwork in the active window to the printer that has been designated with the Chooser (see Chooser command). The keyboard shortcut is Command-P.

Procedure Choose Print from the File menu, or press Command-P. Illustrator displays the Print dialog box, which is specific to the printer you select with the Chooser. The following figure shows the Print dialog box for an Apple LaserWriter NTX printer.

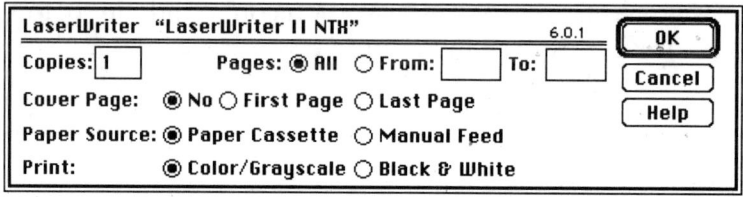

The Print dialog box for an Apple LaserWriter NTX printer

The Copies setting lets you specify the number of copies you wish to print. The Pages settings let you print all pages (by selecting All) or a range of pages (by selecting From and To and specifying the range, for example, from 1 to 3). The page numbers are shown at the corners of pages bordered with dotted lines on the screen display of the artwork, as shown in the following figure.

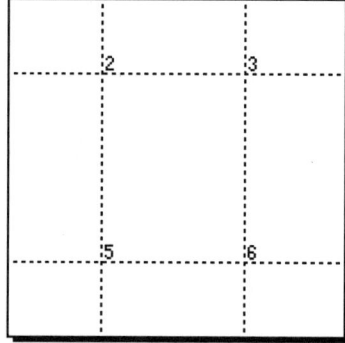

Page numbers shown on screen display

You can choose to print, as either first or last page, a Cover Page. The Cover Page will contain the user name (that you have entered in the Chooser), the application you used to print the document, the document name, the date and time of printing, and the printer name. You will find this feature useful in identifying your printouts when several computers share the same printer over an AppleTalk network. The Paper Source settings let you choose paper cassette or manual feed. By clicking on the Paper Cassette option, you choose to use the paper source in the printer's paper tray. If you click on the Manual Feed option, the system will prompt you to feed paper to the printer one page at a time. You can also choose Help from the Print dialog box. Click on the Help button to get more information on printer settings and options that affect your printed output. Help will display only if the Help files are loaded on your system.

Quit

Overview The Quit command quits Adobe Illustrator and returns you to the desktop. The keyboard shortcut is Command-Q.

Procedure Choose Quit from the File menu or press Command-Q. If you choose to quit Illustrator and have made changes since you last saved any file that is open, Illustrator asks you if you want to save that file, as shown in the following figure. If you click Yes, Illustrator saves the file using the artwork name in the title bar or, if the window is named Untitled art, Illustrator displays the Save As dialog box, prompting you to enter a new name for the file. Once you do this, Illustrator completes the Quit command, returning you to the desktop.

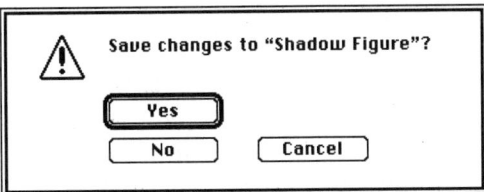

The Quit dialog box, asking if you want to save the file

Release Compound — PART II

Redo (see Undo)

Release All Guides

Overview   The Release All Guides command converts all guide objects, including Ruler Guides, to paths. The keyboard shortcut is Command-6.

Procedure   Choose Release All Guides from the Arrange menu or press Command-6. All guide objects including ruler guides are converted to paths, and are selected. (See Make Guide and Show/Hide Rulers.)

Tip   Because Release All Guides leaves the newly converted guide objects selected, you can quickly delete all guide objects from your artwork when you no longer require them by choosing Release All Guides from the Arrange menu, then immediately pressing the Delete key.

Release Compound

Overview   The Release Compound command converts a selected compound path back to its components, which may also be compound paths. The keyboard shortcut is Command-Option-U.

Procedure   Select the compound path you want to convert back to its components using the Selection tool, then choose Release Compound from the Paint menu, or press Command-Option-U. The compound path is converted back to its component elements, and all the components are selected. (See Make Compound.)

Warning   When a compound path is selected, all the objects that were formerly part of the compound path have the Paint attributes of the backmost object in the compound path. The Paint attributes they had before creating the compound path are not restored.

Release Cropmarks

Overview — The Release Cropmarks command converts crop marks back to a rectangle that defines the bounding area of your artwork.

Procedure — Choose Release Cropmarks from the Arrange menu. The crop marks are converted back to a rectangle that defines the bounding area of your artwork. The rectangle is selected. (See Set Cropmarks.)

Tip — If you want to move existing crop marks, you do not need to release them first. Simply draw a new bounding rectangle using the rectangle tool, then choose Set Cropmarks from the Arrange menu. The new crop marks automatically replace the old ones.

Release Text Wrap

Overview — The Release Text Wrap command applies to grouped objects created with the Make Text Wrap command. It releases the text wrap and ungroups the text object from the graphic object around which the text wraps.

Procedure — Select the grouped object containing the text and the object around which the text wraps using the Selection tool, then choose Release Text Wrap from the Type menu. The text no longer wraps around the graphic object, and the text object and the graphic object become separate objects. Both the text object and the graphic object are left selected. (See Make Text Wrap.)

Reset Toolbox

Overview — The Reset Toolbox command resets the entire toolbox to the default tools.

| Save | PART II |

Procedure Choose the Reset Toolbox command from the Window Menu. All the tools in the toolbox are restored to their defaults. You can also reset the toolbox to its defaults by holding down the Command and Shift keys while double-clicking any tool icon in the toolbox. To reset a single tool to its default, hold down the Shift key while double-clicking the tool's icon in the toolbox.

Save

Overview The Save command saves the latest version of the active Illustrator file. The keyboard shortcut is Command-S.

Procedure Choose Save from the File menu or press Command-S. Illustrator saves the file that is in the active window using the same name as shown in the artwork portion of the title bar. If the Illustrator file name is Untitled art, Illustrator displays the Save As dialog box, prompting you to provide a new artwork file name. (See Save As).

Illustrator saves the file on the current disk and leaves the active file window on the screen. If there is not enough room on the disk, Illustrator notifies you that you do not have enough room with an alert dialog box, and you can then choose Save As from the File menu and save the file on another disk.

Tip You should save frequently to prevent losing the work you have completed. At the very least, always save your work before you print. This is recommended because, when printing, the application accesses the AppleTalk network, thus becoming slightly more vulnerable to failure than when working locally on your Macintosh. And although system crashes may be rare, you can bet that the one system crash you experience per year will happen when you did not save your file and you have a critical deadline to meet. It is much easier to press Command-S frequently than to redraw your work.

Save As...

Overview The Save As command saves the file in the active window under a new name or on a different disk or in a format that will display the artwork when it is imported into a page layout application. There is no keyboard shortcut for the Save As command.

Procedure Choose Save As from the File menu. Illustrator displays a dialog box, shown in the following figure, into which you enter the name for the file you wish to save and from which you specify the disk and file folder in which you wish the file to be saved. Illustrator saves the file and leaves the active file window on the screen so that you can continue working on it.

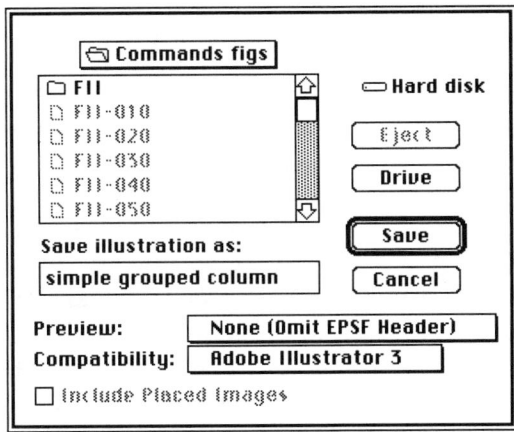

The Save As dialog box

There are five preview modes and three compatibility modes that you can specify through the Save As dialog box. To save a file under more than one of these formats, you must save it under a different name for each format. The following paragraphs describe the five preview modes.

None (Omit EPSF Header)   This mode creates a file that can only be reopened by Adobe Illustrator. To select this file format, choose None (Omit EPSF Header) from the Preview pop-up menu in the dialog box. This format has minimum space requirements and is the default file format. You cannot place files saved in this format in other Macintosh applications, such as PageMaker or QuarkXPress.

None (Include EPSF Header)   This mode saves the file as a complete PostScript language program. To select this file format, choose None (Include EPSF Header) from the Preview pop-up menu in the dialog box. You must use this format if you want to open the document with the Adobe Separator 3.0 program. When placed in other Macintosh applications, such as PageMaker or QuarkXPress, a file saved in this format displays as a gray box, but prints correctly. This format takes up more disk space than the None (Omit EPSF Header) format. If you know how to program in the PostScript language, you can open and edit the PostScript code of documents saved in this format with a word processor or text editor (see Appendix E). You may need to change the file type to TEXT in order to do so.

Black & White Macintosh   This mode saves the file in an EPS format that you can still edit in Adobe Illustrator, but attaches a black and white preview image in Macintosh QuickDraw PICT format. To select this file format, choose Black & White Macintosh from the Preview pop-up menu in the dialog box. This format is designed to be used in conjunction with page layout applications that support the EPS format, allowing you to see a preview image of your artwork after it has been imported into the page layout application. You cannot edit documents saved in this format with word processors or text editors. When placed in other Macintosh applications, such as PageMaker or QuarkXPress, a file saved in this format displays a black and white preview image. However, any color information in the document is preserved. This format takes up considerably more disk space than either of the formats with no preview image, but takes up less space than those saved with a color preview image.

Color Macintosh This mode saves the file in an EPS format that you can still edit in Adobe Illustrator, but attaches a color preview image in Macintosh QuickDraw PICT format. To select this file format, choose Color Macintosh from the Preview pop-up menu in the dialog box. This format is designed to be used in conjunction with page layout applications that support the EPS format, allowing you to see a preview image of your artwork after it has been imported into the page layout application. You cannot edit documents saved in this format with word processors or text editors. When placed in other Macintosh applications, such as PageMaker or QuarkXPress, a file saved in this format displays a color preview image. You should use this format when you know that you will use a color monitor, and that you will import the file into a page layout application such as PageMaker or QuarkXPress.

IBM PC This mode saves the file in an EPS format that you can transfer to an MS-DOS system and place in MS-DOS applications, such as PageMaker and Ventura Publisher. To select this file format, choose IBM PC from the Preview pop-up menu in the dialog box. The artwork will be displayed on the screen either as artwork or as a place-holding box, depending on the application. Both PageMaker for the PC and Ventura Publisher display the actual artwork. To transfer the Macintosh Illustrator file to the IBM PC, use a file transfer program such as MacLink (binary format), transfer the file over a network such as TOPS or Appleshare, or telecommunicate the file in binary format through modems.

The three compatibility modes are described in the following paragraphs.

Adobe Illustrator 3.0 This mode saves the file in a format that can only be edited by Adobe Illustrator 3.0. Earlier versions of the Illustrator program cannot open documents saved in this format. However, if any of the preview options other than None (Omit EPS Header) have been used, you can place a file of this format in page layout applications such as PageMaker or QuarkXPress. To select this file format, choose Adobe Illustrator 3.0 from the Compatibility pop-up menu in the dialog box.

Adobe Illustrator 88™   This mode saves the file in a format that can be opened and edited using Adobe Illustrator 88 or Aldus FreeHand. However, the new features in version 3.0 will not be available. Compound paths, guide objects, and most text objects are saved in a modified form. If any of the preview options other than None (Omit EPS Header) have been used, you can place a file of this format in page layout applications such as PageMaker or QuarkXPress. To select this file format, choose Adobe Illustrator 88™ from the Compatibility pop-up menu in the dialog box.

Adobe Illustrator 1.1   This mode saves the file in a format that can be opened by Illustrator 1.1. However, many of the features in version 3.0 will not be available. Compound paths, guide objects, and most text objects are saved in a modified form; custom colors are converted to process colors; masking is not in effect (though all objects in the mask are present); and patterns and placed images are removed. If any of the preview options other than None (Omit EPS Header) have been used, you can place a file of this format in page layout applications such as PageMaker or QuarkXPress. To select this file format, choose Adobe Illustrator 1.1 from the Compatibility pop-up menu in the dialog box.

If your artwork contains placed EPS images, the Include Placed Images check box is enabled. Clicking this option saves a copy of any EPS files you placed using the Place Art command within your document. To select this option, click in the check box or anywhere on the label. Using this option means that Illustrator no longer requires a copy of the original placed image, but it results in a larger file. Also, placed images cannot be edited in any detail, so it's generally a good idea to keep the placed image file separately. You should always use the Include Placed Images option when you intend to place your artwork in another application such as a page composition application, but you should generally wait until you are sure that the artwork is finalized before you do so.

| COMMANDS | Send To Back |

Tip You can give an Illustrator file a name up to thirty characters long (including spaces), but the list of files displayed in the Open dialog box will display only the first twenty characters. It is a good idea to name related files with the same initial characters (so they will be grouped together in an alphabetical list), but be sure to differentiate among the names within the first twenty characters.

Select All

Overview The Select All command selects all objects that are not locked or hidden. The keyboard shortcut is Command-A.

Procedure Choose Select All from the Edit menu or press Command-A. All objects, except those hidden or locked, will be selected. You may then perform any action on them that will affect the objects as a group.

The most obvious use of the Select All command is to select all of the elements of the artwork at once, especially if the artwork extends past the boundaries of the active window and you cannot select all by dragging a selection tool.

Tip When you wish to select most but not all of the objects in a file, it often saves time to use Select All, then deselect those objects you do not wish to be selected by holding down the Shift key and clicking on them.

Send To Back

Overview The Send To Back command moves selected objects to the backmost layer in the artwork. The keyboard shortcut is Command-(hyphen).

Procedure Select the object or objects you wish to move to the back layer using any of the techniques described under The Selection Tools and choose Send To Back from the Edit menu or press Command-(hyphen). If the selection itself is composed of more than one layer, the selected objects retain their relative positions in layers.

(See Procedure and Warning in Bring To Front.)

Tips Use this command to send an object that you wish to use as a mask to the back, since the mask will not occur unless the path is the backmost object. See the Mask option in Style (Paint Menu), and Masking a Mask in Part III.

Also, use this command on the rectangle that defines a pattern, since that rectangle must be the backmost object. (See Pattern and Patterns: Methods 1–3 in Part III.)

Set Cropmarks

Overview The Set Cropmarks command allows you to set the position of crop marks on the page. Crop marks will print from Illustrator or from the Adobe Separator program if you plan to produce color separations of your artwork.

Procedure To set crop marks, first draw a rectangle to define the boundary of your artwork; then, with the rectangle selected, choose Set Cropmarks from the Arrange menu. Crop marks then replace the selected rectangle. Once you have set crop marks, you cannot select them. However, you can replace crop marks by drawing a new bounding rectangle and choosing Set Cropmarks again. To delete crop marks, use the Release Cropmarks command. (See Release Cropmarks.)

If you have selected the Single Full Page option in the Preferences dialog box, you can use the Set Cropmarks command without first drawing a bounding rectangle. If you have selected either Tile Full Pages or Tile Imageable Areas, the Set Cropmarks command is unavailable unless a rectangle is selected.

Show All

Overview The Show All command shows all parts of the artwork and deactivates the Hide command for all hidden objects. The keyboard shortcut is Command-4.

Procedure Choose Show All from the Arrange menu or press Command-4 to show hidden objects. When you choose this command, all hidden objects display and are automatically selected. Previously selected objects are deselected. If you have not hidden any objects, choosing Show All has no effect.

Tip To glimpse all hidden elements and then hide them again, choose Show All (or press Command-4), then choose Hide (Command-3) while the previously hidden objects are still selected, before clicking any other selections. To add a group of elements to a hidden set, first group the new elements, then choose Show All, Shift-click on the new group to add it to the selection, then choose Hide (see also Hide).

Show/Hide Clipboard

Overview The Show/Hide Clipboard command opens (or closes) the Clipboard window and displays its contents.

Procedure Choose Show Clipboard from the Window menu to make the contents of the Clipboard become the active window. This command becomes Hide Clipboard if the Clipboard is already the active window. Choose Hide Clipboard to hide the contents of the Clipboard, close the Clipboard window, and show the previously active window. You can also close the Clipboard window, or any active window, by clicking in the close box in the upper left corner of the window.

The phrase *<n> artwork objects* appears in the Clipboard window when you choose the Show Clipboard command, where *<n>* is the number of objects in the Clipboard. If you cut or copy any text into

Show/Hide Clipboard — PART II

the Clipboard while editing text, the text itself appears in the Clipboard window. If you hold the Option key down while you use the Copy command, the Clipboard window displays a bitmapped version of the objects (see Copy for more details; see *bitmap* in the Glossary). You cannot edit the contents of the Clipboard window.

Illustrator uses the Clipboard as temporary storage for artwork or text that you cut, copy, or paste. Illustrator artwork objects from the Clipboard can be pasted only into an Illustrator file window. Text can be pasted only into the text area of a dialog box. The following figure shows how the Clipboard works as a temporary storage in memory for objects that you cut, copy, or paste.

Use the Copy command while holding down the Option key to place a bitmapped image of your Illustrator artwork into the Clipboard

To close the Clipboard, click the close box of the Clipboard window, choose Close from the File menu, or choose Hide Clipboard from the Window menu.

Tip You can resize the Clipboard window and move it around the screen just like any other Mac window. This can be helpful if you want the Clipboard window always open but out of the way of your artwork.

| COMMANDS | Show/Hide Toolbox |

Show/Hide Rulers

Overview   The Show/Hide Rulers command displays (or hides) rulers along the inside of the scroll bars in the active window. The keyboard shortcut is Command-R. When the rulers are displayed, you can drag horizontal and vertical guides from them into the artwork window. These appear as dashed lines and exhibit the same properties as guide objects created with the Make Guide command. (See Make Guide.)

Procedure   When you choose Show Rulers from the View menu, two rulers appear, one along the bottom edge and one along the right edge of the window.

As you move the pointer, dotted lines in the rulers track your movements to indicate the current position. To remove rulers, choose Hide Rulers from the View menu or press Command-R.

To create a horizontal or vertical guide, move the mouse pointer over the appropriate ruler, then hold down the mouse button and drag into the artwork area. A ruler guide appears as a dashed line. Release the mouse button when the guide is in the desired position. Hiding the rulers has no effect on existing ruler guides, but you must show the rulers again to create new guides.

Tip   Set the type of measurement system desired using Preferences on the Edit menu (Inches, Centimeters, or Picas/Points). When the unit of measure is points (the default), the rulers display either picas or picas and points, depending on the zoom scale.

Show/Hide Toolbox

Overview   The Show/Hide Toolbox command shows (or hides) the Toolbox palette, which normally appears along the left side of the Illustrator screen.

Procedure   Hide the toolbox by choosing Hide Toolbox from the Window menu or by clicking the toolbox's close box. Display the toolbox by choosing Show Toolbox from the Window menu.

Size   PART II

Tips   Hiding the toolbox lets you use the full screen for your drawing area. You can also move the toolbox around the screen by clicking on the top border of the toolbox window and dragging it with the mouse. (Note that you can choose the selection tools, the Hand tool, and the zoom tools from the keyboard as well as from the toolbox. See descriptions of those tools in Part I for details.)

Show/Hide Unpainted Objects

Overview   The Show/Hide Unpainted Objects command shows (or hides) all objects in your artwork that have both fill and stroke set to none. When they are visible, the command reads Hide Unpainted Objects. If you use this command to hide the unpainted objects, the command then changes to read Show Unpainted Objects. You do not need to select the objects to apply this command. This command is only applicable to Artwork views—unpainted objects are always invisible in Preview mode.

Procedure   To hide all unpainted objects in your artwork, choose Hide Unpainted Objects from the View menu. To make them visible again, choose Show Unpainted Objects from the View menu.

Size

Overview   The Size command gives access to the Size submenu, from which you can specify the font size of selected text. Font size is measured in points. The Size submenu offers a choice of eleven preset font sizes, and the Other command, which lets you specify sizes that do not appear on the submenu. The keyboard shortcut for the Other command is Command-Shift-S.

Procedure   Choose this command to change the font size of selected text. If the size you wish to use appears on the submenu, you can choose it directly. If you want to use a different value, choose Other, or press

Command-Shift-S. The Font Size dialog box appears, showing the current settings for both font size and leading. You can enter values in points for both font size and leading in the Font Size dialog box, to an accuracy of one one-hundredth of a point.

Tips   If you want to change only the font size and/or leading of selected text, use the Command-Shift-S keyboard shortcut to open the Font Size dialog box. To change other attributes in addition to the size or leading, use the Type Style command, or press Command-T, instead. You can also increase or decrease the point size of selected text by pressing Command-Shift-> or Command-Shift-<. The size changes by the increment specified in the Type Preferences dialog box using the Preferences command. (See Preferences.)

Spacing Options...

Overview   The Spacing Options command lets you specify the amount of space between words and between characters in selected text. If the text is justified, you can specify minimum, desired, and maximum space between both words and letters. Spacing options apply to entire paragraphs of text. The values are expressed as percentages of the width of a space. The keyboard shortcut is Command-Shift-O.

Procedure   Select an entire text object using the Selection tool, or select a range of text using the Type tool. Then choose Spacing Options from the Type menu or press Command-Shift-O. The Spacing Options dialog box appears. In the dialog box, you can specify values for both Word Spacing and Letter Spacing.

Word Spacing controls the amount of white space between words. For justified type, you can set minimum, desired, and maximum values for word spacing. The default values are 100 percent minimum, 100 percent desired, and 150 percent maximum. At 100 percent, no additional space is added between words. With nonjustified type, you can specify the desired value only.

Style...(Paint Menu) — PART II

Letter Spacing controls the amount of white space between letters. For justified type, you can specify minimum, desired, and maximum values. The default values are 0 percent minimum, 0 percent desired, and 25 percent maximum. At 0 percent, no extra space is added between letters. (The actual amount of space is built into each font by the font's designers.) You can enter negative amounts to reduce letter spacing. With nonjustified type, you can specify the desired value only.

Tips Spacing options apply to entire paragraphs. If you want to adjust the spacing in a smaller amount of text, use the Tracking/Kerning command instead. (See Tracking/Kerning.)

Use the Spacing Options command when the word and letter spacing are the only type attributes you want to adjust. If you want to adjust other type attributes at the same time, use the Style command from the Type menu instead.

Style... (Paint Menu)

Overview The Style command under the Paint menu displays the Paint Style dialog box, which lets you set attributes for existing objects or for new objects you create, including settings for how paths or text characters are filled and stroked. Fills can be None (transparent), White, Black, Process Color, Custom Color, or Pattern. Strokes can be dashed or solid lines, with a line weight of 0 to 1296 points, in None (transparent), White, Black, Process Color, Custom Color, or Pattern. The keyboard shortcut is Command-I.

Procedure Select an object or objects with a selection tool, then choose Style from the Paint menu or press Command-I to display the Paint Style dialog box, shown in the following figure.

COMMANDS   Style...(Paint Menu)

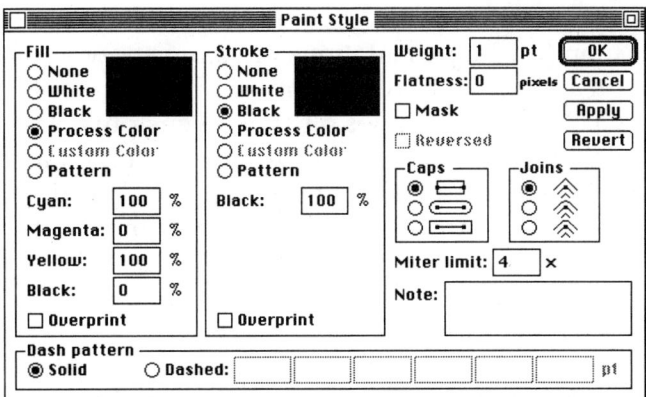

The Paint Style dialog box

The Paint Style dialog box allows you to change the following attributes by clicking on the appropriate option or by typing in the desired values.

Fill The fill options are as follows:

- None designates no fill or a transparent fill.
- White designates a white or opaque fill.
- Black designates a black fill, which can be set to percentages (shades of gray) by entering a value in the text box next to Black. The following figure shows examples of fill percentages, from 100 percent to 10 percent in increments of 10 percent.

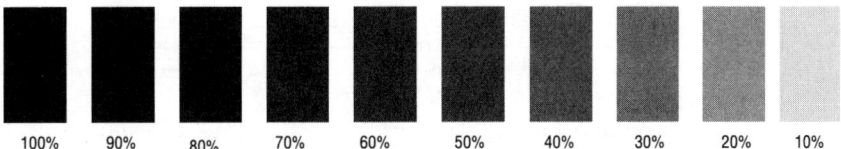

Examples of fills in various percentages

- Process Color yields virtually any color when you enter percentages for Cyan, Magenta, Yellow, and Black. Percentages can include one decimal place. As you define each color, it

143

Style...(Paint Menu) — PART II

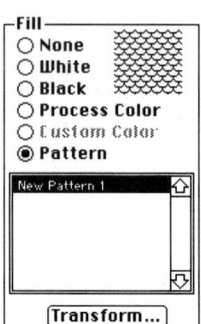

appears in a rectangle to the right of the list on your color monitor. Representations of colors show as shades of gray on a black-and-white monitor.

- Custom Color shows a list of all custom colors you created using the Custom Color command in the Paint menu, or it shows a list of all Pantone colors. The file PANTONE® Colors (coated paper) (which comes with Illustrator) must be open to show the Pantone color list. You can screen custom colors, including Pantone colors, by various percentages.

- Pattern shows the list of patterns that have been defined with Pattern under the Paint menu. As you click on each item in the list, a miniature view of the pattern appears to the right of the list. You can have access to patterns created in another file simply by opening the other file. As long as the other file is open, you will have access to all its patterns in the current file.

- When you click on Transform, the Transform Pattern Style dialog box appears. Transformations include moving, scaling, rotating, reflecting, and shearing the pattern. The pattern swatch in the Paint Style dialog box does not change, but the objects filled with the transformed pattern will show when you preview them. You can use Transform Pattern Style as a style sheet, in that if you make a change in the Transform Pattern Style dialog box, all objects painted with that pattern change.

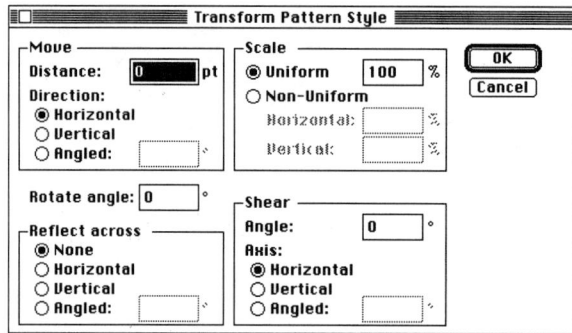

The Transform Pattern Style dialog box

144

- Overprint results in the selected object overprinting colors and percentages of black on the objects below the selected object. The default is for a knockout, a term for an overlay that "knocks out" part of an image from another image. For example, in printing white type on a black background, the white type is knocked out of the background.

Stroke A stroke (border) of an object can have any of the attributes described under Fill, as well as a weight (thickness), miter limit, end cap, join style, and dashed pattern. These features are described shortly.

Mask When you turn this option on by clicking in the check box in the Paint Style dialog box, the selected objects become a mask for viewing parts of the object or objects in your drawing. In PostScript programming this is called clipping. You can view your drawing through any shape you draw.

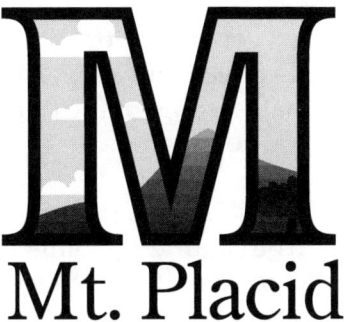

Mt. Placid

Example of a letter shape masking a mountain scene

The object assigned as the mask must be in the backmost layer. The figure on the following page outlines the procedure for masking. See Masking in Part III for further explanation of how to create masks.

Style...(Paint Menu) PART II

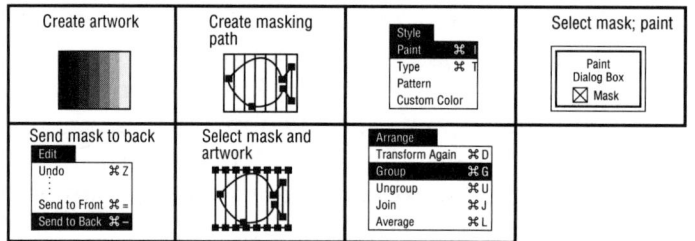

Procedure for masking

Reversed This option is dimmed unless a compound path is selected. When a compound path is created, the Reversed option is automatically applied to the foreground objects in a compound path where they overlap the background object. The result is that the foreground objects create a "hole" in the background object. If you combine compound paths into a single compound path, the objects keep their Reverse options. Illustrator reverses objects only when they first become part of a compound path.

To reverse a path within a compound path, use the Direct-selection tool to select the path; then choose Style from the Paint menu and click to turn the Reverse option on or off.

If the Reversed check box is filled with gray, this indicates that you have a mixed selection; that is, some of the objects in the selection are reversed and others are not.

Weight You can set the line weight of the stroke in points or decimal fractions of a point, from 0 to 1296 points in quarter-point increments, when Stroke is set to something other than None. This option is not available when Stroke is set to None. Lines are stroked from the center of the line that is displayed in Artwork view, outward in both directions.

Miter Limit The miter limit determines the point at which, when two lines meet at a sharp angle, Illustrator switches from a miter (pointed) to a bevel (squared-off) join. You can set the miter limit only if you have specified a miter join, otherwise the option is disabled. The miter limit default value is 4, which means that when the length of the spike formed by the miter join reaches 4 times the line weight, Illustrator switches from a miter to a bevel join. You can set the miter limit from 1 to 10. A value of 1 always creates a bevel join. See the next figure for examples of miter settings.

Caps You have a choice of three end caps for lines. This refers to the shape of the end of the line. Butt caps (the default) are squared off perpendicular to the path; the cap does not extend beyond the path. Round caps end the line in a semicircular cap with a diameter equal to the line weight. Projecting caps have square ends that project half the line weight beyond the end of the path.

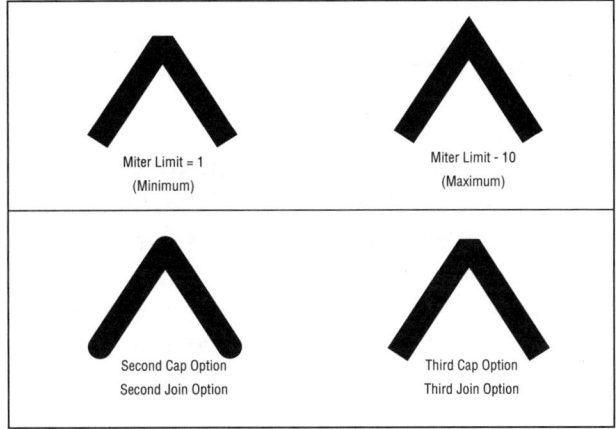

Examples of miter limit, end cap, and joins settings

Joins You have a choice of three joins for corners. Miter joins (the default) extend the edges of two converging strokes until they meet. (See Miter Limit.) Round joins connect corners with a circular arc whose diameter is equal to the line weight. Bevel joins finish the converging lines with butt caps and fill the resulting notch with a triangle, giving the corner a squared-off appearance. (See the preceding figure.)

Flatness This feature determines the precision with which Illustrator calculates curves. Illustrator constructs curves by linking anchor points with a series of very short straight line segments (though the resulting curves appear smooth to the naked eye). A

Style...(Paint Menu) PART II

low flatness value causes Illustrator to use a greater number of short line segments to create a more accurate curve. The default value is zero. Normally you do not need to adjust this value. But if you draw a very long curve, you may get a PostScript language *limitcheck* error, or your artwork may not print due to the large number of anchor points. Increasing the flatness value can prevent this error.

Note that flatness settings are device dependent. A flatness setting that works with a laser printer may not work with a Linotronic typesetter. With the flatness at the default value of zero, the screen uses a flatness setting of one and the printer uses its own preset value. You can also use a high flatness value while working to speed up screen redrawing, then change it back to a low value for final printing.

Note You can type descriptive notes about a particular set of Paint settings as shown in the Note area of the dialog box. These notes do not print out, but you can use them as production aids or descriptions of when the specified Paint attributes are to be used. They appear as comments in the generated PostScript code, so you can also use the Note area for comments that will help you find specific portions of code if you will be modifying the PostScript code directly.

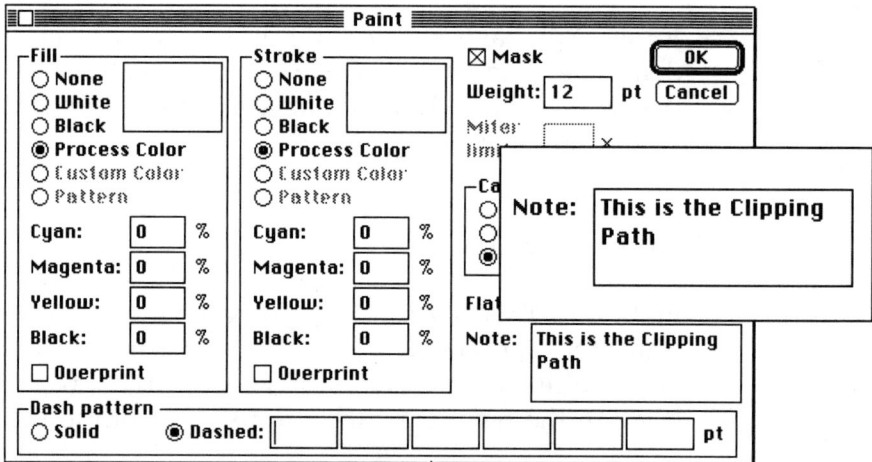

Example of Note text describing a Paint setting

Dash Pattern This is enabled when Stroke is set to any weight. When stroke is set to None, the Dash pattern option is disabled.

You can set up custom dashed lines by clicking on Dashed. If you want an evenly dashed line with black dashes the same length as the white gaps, as shown in the first example in the following figure, enter one value (in points) for the interval in the first box provided. If you want two different measurements for the black and white portions of a line with a black stroke, which produces variations of dashed and/or dotted lines, enter the length of the black intervals in the first box and the length of the white intervals in the second box. You can create complex dashed lines by entering up to six values for intervals. The fourth example in the figure shows three values for intervals; the fifth example shows values entered in all six interval boxes.

■ ■
Dash pattern: [5]

■■ ■■ ■■ ■■ ■■ ■■ ■■ ■■ ■■ ■■ ■■ ■■ ■■
Dash pattern: [5] [2]

. . . .
Dash pattern: [2] [5]

■■ . ■■ . ■■ . ■■ . ■■ . ■■ . ■■ . ■■
Dash pattern: [5] [2] [10]

■■■ ■■■ ■■■ ■■■ ■■■ ■■■ ■■■ ■■
Dash pattern: [5] [2] [10] [1] [8] [8] [4]

Examples of dashed line settings

The Paint Style dialog box has four control buttons. Click OK to apply the changes you have made and close the dialog box. Click Cancel to close the dialog box and discard any changes you have made. Click Apply to apply the changes you have made and leave the dialog box open. Click Revert to restore all settings to the state they were in when you opened the dialog box and leave the dialog box open.

Style... (Type Menu)

Overview   The Style command under the Type menu displays the Type Style dialog box, shown in the next figure. The Type Style dialog box lets you specify the font style, size, leading, spacing, and alignment of selected type, and lets you type text in the bottom box. The keyboard shortcut is Command-T.

Procedure   Select the text you wish to format using any of the techniques described under The Selection Tools and The Type Tools, then choose Style from the Type menu or press Command-T to display the Type Style dialog box. If you choose Style from the Type menu when more than one text object is selected, you will globally change type attributes for all selected text objects.

The Type Style dialog box

The Type Style dialog box lets you set the following character-level type specifications:

Font   The Font pop-up menu lets you choose a font for the selected text. The pop-up menu is identical to the Font submenu obtained from the Font command on the Type menu. (See Font.)

Size   The Size field lets you enter a font size, in points, for the selected text. (See Size.)

Style...(Type Menu)

Leading The Leading field lets you enter a leading value, in points, for the selected text. (See Leading.)

Tracking/Kerning The Tracking/Kerning field lets you enter a tracking value for the selected text in units of 1/1000 of an em space. Negative numbers reduce the space between characters; positive numbers increase it. The label reads Kerning if there is an active insertion point between two characters, otherwise it reads Tracking. (See Tracking/Kerning.)

Vertical Shift The Vertical shift field lets you shift the selected text above or below the baseline. The units used are those you specified in the Vertical Shift units field in the Type Preferences dialog box using the Preferences command. (See Preferences.) Positive increments shift the type above the baseline; negative increments shift it below the baseline.

Horizontal Scale The Horizontal scale field lets you condense or expand the selected type by entering a percentage. Unscaled type is 100 percent. Percentages greater than 100 percent expand the type; percentages less than 100 percent condense it. Scaling is different from tracking: with tracking, only the space between the characters is adjusted, while with scaling, the vertical and horizontal proportions of the letterforms themselves are changed.

Auto Leading Turning this option on causes Illustrator to apply Auto leading, which is 120 percent of the font size.

Auto Kerning Turning this option on causes Illustrator to use the pair-kerning tables built into the font. Any manual kerning values you set override auto-kerning values.

In addition to character-level type attributes, the Type Style dialog box lets you set the following paragraph-level attributes:

Indentation You can enter left, right, and first line indent values. The Left indent indents the left edge of the paragraph from the left side of the baseline by the specified amount. The Right indent in-

Style...(Type Menu) — PART II

dents the right edge of the paragraph from the right side of the baseline by the specified amount. The First Line indent indents the beginning of the first line of the paragraph from the left edge of the paragraph. The units used are those you specified in the Indent/Shift units field in the Type Preferences dialog box using the Preferences command. (See Preferences.)

Alignment   You can specify Left, Right, Centered, or Justified alignment. If you specify Justified alignment, you have the option of whether or not to justify the last line in a paragraph. If you choose to justify the last line it stretches the full width of the paragraph.

Hanging Punctuation   Turning this option on places punctuation marks that fall at the ends of lines outside the paragraph margins.

Leading Before   The Leading before field lets you enter a value, in points, for extra leading (vertical space) before paragraphs.

Spacing Options   Clicking this button opens the Spacing Options dialog box, where you can specify the amount of space between words and between characters in the selected paragraph or paragraphs. If the text is justified, you can specify minimum, desired, and maximum space between both words and letters. This is the same dialog box as that opened by choosing Spacing Options from the Type menu. (See Spacing Options.)

   The Type Style dialog box has four control buttons. Click OK to apply the changes you have made and close the dialog box. Click Cancel to close the dialog box and discard any changes you have made. Click Apply to apply the changes you have made and to leave the dialog box open. Click Revert to restore all settings to the state they were in when you opened the dialog box and to leave the dialog box open.

| COMMANDS | Tracking/Kerning |

Template Only

Overview   The Template Only command displays only the template in the active window.

Procedure   Choose Template Only from the View menu when you wish to examine a template without seeing your artwork.
You cannot make changes to the artwork in Template Only mode.

Tracking/Kerning

Overview   The Tracking/Kerning command lets you control the space between adjacent text characters. The appearance of this command on the menu differs according to what is selected. If you place an insertion point between two characters, the command is Kern. If a range of text or an entire text object is selected, the command is Tracking. The keyboard shortcut is Command-Shift-K.

Procedure   Select the text for which you want to adjust the tracking or place an insertion point between two characters that you want to kern. Then choose Tracking/Kerning from the Type menu or press Command-Shift-K. The Tracking or Kerning dialog box appears, according to the selection. Type a value in the dialog box, then click OK to apply the adjustment and close the dialog box. The units used are 1/1000 of an em space. (An em space is the same width as an upper-case M.) Positive values increase the space between characters; negative values reduce the space between characters.

Tips   To view the kerning value between two characters, click a text tool to place an insertion point between the two characters and press the Option key. The information bar at the lower left corner of the screen displays the kerning value.
To move two characters closer together, place an insertion point between them, then press the Option key and the left arrow key. To

153

move them apart, press the Option key and the right arrow key. The characters move by the increment specified in the Type Preferences dialog box using the Preferences command. (See Preferences.) To move characters by 5 times this increment, use Command-Option-left arrow or Command-Option-right arrow.

Transform Again

Overview   The Transform Again command repeats the most recent transformation. The keyboard shortcut is Command-D. Transformations that can be repeated are those created using the Scale, Rotate, Reflect, and Shear tools. Moving of objects can also be repeated using Transform Again. Blending cannot be transformed again. If the last transformation also made a copy of the object, Transform Again will transform and make another copy.

Procedure   After transforming an object, choose Transform Again from the Arrange menu or press Command-D to repeat the transformation.

There are numerous applications for Transform Again. For example, you can draw a single object, use the Rotate tool to rotate a copy around a central point, then press Command-D as many times as needed to make a radially symmetrical object. (See also The Rotate Tool and Radial Symmetry: Methods 1 and 2 in Part III for examples of objects created this way.)

Another common application is the creation of a shaded effect. You can draw a single object, use the Scale tool to scale a slightly smaller copy inside the first object's closed path, then use Paint from the Style menu to set a lighter fill for the second object. Press Command-D as many times as you need to make a series of progressively smaller objects of the same shape, each time following Command-D with Command-I (for the Paint command). You can intersperse other commands with Command-D in this way, as long as only one of the commands is a transformation (Scale, Rotate, Reflect, Shear, or Move). (See The Scale Tool for examples of objects shaded in this way, The Blend Tool, and Highlights in Part III.)

Tip Each newly transformed copy will appear on the top layer of the artwork. When creating a series of objects, always start with the one that will end up on the bottom layer.

Undo/Redo

Overview The Undo/Redo command reverses the last operation you performed. The keyboard shortcut is Command-Z.

Procedure Choose Undo or Redo from the Edit menu or press Command-Z. The text of the command that is displayed in the menu varies depending on the last operation. If the operation can be undone, the command becomes Undo, followed by the name of the action—for example, Undo Clear. If the action cannot be undone, Undo appears dimmed, indicating that the Undo command is disabled.

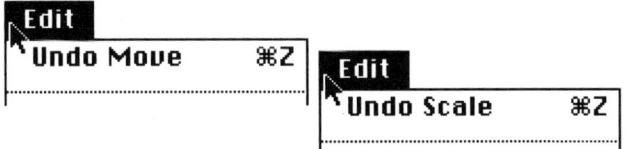

Examples of the Undo command

After you undo an action, the Undo command becomes Redo, followed by the name of the action—for example, Redo Clear. This way, you can redo undone actions. The specific Undo/Redo command remains on the Edit menu until you choose another command.

Ungroup

Overview The Ungroup command breaks a group into independent objects, ungrouped paths, or subgroups (if a group has grouped objects within it). The keyboard shortcut is Command-U.

Procedure   Select a grouped path or a group of objects with the Selection tool and choose Ungroup from the Arrange menu or press Command-U. If a group consists of other grouped objects, you must ungroup the subgroups repeatedly to reduce them into individual objects.

Unlink

Overview   The Unlink command unlinks linked text paths that make up a text object. The keyboard shortcut is Command-Shift-U.

Procedure   Select the text object you want to unlink using the Selection tool, then choose Unlink from the Type menu, or press Command-Shift-U. All the component text paths in the text object are unlinked and selected. The text remains in the individual text paths, but no longer flows from one path to the next. You cannot unlink only one text path from a text object that contains multiple paths. All the paths in the text object become separate unlinked text objects when you choose Unlink.

Unlock All

Overview   The Unlock All command unlocks all locked objects so they can be selected and modified. The keyboard shortcut is Command-2.

Procedure   Choose Unlock All from the Arrange menu or press Command-2. This action unlocks all locked objects and automatically selects them. You do not need to select objects before unlocking them. Previously selected objects are deselected. If you have not locked any objects, Unlock All has no effect.

Tip   If you inadvertently select the Unlock All command, immediately select Lock again. (See also Lock.) Since invoking Unlock All results in all locked objects being selected, this quick recovery makes it easy to restore the locked status of the selected objects.

Use Column Design...

Overview The Use Column Design command lets you use any graph design created with the Define Graph Design command in a column graph. This command is only available if a graph design has been defined in an open document *and* one or more columns in a column graph are currently selected. The keyboard shortcut is Command-Shift-Option-C.

Procedure Select the entire column graph using the Selection tool, or select those columns and legends for which you want to substitute the design using the Direct-selection tool. Then choose Use Column Design from the Graph menu or press Command-Shift-Option-C. The Graph Column Design dialog box appears as shown below.

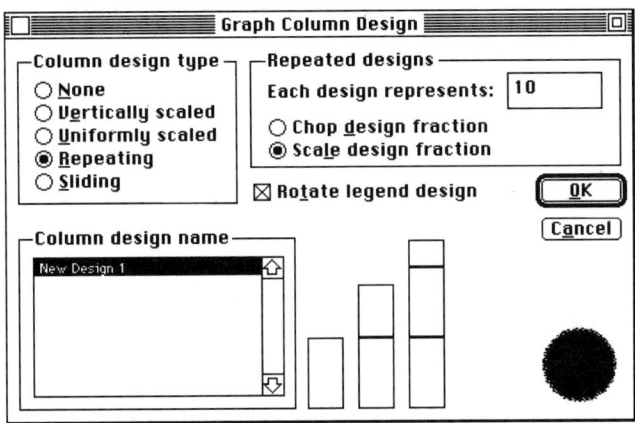

The Graph Column Design dialog box

The Graph Column Design dialog box lets you control how graph designs appear in your graph. The Column design type options are as follows:

None Click None to convert a graph or column that uses a graph design back to regular columns.

Vertically Scaled   Click this button to scale the graph design vertically to the height of the selected column or columns.

Uniformly Scaled   Click this button to scale the graph design uniformly to the height of the selected column or columns.

Repeating   Click this button to create columns of repeating graph designs. If you use this option, you must also enter a value in the Each design represents field, and click either the Chop design fraction or Scale design fraction button, under the Repeated designs options. These options are dimmed unless you choose the Repeating option from Column design type. Chop design fraction places a truncated design at the top of columns where the column value is not an exact multiple of the unit specified in the Each design represents field. Scale design fraction uses a vertically scaled design instead.

Sliding   Click this button to use sliding column designs. To use this option, the graph design you choose must contain a guide that indicates the sliding point. (See Define Graph Design.)

Rotate Legend Design   Click this option to rotate the design that appears in the legend 90 degrees.

The Column design name area shows a scrolling list of all available graph designs. You can make any graph design available by opening a document that contains the design.

If you want a set of graph designs to be available automatically whenever you use Illustrator, create an Illustrator file containing all the graph designs you want, then name it Adobe Illustrator Startup, and place it in the folder containing the Illustrator application. (If you keep the application on the desktop, place the Adobe Illustrator Startup file in your startup disk's disk window.) You can also include custom colors, fonts, and patterns in the Adobe Illustrator Startup document. These elements will automatically be available whenever you use Illustrator.

Use Marker Design...

Overview   The Use Marker Design command lets you use any graph design created with the Define Graph Design command in a line or scatter graph. This command is only available if a graph design has been defined in an open document *and* one or more data points in a line or scatter graph are currently selected. The keyboard shortcut is Command-Shift-Option-M.

Procedure   Select the entire graph using the Selection tool or select those data points and legends for which you want to substitute the design using the Direct-selection tool. Then choose Use Marker Design from the Graph menu or press Command-Shift-Option-M. The Graph Marker Design dialog box appears.

The Graph Marker Design dialog box lets you control how graph designs appear in your graph. Click None to convert an existing data point that uses a marker design back to the default square marker design. Click on data point to replace the selected data point markers and legends with a graph design. Choose the graph design from the scrolling list under Marker design name.

Window Titles

Overview   The last section of the Window menu contains a list of all currently open windows. Selecting a window name from the menu places a check mark beside its name in the Window menu and makes that window the active window.

Procedure   Using the usual techniques of selecting from a menu, choose the name of the window you wish to make active from the Window menu.

Tip   If you can see part of a window behind the active window, you can activate it by clicking on it on the screen; you need not use the Window menu.

Part III:
Techniques

| TECHNIQUES | Introduction |

Introduction to Techniques

This part of the book presents over fifty different techniques for achieving specific effects that can be applied to a wide range of applications. Variations of these techniques can be used to create the particular effects you want to apply in your own artwork.

The techniques are divided into seven basic categories:

CATEGORY	DESCRIPTION
Alignment	Techniques for aligning objects, measuring objects, and creating grids as backgrounds for artwork that requires careful alignment.
Text	Techniques for aligning text in tabular columns, horizontally and vertically, and on a curved path.
Fills and Patterns	Techniques for creating custom fill patterns, blending colors, and using a custom paint palette for quickly selecting the fill and stroke settings you want to use repeatedly in developing complex or multiple pages of artwork.
Layering	Techniques for working in layers, including creating compound lines, masking, and creating overlays.
Lines	Techniques for creating dotted lines, lines with a hand-drawn look, and parallel curves.
Shapes (Closed Paths)	Techniques for selecting and editing parts of generated charts, creating arrows, organization charts, polygons, symmetrical designs, objects that share irregular borders, star shapes, and solid objects with "see-through" holes cut out of the center.
Three-Dimensional Effects	Techniques for drawing cubes, coils, drop shadows, flowers, and highlights.

Within each of these categories, you will find each technique listed alphabetically. The results of each technique are shown at the top outside corner of each page for easy reference.

PART III: TECHNIQUES

Alignment

Aligning Objects: Method 1

There are two approaches to aligning objects: (1) aligning them as you create them (described here), and (2) aligning them after you create them (described in the next technique).

Any illustration that is composed of more than one object, such as the series of squares illustrated in the accompanying figure, probably calls for careful alignment procedures.

There are two strategies you can use to align objects. The first strategy is to drag the original object while holding both the Shift key (to force alignment along the horizontal or vertical axis) and the Option key (to create a copy of the object). You may then edit the copied object if you desire.

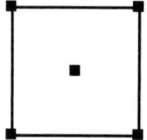

1

Create the first object using whatever tool is appropriate (Freehand tool, Autotrace tool, Pen tool, Type tools, Rectangle tools, or Oval tools). For example, use a Rectangle tool to create a rectangular object, as shown in the figure on the left.

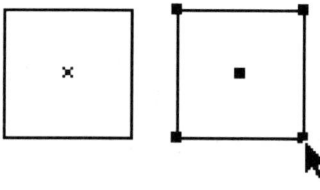

2

If subsequent objects are to be identical, drag the first object to the new position, and hold the Shift and Option keys to align and copy the object as you release the mouse button.

ALIGNMENT

3

Select Transform Again from the Arrange menu (Command-D) to align another copy of the object the same relative distance apart. Press Command-D for each additional copy you wish to make.

4

Modify the copied objects as appropriate *after* you have used the Transform Again command.

5

Once you have positioned all the objects, you can select them all and use the Group command under the Arrange menu (Command-G) to group them and thereby keep them in alignment when you want to move them as a unit.

See also Aligning Objects: Method 2, Aligning Text: Methods 1 and 2, and Tabular Text.

PART III: TECHNIQUES

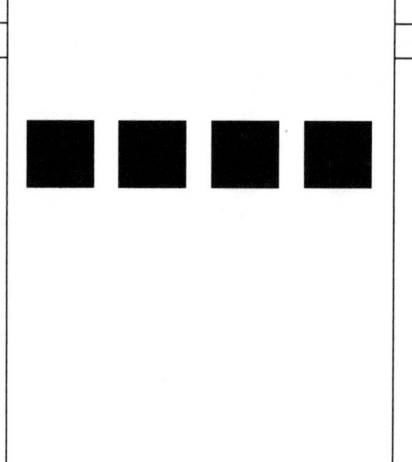

Aligning Objects: Method 2

The second strategy for aligning objects, to align objects after you create them, is to draw nonprinting guidelines on the page. You can also use this technique to align scissor cuts when cutting an object in half.

1

Create the objects using whatever tools are appropriate, positioning them roughly where you want them to be on the screen.

The figure on the left shows four squares created with the Rectangle tool. Notice that they are not exactly aligned.

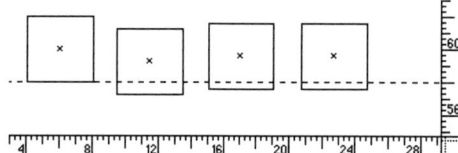

2

Choose Show Rulers (Command-R) from the View menu (if they are not already displayed) and drag a horizontal guide from the horizontal ruler onto the page.

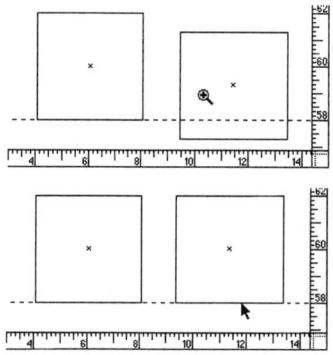

3

Select the Zoom-in tool (or hold down the Command key and Spacebar) and click on the objects you want to align, to invoke a magnified view. Press the Command key to get the Selection tool, and drag each object to touch the ruler guide.

ALIGNMENT

4

Once you have positioned all of the objects, you can select them all and use the Group command under the Arrange menu (Command-G) to group them and thereby keep them in alignment when you want to move them as a unit.

See also Grid: Methods 1–3.

PART III: TECHNIQUES

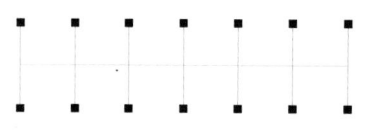

Dividing Equally

You may find that it is necessary to divide a shape or a line into a specific number of segments. Even dividing something in half can be difficult if you rely on the rulers or the Measure tool as your only aids. With the following technique, you do not need to actually calculate the divisions; Illustrator does it for you.

Common applications for this technique include dividing lines and shapes for technical or architectural drawings or creating grids and guidelines for templates and artwork. This is also an easy way to create forms.

1

For this demonstration, first use the Pen tool with the Shift key to draw a horizontal line of any length. This is the line you will divide into equal segments.

2

Select the Pen tool and draw a short vertical line. With the Snap to Point option turned on, snap this vertical line to one endpoint of the horizontal line. Hold down the Command key to get the Selection tool and drag this vertical line to the opposite endpoint of the horizontal line and snap once again, holding down both the Shift key (to align the second tick relative to the first tick along the horizontal axis) and the Option key (to create a copy) as you release the mouse button.

ALIGNMENT	

3

Using the Object-selection tool, Shift-click (or using the Selection tool, Option-Shift-click) both vertical lines to select both lines and their anchor points.

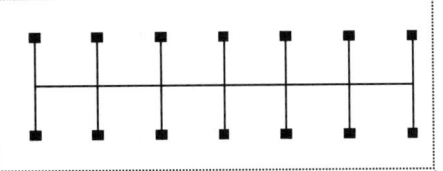

4

Choose the Blend tool and click once on the top point of each of the vertical lines. When the Blend dialog box appears, type in a number that is one less than the number of parts you would like. For example, if you would like to divide the line into six equal parts, type in 5 for number of steps. Click OK. In this example, five dividers are added at six equal intervals between the two end lines.

This procedure adds dividers but does not actually break the horizontal line into segments. If you want to break up the horizontal line into separate parts, you can use the Scissors tool.

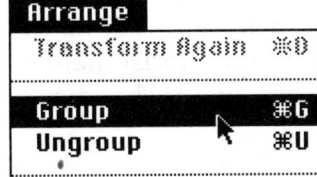

5

If the divisions look correct, drag the Selection tool to display the selection marquee over all of the lines and choose Group from the Arrange menu (Command-G). This way the dividers will retain their relative positions if you move them later.

See also The Measure Tool, Measuring with a Point, and Grid: Methods 1–3.

Grid: Method 1—Quadrille Rules

Often you will need to have an accurate grid or guidelines to follow in an illustration. For instance, some artists like to create custom perspective guidelines and use them as templates. Or maybe you have a custom grid for your newsletter.

If you have a drawing of the grid or guidelines and you have a scanner, you can scan the printed grid and use the scanned template as a background while you work. But you may find the lines on a scanned template are too coarse for your needs. Using the grid as the template also precludes using other images as the template.

This grid technique shows you how to create a grid of squared rules at a scale you choose. You can use this type of grid as a template for any illustrations that require a squared grid for alignment.

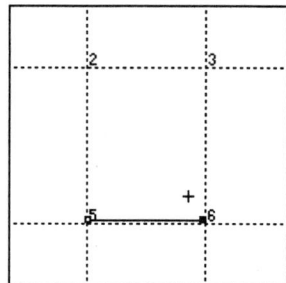

1

Select the Pen tool and hold down the Shift key as you click the mouse on two endpoints to draw a straight horizontal line across the bottom of the page, as shown in the figure on the left.

Note that in steps 1 and 3, the page area can be the entire 18-inch Illustrator page, or the smaller paper size ($8\frac{1}{2}$" by 11"). For large pages, perform steps 1 and 3 in the Fit In Window view, which you select from the View menu or by pressing Command-M.

ALIGNMENT

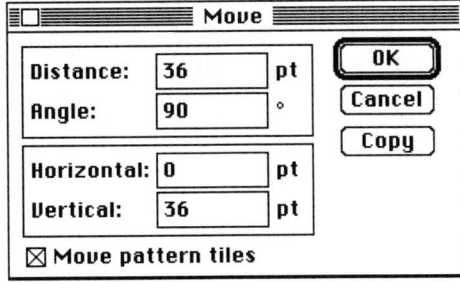

2

Hold down the Command key to get the current Selection tool, and Option-click on the line to select the entire path. Option-click the Selection tool in the toolbox to get the Move dialog box. Select Vertical move by clicking this option, and enter a value in the Distance box (in points) that matches your desired grid size—for example, 36 points (one-half inch). Click Copy to close the box and make a copy of the first line.

Use Tranform Again (Command-D) as many times as you need to fill the image area with grid lines.

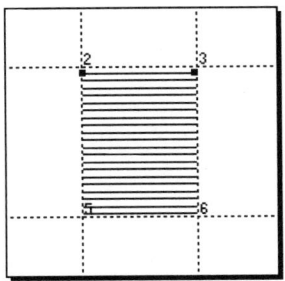

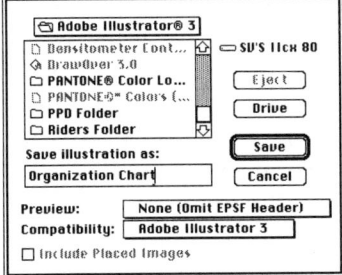

3

Choose Select All from the Edit menu (Command-A), then select the Rotate-dialog tool and click (or select the Rotate tool and Option-click) on the center of the grid to get the Rotate dialog box. Type 90 (degrees) in the Angle box, and click Copy to close the box and rotate a copy of the horizontal lines, to create a vertical grid.

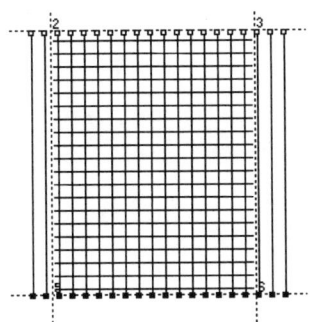

171

PART III: TECHNIQUES

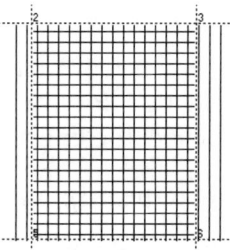

4
While the vertical grid lines are still selected, move them if necessary to center over the horizontal grid lines.

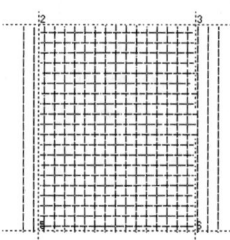

5
Choose Select All from the Edit menu (Command-A), then choose Make Guide (Command-5) from the Arrange menu.

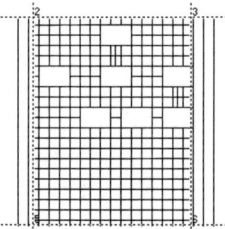

6
Save the grid as a boilerplate document that you can use repeatedly.

When you open the master to start a new document, use the Save As command (from the File menu) to give it a new name so the original grid boilerplate document will remain unchanged.

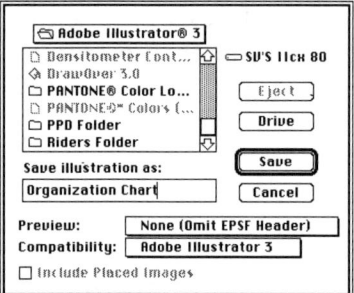

| ALIGNMENT |

Tip: Using the grid as part of the artwork will give you the possibility of more precision in positioning objects relative to the grid, but it will also increase the overall size of files. You can reduce file size by deleting the grid when the artwork is finished.

PART III: TECHNIQUES

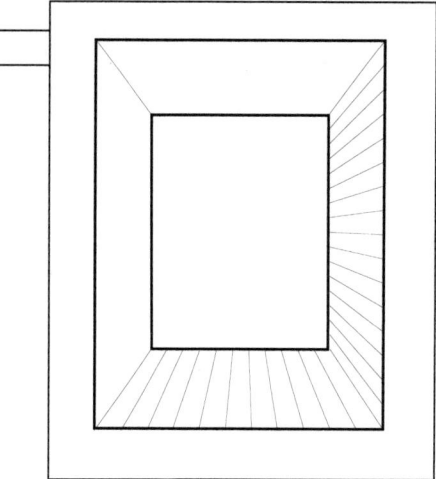

Grid: Method 2—Perspective

Grid: Method 1 showed you how to create a simple squared grid. This technique enables you to create a grid that shows perspective, like the one shown in the accompanying figure.

You can use this grid as a template for any illustrations that show three-dimensional perspective of single objects, or for several objects that will appear to be standing beside each other.

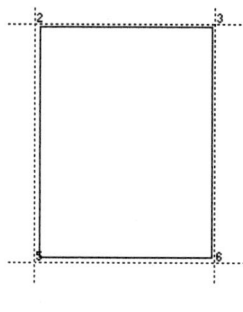

1

Use the Rectangle tool or the Centered-rectangle tool to draw a rectangle the size of the finished illustration. In the figure on the left, the size of the rectangle is the size of the page. Delete the center point by direct-selecting it and pressing the Delete or Backspace key.

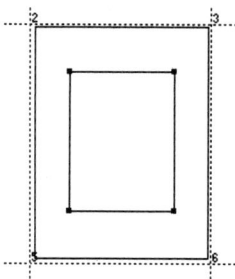

2

Use the Scale tool to make one smaller copy of the rectangle (see The Scale Tools in Part I). Position the smaller rectangle inside the first rectangle.

The smaller the copy, the deeper the perspective will seem. Also, the positioning of the smaller rectangle will determine the viewer's perspective.

| ALIGNMENT |

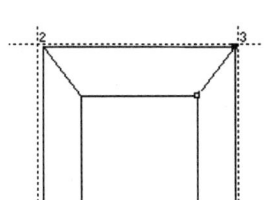

3

Use the Pen tool with the Shift key to connect corresponding corners of each rectangle with straight lines, as shown in the figure on the left.

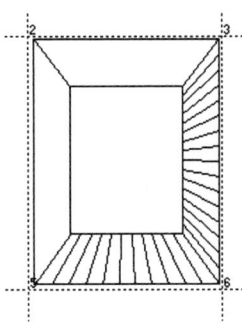

4

Use the Blend tool to add more grid lines for depth (see The Blend Tool in Part I). To keep the grid as simple as possible, add grid lines only to two sides, such as the bottom and right sides of the field, as shown in the figure on the left.

Use Select All (Command-A) and choose Make Guide (Command-5) from the Arrange menu.

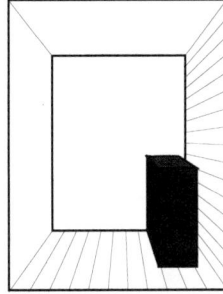

5

In drawing three-dimensional objects, use the diagonal depth lines as guides in drawing the side walls of the object, but maintain horizontal and vertical lines for the front face of the object. For example, in the figure on the left, the front and back faces are normal rectangles, but the side walls follow diagonal grid lines.

PART III: TECHNIQUES

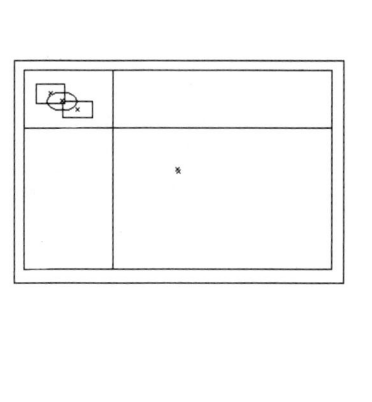

Grid: Method 3—Page Layout

You can use the grid shown in the accompanying figure in creating a series of illustrations that must all conform to the same page layout specifications. Then use this grid as a template for creating each document.

You can use this technique to create any template system for consistent page layout, such as a series of ads, a series of overheads or slides, or a series of charts.

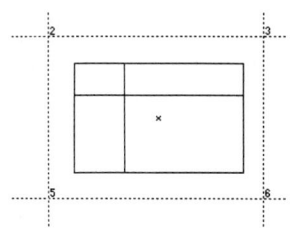

1

Determine the basic grid of the page layout and sketch it with the Pen tool and/or the Rectangle tool.

2

Use the Select All command to select the entire grid and choose Make Guide (Command-5) from the Arrange menu.

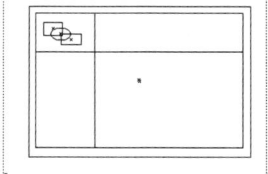

3

Add ruled lines and standing text that are intended to print on every page. Use Select All (Command-A) and Lock (Command-1) to lock the objects in place so they will not be selected or moved as you work.

ALIGNMENT

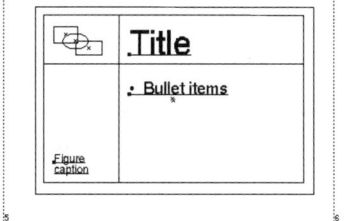

4

Add dummy text blocks that will change on each page and move them into their fixed positions. The figure on the left shows dummy text blocks.

The content of the dummy text blocks will be altered for each page, but their positioning will not.

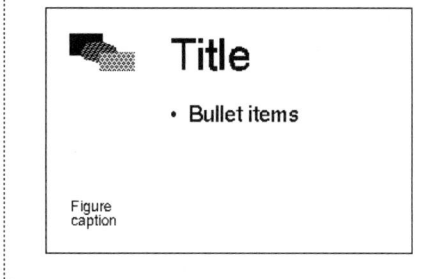

5

Save the grid as a boilerplate document that you can use repeatedly.

Tip: When you open the boilerplate to start a new document, immediately use Save As from the File menu to give it a new name so the original grid boilerplate document will remain unchanged.

See also Spacing Guides.

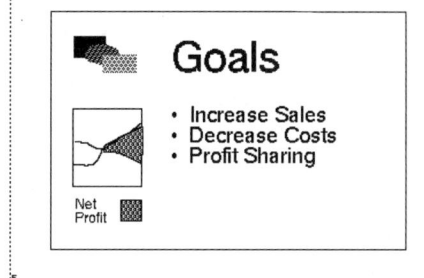

PART III: TECHNIQUES

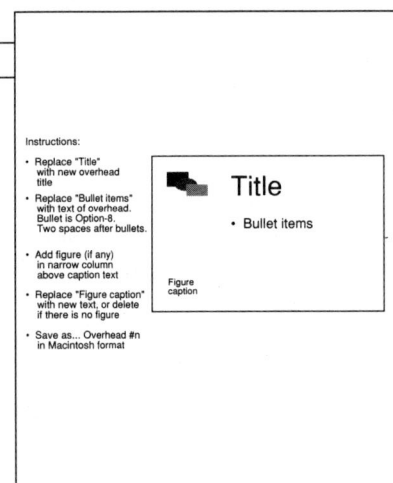

"Hidden" Notes

In working with complex illustrations that involve many grouped objects and layers, you can type notes about how the file is organized for your own reference or for others who might need to edit the artwork later.

This technique is especially useful if you are working in a group where work on a single illustration is shared among several people, or when you are working on many different, complex illustrations that you must modify over a period of time. Hidden notes can also be helpful on a boilerplate document that will be "cloned" to create many illustrations in a series, as in this example.

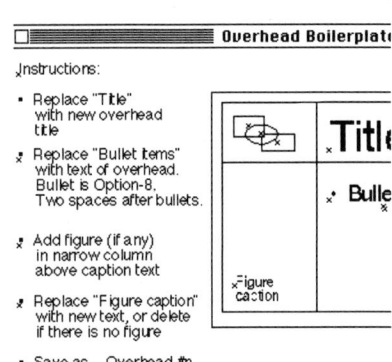

1

Use the Type tool to type notes (such as instructions about alignment or how the artwork is organized) as text, directly on the artwork. These can be typed in one area on a page of the document that is not used by the artwork, or they can be scattered around on the artwork, with each note close to the objects it addresses.

ALIGNMENT	

	Instructions:
	• Replace "Title"
	  with new overhead
	  title
	• Replace "Bullet items"
	  with text of overhead.

```
┌─Fill──────────┐   ┌─Stroke────────┐
│ ⦿ None        │   │ ⦿ None        │
│ ○ White       │   │ ○ White       │
│ ○ Black       │   │ ○ Black       │
│ ○ Process Color│  │ ○ Process Color│
│ ○ Custom Color│   │ ○ Custom Color│
│ ○ Pattern     │   │ ○ Pattern     │
│               │   │               │
└───────────────┘   └───────────────┘
```

2

Select all notes, group them (Command-G), and use the Style command from the Paint menu (Command-I) to give them a Fill and Stroke of None so they do not print out as part of the artwork.

If the notes are grouped, you can easily change the paint specifications from Fill Black (for drafts on which the notes will print out) to Fill None (so the notes will not print out).

Tip: Use a small font that is easy to read on the screen. To fit many notes in a small space, you can make the font as small as 1 point so the notes will be readable on the screen only at the highest magnification.

PART III: TECHNIQUES

■ 1 inch ■

Measuring with a Point

Here is a quick and effective way to measure distance and angle, as a supplement to Illustrator's Measure tool.

You can use this technique on any artwork. By keeping your measuring point handy, you will not need to select the Measure tool.

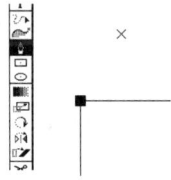

1

Create a single anchor point by clicking the Pen tool once on the page, as the figure on the left shows. This point will be your measuring point.

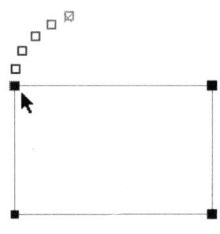

2

Using any selection tool, click on and move the point to a starting place for measuring, as shown in the figure on the left. You can measure an actual object you have drawn or measure empty space in the drawing window.

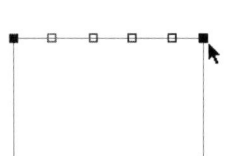

3

Select the point again and move it across the page the distance you would like to measure. If you are measuring a horizontal or vertical distance, hold down the Shift key to constrain your movement and measurement along 45-degree angles.

ALIGNMENT

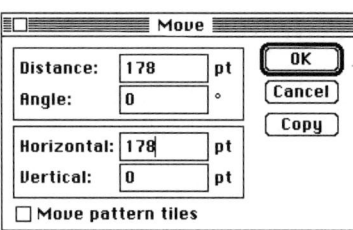

4

Option-click on the Selection tool to view the Move dialog box. The distance and angle that you moved the point will be shown here.

See also The Measure Tool in Part I and Grid: Methods 1–3.

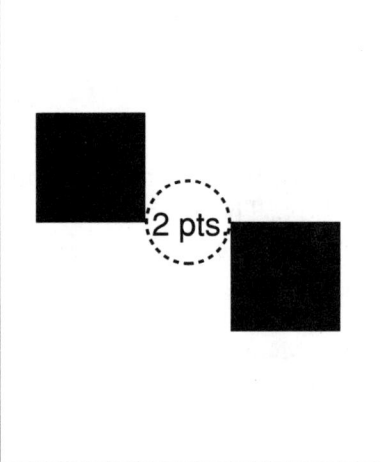

PART III: TECHNIQUES

Spacing Guides

It is a good idea to apply consistent standards for spacing between objects in an illustration. Here is one technique that supplements the Measure tool by storing the spacing information as part of the artwork, in the form of a graphic object with Fill and Stroke of None.

This technique is especially useful when you need to create a series of illustrations that meet consistent standards for spacing between objects or between graphic elements and text elements.

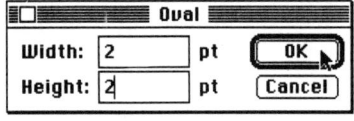

1

Select either Oval tool and click once in the active window to get the Oval dialog box. Enter the same value for the Height and Width of the oval to draw a perfect circle. The value should match the space that you wish to make consistent between objects.

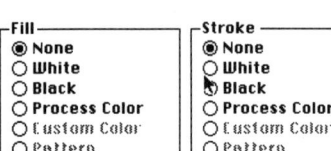

2

Choose Style from the Paint menu (Command-I). Set the Stroke and Fill options of the circle to None. Click OK to close the dialog box.

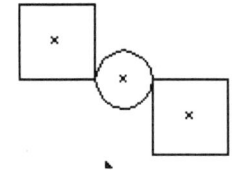

3

Whenever you need to position two objects next to each other, drag the circle to meet one edge of one object, then bring the second object to meet the opposite edge of the circle.

ALIGNMENT

4

If you need more than one spacing guide to measure different distances, type a text label for each guide using the Type tool, group the label with the circle by selecting the guide object and the text and choosing Group from the Arrange menu (Command-G), and set the Stroke and Fill of the text to None using Style from the Paint menu (Command-I).

Tips: By using a circle instead of a line or a rectangle as a measuring guide, you can measure distances consistently at any angle—not only vertical and horizontal distances.

By setting Stroke and Fill to None, you can keep the circle as part of the artwork but it will not display in Preview or print out. This technique also lets you move the spacing guide around on the page as needed; you could not move it if you used the Make Guide command to set it as a nonprinting guide.

See also Grid: Methods 1–3, Measuring with a Point, The Measure Tool, "Hidden" Notes.

PART III: TECHNIQUES

Text

Aligning Text: Method 1

Adobe Illustrator 3.0 provides enhanced features for handling text that enable you to create long text blocks and to mix fonts within a text block—you are no longer forced to create separate text blocks for long text or mixed fonts. However, if you choose to create a series of separate text blocks, you can align them using one of the next two techniques. The first technique involves aligning text along the same vertical grid line. The basic strategy in aligning text along a vertical grid is to drag the first text object while holding both the Shift key (forcing alignment) and the Option key (creating a copy of the block). You can then edit the copied block.

1
Select the Type tool and click or drag on the screen where you want the text to start. Type in the text; the characters appear onscreen as you type.

2
Hold down the Command key to get the current Selection tool, and drag the text block down. Hold the Shift and Option keys to align and copy the text as you release the mouse button.

| TEXT | | Text
Text
Text |

3

Select the text with the I-beam pointer to edit the new block of text and change the text content or style.

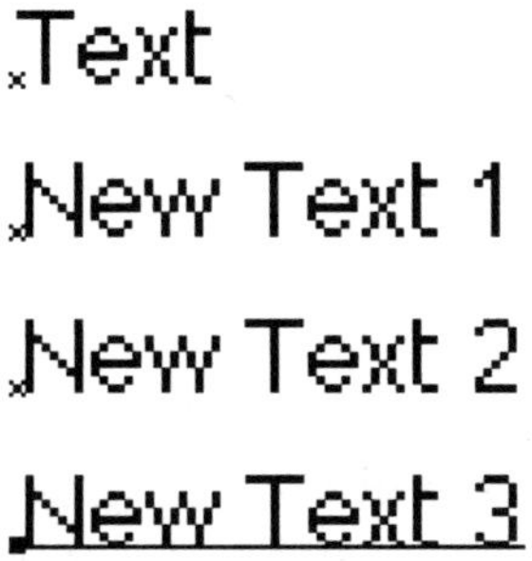

4

Continue creating new blocks by copying and aligning the most recently changed block with the Option and Shift keys, or use the Transform Again command to create new text objects based on the distance of the second text object from the first.

Warning: Be sure to choose the correct type specifications (font size, style, and so on) before you perform this procedure. If you change the specifications of the blocks *after* you align them, you may have to realign each one.

PART III: TECHNIQUES

Aligning Text: Method 2

This technique involves the Average command; it can be used to align a series of text blocks vertically or horizontally. The technique cannot be used to adjust the spacing between text blocks.

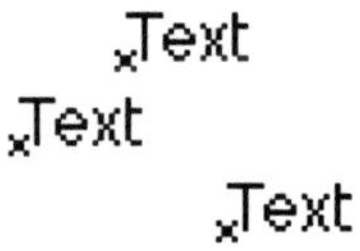

1

Create the text blocks using either Type tool, roughly positioning them where you want them to be on the screen.

The figure on the left shows three separate text blocks. Notice that they are not exactly aligned.

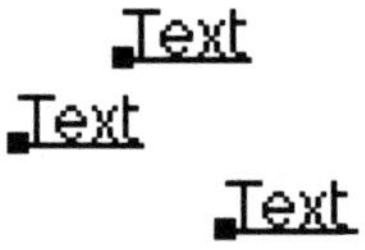

2

Select all of the text blocks using the Selection tool or the Select All command under the Edit menu (Command-A), or by dragging the selection marquee around the baselines of the type (see The Selection Tools in Part I).

TEXT

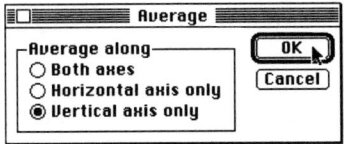

3 With all of the text blocks selected, choose Average from the Arrange menu (Command-L). In the Average dialog box, click Horizontal axis only if the text blocks are already arranged beside each other; or click Vertical axis only if the text blocks are already arranged one above the other; then click OK or press Return to close the dialog box and align the text blocks.

See also Average in Part II, and Aligning Objects: Methods 1 and 2 and Grid: Methods 1–3 in Part III.

Year	Sales	%	Goals Met
1986	15,356	16%	NO
1987	21,872	19%	YES
1988	29,845	23%	YES

Tabular Text

Adobe Illustrator does not have tab settings like those of word processors, but the technique described here can be used to create the appearance of tabular material. The different columns of text need not be set in the same font.

This technique is useful whenever you need to create columns and rows of text that are aligned horizontally as well as vertically.

The basic strategy in setting up columns of text is to create the column that will use the largest font first, and then copy that column and change the type specifications (if necessary) to create all other columns.

1

Select the Type tool and click or drag on the screen where you want the text to start. Type the first column of text. Select the text with the Selection tool or the Object-selection tool, and set the alignment to left, centered, or right, as appropriate for this column.

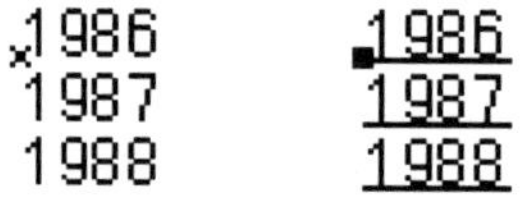

2

Hold down the Command key to get the current Selection tool, and drag the text block to the right to form the second column. Hold the Shift and Option keys to align and copy the text as you release the mouse button.

TEXT

3

Select the text with the I-beam pointer to edit the new block of text and change the text content or font specification. You can change alignment (left, centered, right) and the font and the point size of the type, but do not change the leading between lines if you wish to maintain horizontal alignment between columns of text.

4

Continue creating new columns by copying and aligning the last changed block with the Option and Shift keys, respectively.

5

After you have typed all columns, adjust the space between columns using the Selection tool or the Object-selection tool with the Shift key depressed to drag each column left or right to refine the overall layout of the columns.

Tips: Be sure to set up the column with the largest font size before you go through this procedure. Otherwise, the lines of text might run into each other when you set up columns that call for larger type, and you will have to change the leading for all of the columns.

Once you have typed and aligned all of the text blocks, select them all and use the Group command under the Arrange menu (Command-G) to group them to keep them in alignment when you move them. You can still edit individual elements of the group using the Direct-selection tool.

PART III: TECHNIQUES

Text on a Curved Path

This technique explains the basic steps to set text along a curved path. In this section you will learn to set text along the boundary of a circle, as shown in the figure. But you can apply the technique to a path of any shape.

This technique is especially useful for logos, labels, maps, and other applications that require text to follow an arbitrary path.

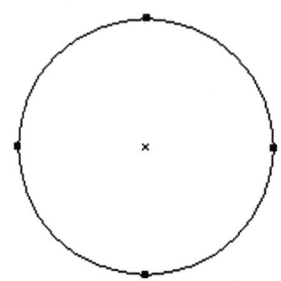

1

Use either Oval tool from the toolbox with the Shift key to draw a perfect circle. (Recall that the Shift key constrains the Oval tool to creating perfect circles.) The curvature of the circle can be adjusted now or changed at any time by selecting points with the Direct-selection tool.

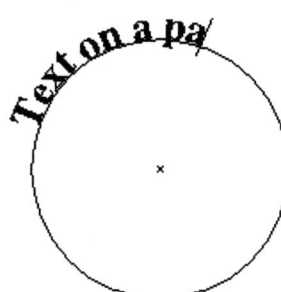

2

Choose the Path-type tool from the toolbox. Then click on the circle and begin typing. The text will appear on the circle as you type.

| TEXT |  |

3

Once you have typed the text you can edit the contents or type specifications by selecting it with the I-beam pointer.

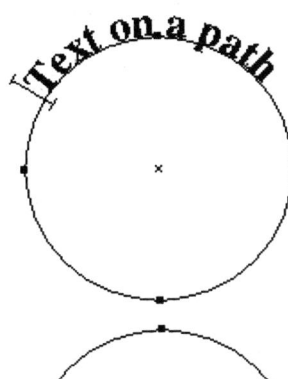

4

To reposition the text on the path, use the Selection tool and move the I-beam pointer, which appears at the beginning of the text. To flip the text into the circle, double-click the I-beam.

PART III: TECHNIQUES

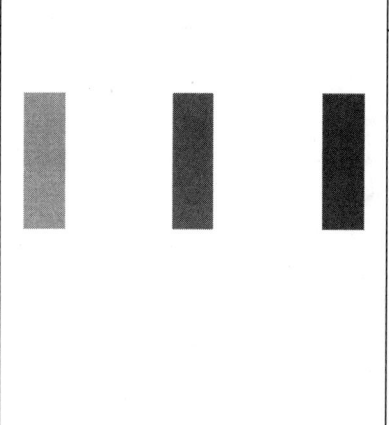

Fills and Patterns

Blending Colors or Grays

You may want a color that is exactly halfway between two PMS colors, two process colors, or two gray fills. This technique uses the Blend tool to generate the color automatically. The result of the example you create here appears as shades of gray in the accompanying figure.

This is a good alternative to defining a new color numerically or visually through the Custom Color dialog box (from the Paint menu), especially if you do not have a color screen.

Draw two objects (closed paths) and use Style from the Paint menu (Command-I) to assign them the two Fill colors (or grays) you wish to blend. In the figure on the left, the two rectangles are assigned different percentages of black fill. If you are using color, you must already know the cyan, magenta, yellow, and black percentages of the two starting colors, or use custom colors that have already been created (either your own custom colors or the PMS colors provided by Adobe).

192

FILLS AND PATTERNS

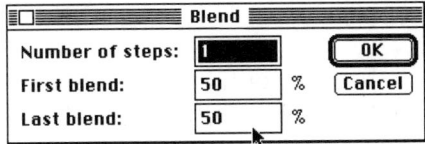

2

Select two corresponding points on each of the objects, and use the Blend tool to specify one step of blending between your two colors. (See The Blend Tool in Part I. Remember that objects must be ungrouped in order to be blended.) By leaving the defaults, the first blend to 50 percent, and the last blend to 50 percent, you will produce a new color that is exactly halfway along the spectrum between the two starting colors. This same procedure can be used to create automatically colors that are one-third, one-fourth, one-fifth, or even one-four hundredth of each other simply by increasing the number of steps or by adjusting the percentages entered in the Blend dialog box.

Click OK in the Blend dialog box. The Blend tool will produce the midway color and fill a new object with that color automatically in the active window.

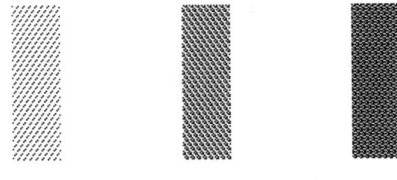

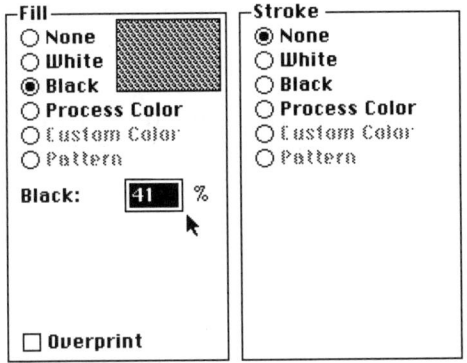

3

Select the new object created by the Blend tool using the Selection tool, then choose Style from the Paint menu (Command-I) to view the cyan, magenta, yellow, and black percentage attributes of the new color fill.

See also Paint Palettes.

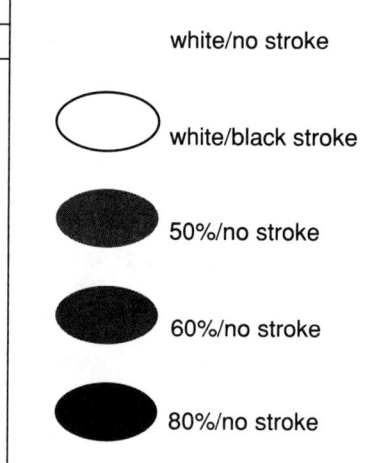

Paint Palettes

If you know that you will be using certain attributes—such as colors, fills, or stroke combinations—repeatedly in a drawing, it is useful to create a paint palette containing your choices as part of the working artwork in your file. Before you draw a new object, you can set the paint attributes with a click and three keys: click, Command-I, Return.

This is useful when you are creating artwork that uses different paint attributes.

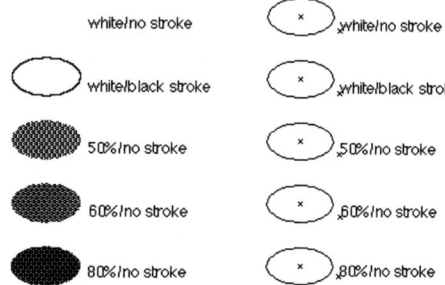

1

Draw a series of ovals with either Oval tool and line them up off to the side of your drawing. Paint each oval with the paint attributes you want using Style from the Paint menu (Command-I), and label each oval using the Type tool. In this example, five ovals are set up as the palette, each with different fill and stroke attributes: (1) white fill, no stroke; (2) white fill, black stroke; (3) 50 percent black fill, no stroke; (4) 60 percent black fill, no stroke; and (5) 80 percent black fill, no stroke. (Another common setting, not used in this example, is no fill and no stroke.)

FILLS AND PATTERNS

2

Once this palette is set up, simply click on a palette oval to select it, choose Style from the Paint menu (Command-I), and press Return. In other words, click, Command-I, Return. The next object you draw will have the attributes of the chosen palette oval.

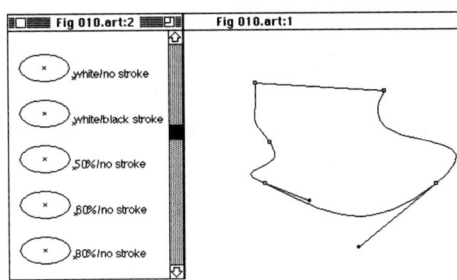

3

When working in close-up views of the artwork, you can keep the palette visible in a second open window. To do this, choose New Window from the Window menu. Size the windows so they do not overlap. The palette window can be small and show a reduced view of the palette artwork.

PART III: TECHNIQUES

Patterns: Method 1— Discrete Objects

The nuances of a repeating pattern can be difficult to visualize. Until you can see the result of a simple graphic repeat, you are not sure it is what you want. With traditional pen-and-ink methods, creating a pattern repeat is a costly and time-consuming exercise, often producing unusable results. Adobe Illustrator automatically generates repeating *tiles* of a pattern for you to see. The program does the tough work and all you have to do is decide if you like the results.

Here is one example of how to build a simple pattern of geometric shapes. Besides creating your own custom fill patterns for charts or graphs or any shape, you can use Illustrator's pattern feature in designing fabrics or wallpapers.

1

Build a basic shape with one of the drawing tools. The figure on the left shows a circle shape customized in a particular color and stroke. This is the shape that will be repeated in a pattern.

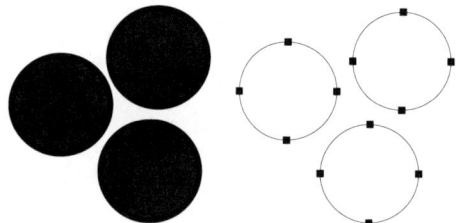

2

Repeat the shape by Option-dragging to make copies. The goal is to arrange a small area as the basic tile that will be repeated as a fill pattern later.

FILLS AND PATTERNS

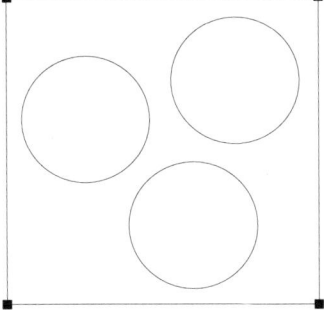

3

Using either the Rectangle tool or the Centered-rectangle tool, draw a nonfilled, nonstroked rectangle over the area you would like to serve as a pattern fill. To have the repeat line up well, position your rectangle (called the *tiling rectangle*) to surround all of the graphics, without letting any graphic cross the border of the rectangle, and with the space between the rectangle and the graphics roughly half the space you intend between graphics when the pattern is used to fill a shape. (See Patterns: Method 2 for a description of how to create tiles with crossover patterns.)

4

Send the tiling rectangle to the back by selecting it and choosing Send To Back from the Edit menu (Command-hyphen).

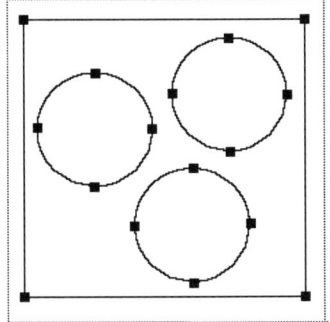

5

Select all the geometric shapes and the tiling rectangle by dragging the selection marquee over them (see The Selection Tools in Part I).

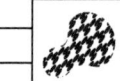

PART III: TECHNIQUES

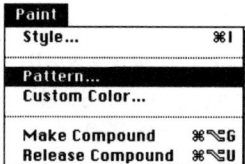

6

Choose Pattern from the Paint menu and click New to define the new pattern in the Pattern dialog box. You can use Illustrator's default pattern name (New Pattern 1), or type a name that you will recognize as describing this particular design. Click OK to close the dialog box and save the pattern.

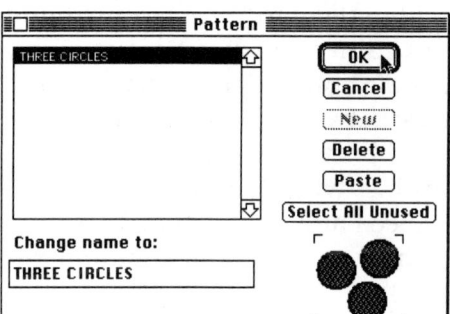

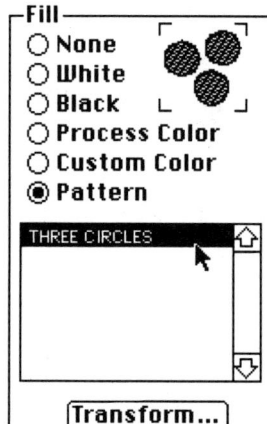

7

Now that you have created the pattern, you can fill any new shape with it by choosing Style from the Paint menu (Command-I) and clicking Pattern under the Fill or Stroke option. The new pattern name should appear in the scrolling window that lists any patterns you have created in the current window or in any other artwork that is open in other windows.

FILLS AND PATTERNS

8

In order to preview the pattern, you need to be sure that the Preview and print patterns option is checked in the Preferences dialog box.

(This is the normal default setting, but some illustrators turn this off because patterns slow screen processing time and printing time considerably. When this option is off the preview and printed versions will represent any pattern simply as a gray fill. As a rule, you will want to work with the Preview and print patterns option on when you are creating a new pattern, but then turn it off while you work to build a complex illustration that uses the pattern.)

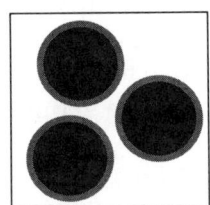
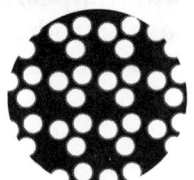
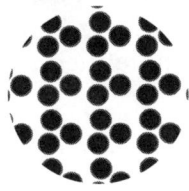

9

You can edit the pattern by changing the artwork that you used originally to create the first pattern tile, then choosing Pattern from the Paint menu, selecting New, and giving the revised pattern a new name. You will have to use the Style command from the Paint menu (Command-I) to apply the revised pattern to the artwork. You cannot edit a pattern and change the artwork simultaneously (as you can with custom colors).

PART III: TECHNIQUES

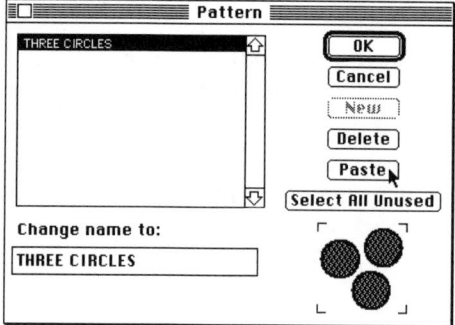

10

When you are satisfied with the pattern design, you can delete the tile artwork; the pattern will remain stored with the current file. If you want to edit the tile later, you can retrieve it by choosing Pattern from the Paint menu, selecting the pattern name from the list, and clicking Paste. This creates a copy of the original tile artwork, which you can edit to create a new pattern.

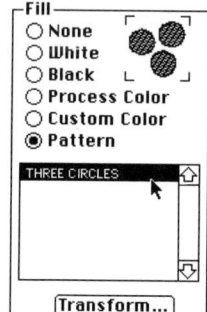

11

You can change many aspects of your fill without redrawing a tiling element. To do so, return to the Paint Style dialog box from the Paint menu. Click Transform... at the bottom of the Fill box. After the Transform Pattern Style dialog box appears, as shown in the figure on the lower left, make any changes you would like to the pattern (such as changing the size of the geometrics or the angle of the pattern).

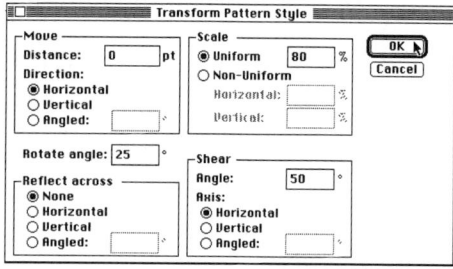

Warning: The Transform... button appears in the Paint dialog box only if a pattern has already been defined and the Pattern option is selected.

FILLS AND PATTERNS

12

Click in the Transform Pattern Style dialog box. When you return to the Paint dialog box you will notice a check mark next to the Transform... button, indicating the pattern has been altered. Click in the active window and choose Preview Illustration from the View menu (Command-Y) to see the transformed pattern.

Tip: In this example we did not fill or stroke the tiling rectangle; this left our background transparent. To produce an opaque background, you can assign a color or fill to the tiling rectangle.

See also Patterns: Method 2.

PART III: TECHNIQUES

Patterns: Method 2— Continuous Symmetry

The previous technique described how to create a simple pattern that is not continuous. In other words, the graphics of the pattern did not overlap the edges of the tiling rectangle. The process is a bit more complicated if you want to create continuous patterns, requiring that the graphics flow in a continuous connection from one tile to another. The technique described here can be used to create tiles that form a continuous, symmetrical pattern.

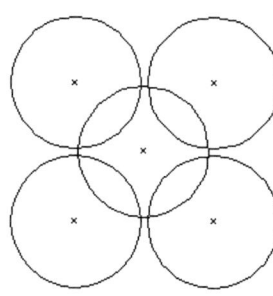

1

Create a symmetrical design with one of the drawing tools. A symmetrical design is one in which the top half is a mirror image of the bottom half, and the left half is a mirror image of the right half. The figure on the left shows a symmetrical design composed of five interlocking circles.

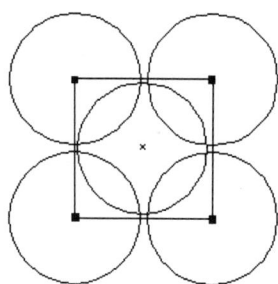

2

Using the Rectangle tool or the Centered-rectangle tool, draw a nonfilled, nonstroked rectangle over the area you would like to create as a pattern fill. To have the design cross over from one tile to another and line up well, position your rectangle so that its center point precisely matches the center of the symmetrical design. Send the tiling rectangle to the back by selecting it and choosing Send To Back from the Edit menu (Command-hyphen).

FILLS AND PATTERNS

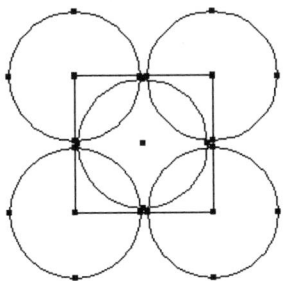

3

Select all the geometric shapes and the tiling rectangle by dragging the marquee over them or choosing Select All from the Edit menu (Command-A).

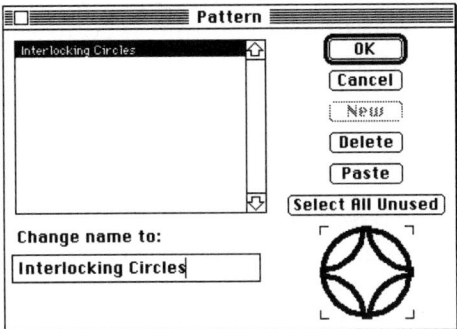

4

Choose Pattern from the Paint menu and click New to define the new pattern in the Pattern dialog box. You can use Illustrator's default pattern name (New Pattern 1), or type a name that you will recognize as describing this particular design. Click OK to close the dialog box and save the pattern.

5

Now that you have created the pattern, you can fill any new shape with the pattern by choosing Style from the Paint menu (Command-I) and clicking Pattern under the Fill or Stroke option. The new pattern name appears in the window that lists patterns you have created in this or any other artwork that is open in other windows.

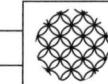

PART III: TECHNIQUES

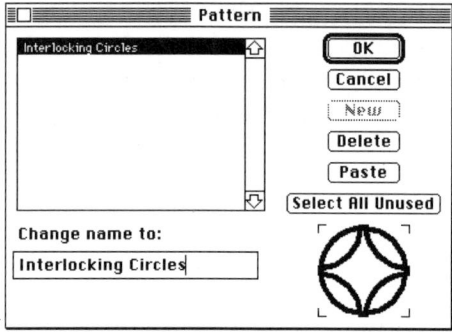

6

In order to preview the pattern, you need to be sure that the Preview and print patterns option is checked in the Preferences dialog box (Command-K).

Tip: As a general rule, you will want to work with the Preview and print patterns option on when you are creating a new pattern, but then turn it off to speed screen redraw while you work to build a complex illustration that uses the pattern.

7

When you are satisfied with the pattern design, you can delete the tile artwork; the pattern will remain stored with the current file. If you want to edit the tile later, you can retrieve it by choosing Pattern from the Paint menu, selecting the pattern name from the list, and clicking Paste. This creates a copy of the original tile artwork, which you can edit to create a new variation.

FILLS AND PATTERNS

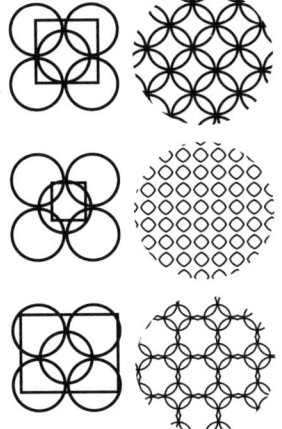

8

Edit the pattern by clicking Paste in the Pattern dialog box to copy the artwork that you used originally to create the first pattern tile, changing it, then choosing Pattern from the Paint menu and selecting New, giving the revised pattern a new name. Use the Style command from the Paint menu (Command-I) to apply the new pattern to the artwork. You cannot edit a pattern and change the artwork simultaneously (as you can with custom colors).

Notice that you can achieve different results in the overall pattern by changing the size of the rectangle. The figure at left shows three variations in the size of the rectangle and the resulting patterns.

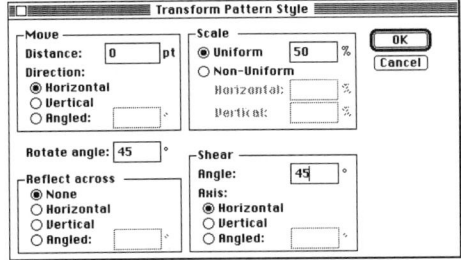

9

You can change many aspects of your fill without redrawing a tiling element. To do so, return to the Paint Style dialog box from the Paint menu (Command-I). Click Transform... at the bottom of the Fill box. After the Transform Pattern Style dialog box appears, make any changes you would like to the pattern (such as the size of the geometrics or the angle of the pattern).

Click in the Transform Pattern Style dialog box. When you return to the Paint dialog box you will see a check mark next to the Transform button, indicating the pattern has been altered. Choose Preview Illustration from the View menu to see the transformed pattern.

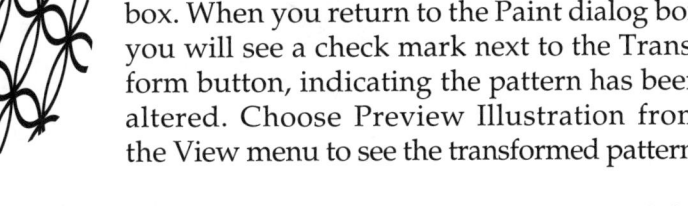

Tip: Create more intricate symmetrical designs by drawing one quadrant of the design and using the Reflect tool to create the other four quadrants.

PART III: TECHNIQUES

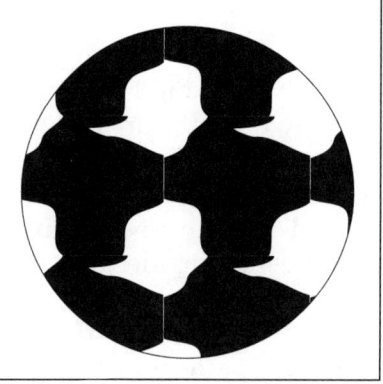

Patterns: Method 3— Continuous Asymmetry

The previous technique described how to create a continuous, symmetrical pattern. The technique described here can be used to create a continuous pattern from an asymmetrical or amorphous design.

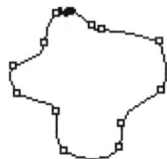

1

Create a design with one of the drawing tools. The figure at left shows a design composed of an amorphous shape.

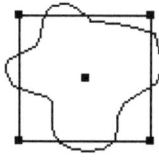

2

Using the Rectangle tool or the Centered-rectangle tool, draw a nonfilled, nonstroked rectangle over the area you would like to serve as a pattern fill. Send the tiling rectangle to the back by selecting it and choosing Send To Back from the Edit menu (Command-hyphen).

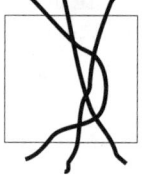

The trick in this step is to make sure that the same number of lines cross the top of the tiling rectangle as cross the bottom, and that the same number of line segments cross the left edge of the tiling rectangle as cross the right edge. In other words, if the design crosses the top edge at three points, you want the bottom of the rectangle to be crossed at three points also.

FILLS AND PATTERNS

Additional precautions are required if all the design elements do not share the same stroke and fill. For example, if three lines cross the top border and use three different strokes, then the three lines that cross the bottom border must have the same sequence of strokes.

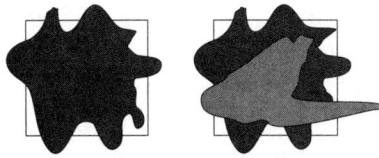

If any fill patterns will be used, then the edges of any filled shape must cross over a border an even number of times and cross the same number of times on the opposing sides of the tiling rectangle.

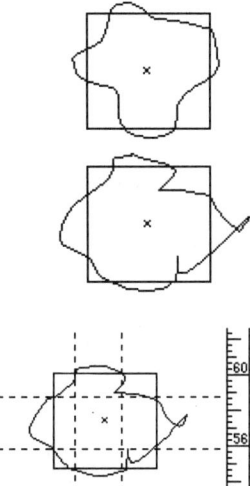

3

Next, make the lines that cross from one tile to the next meet. That is, you want lines that cross the left edge of the rectangle to match the vertical position of lines that cross the right edge, and lines that cross the top edge of the rectangle to match the horizontal position of lines that cross the bottom edge. You can move points visually on the screen.

Or, you can choose Show Rulers (Command-R) from the View menu (if the rulers are not already displayed) and drag ruler guides across the tile as guides for adjusting corresponding points.

PART III: TECHNIQUES

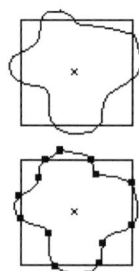

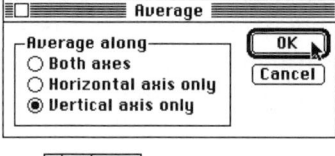

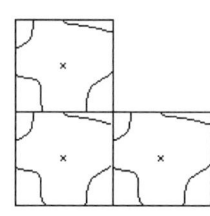

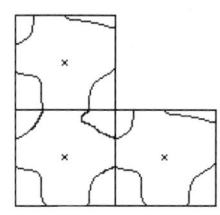

Or, you can adjust the design so that an anchor point falls anywhere the design crosses the tiling rectangle, or use the Scissors tool with the Option key to add anchor points to the line segments of the design where they cross the tiling rectangle. Then select corresponding pairs of endpoints on opposite sides of the tiling rectangle and choose Average from the Arrange menu to move corresponding points from the left and right edges along the vertical axis and to move corresponding points from the top and bottom edges along the horizontal axis.

A fourth alternative is to use the Scissors tool to cut the line segments of the design where they cross the tiling rectangle and delete the segments that extend beyond the rectangle. Select the remaining design elements and the tiling rectangle by dragging the marquee over them, or choose Select All (Command-A), then use any Selection tool to Option-Shift-drag copies of the design and rectangle to form a matrix of three identical tiles, then move the endpoints of the lines that cross *two adjacent sides of the center tile* so they meet the ends of corresponding lines in the adjacent tiles. In this example, the endpoints along the top and right sides of the center tile have been dragged to meet the ends of lines in the adjoining tiles.

FILLS AND PATTERNS

4

Regardless of which method is used in step 3, it is a good idea to check your tiles visually by selecting the whole design and the tiling rectangle, grouping the objects (Command-G), then Option-Shift-dragging copies to form a matrix of nine tiles on the screen to check the alignment of adjacent tiles and to preview the pattern. Besides verifying that the design lines up across tiles, you want to be sure that the fill patterns and strokes assigned to crossing lines match up. In this example, the Join command (Command-J) is used to connect the endpoints that cross each edge of the tile in order to create a solid shape with a fill.

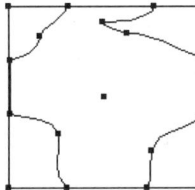

5

When you have achieved the effect you want, delete all but one tile and design set, then select all the geometric shapes and the tiling rectangle by dragging the marquee over them, or choose Select All from the Edit menu (Command-A).

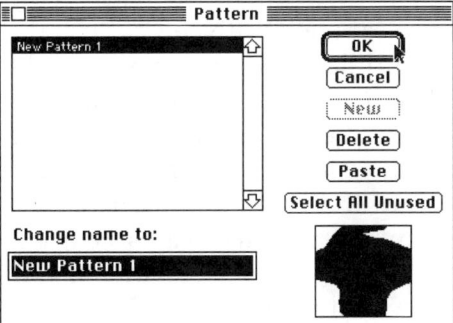

6

Choose Pattern from the Paint menu and click New to define the new pattern in the Pattern dialog box. You can use Illustrator's default pattern name (New Pattern 1), or type a name that you will recognize as describing this particular design. Click OK to close the dialog box and save the pattern.

209

PART III: TECHNIQUES

7

Now that you have created the pattern, you can fill any new shape with the pattern by choosing Style from the Paint menu (Command-I) and clicking Pattern under the Fill or Stroke option. The new pattern name should appear in the scrolling window that lists any patterns you have created in the current window or in any other artwork that is open in other windows.

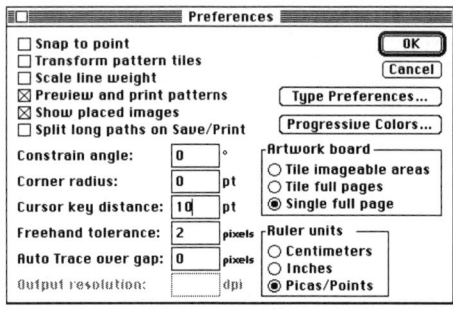

8

In order to preview the pattern, you need to be sure that the Preview and print patterns option is checked in the Preferences dialog box (Command-K).

Tip: As a general rule, you will want to work with the Preview and print patterns option on when you are creating a new pattern, but then turn it off while you work to build a complex illustration that uses the pattern.

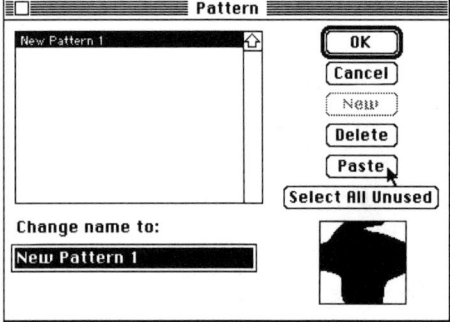

9

When you are satisfied with the pattern design, you can delete the tile artwork; the pattern will remain stored with the current file. If you want to edit the tile later, you can retrieve it by choosing Pattern from the Paint menu, selecting the pattern name from the list, and clicking Paste. This creates a copy of the original tile artwork, which you can edit to create a new pattern.

FILLS AND PATTERNS

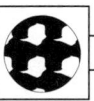

10

You can edit the pattern by pasting the artwork that you used originally to create the first pattern tile, changing it, then choosing Pattern from the Paint menu and selecting New, giving the revised pattern a new name. You will have to use the Style command from the Paint menu to apply the revised pattern to the artwork. You cannot edit a pattern and change the artwork simultaneously (as you can with custom colors).

11

You can change many aspects of your fill without redrawing a tiling element. To do so, return to the Paint Style dialog box from the Paint menu (Command-I). Click on the Transform... button at the bottom of the Fill box. After the Transform Pattern Style dialog box appears, make any changes you would like to the pattern (such as the size of the geometrics or the angle of the pattern).

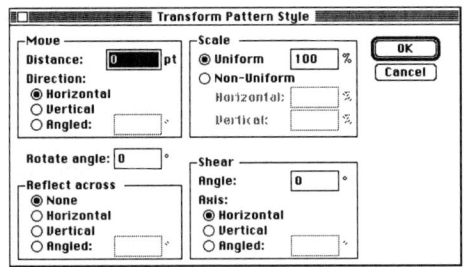

Then click in the Transform Pattern Style dialog box. When you return to the Paint dialog box you will notice a check mark next to the Transform... button, indicating that the pattern has been altered. Click in the active window, and choose Preview Illustration from the View menu (Command-Y) to see the transformed pattern.

See also Patterns: Methods 1 and 2.

PART III: TECHNIQUES

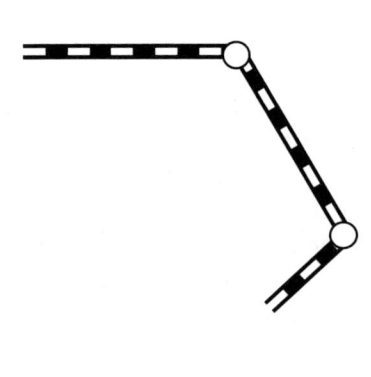

Layering

Compound Lines: Method 1

The distinguishing feature of the lines created by this technique (and the next technique) is that the lines have a fill different from the stroke at the outer edge of the line. This makes the task of creating the effect shown in the accompanying figure a bit more complicated than using Illustrator's dashed line feature. The basic element of the compound line consists of two overlapping lines: a solid black line on the bottom layer, and a slightly thinner, dashed white line on top, as shown in the figure. This unit was created once, then duplicated and pieced into routes on a map. There are really several approaches to this task. The method explained here is a "building block" approach; the method described in the next entry is a "systems" approach.

You can use these types of lines in maps to represent roads, trails, or railway lines. You can also use them in line graphs, floor plans, and other schematic drawings. You can apply the same technique to the borders (strokes) of two-dimensional shapes (such as rectangles, circles, or polygons).

In the building-block technique you simply create one short length of track composed of the two layered lines and then assemble copies of it into extended routes.

LAYERING

1

With the Pen or Freehand tool, draw a short line—a manageable size for your basic building block. This should be close to the most common size you will need for a straight segment of track or road in your design. Use Style from the Paint menu (Command-I) to open the Paint dialog box, and set the attributes for the lower layer of the compound track. For this example, set Fill to None, Stroke to 100 percent Black, and Weight to 8 points. When you are done, click OK.

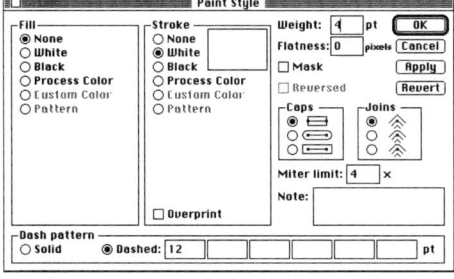

2

Select the line, if it is not already selected, copy it with Copy (Command-C), and use Paste In Front (Command-F) to add a copy of the line to the top layer. Choose Paint (Command-I) to set the attributes for the upper layer of the compound track. The stroke weight should be smaller than that of the bottom line.

In the example, set Fill to None, Stroke to White, and Weight to 4 points. Click on Dashed in the Dash pattern box, and type 12 in the first box to create a dashed line with 12-point dashes and 12-point spaces between dashes. Click OK when you are done.

Choose Preview Illustration from the View menu (Command-Y) to view the results. Then choose Artwork Only (Command-W) to continue working.

PART III: TECHNIQUES

3

Option-drag over this basic building block to select it, and use the Object-selection tool and Option key to move copies into position along the path of the railway route (or whatever you are representing with the lines). Use the Rotate tool to change the angle of the line.

4

Drag over an endpoint to select one end of a straight line and stretch it or make it shorter. After you have finished editing, group the whole route using Group (Command-G). You can direct-select elements within the group if you later need to edit lines or to stretch copies of the basic set to different lengths.

5

Add circles for station markers at each bend in the path.

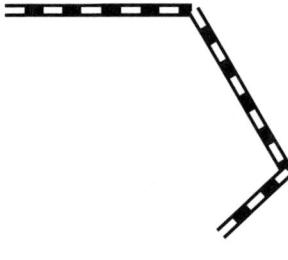

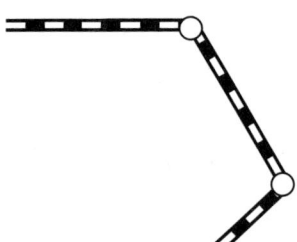

LAYERING

Warning: Under this procedure you cannot globally change the attributes of the layers very easily, but it is easy to add, delete, or move part of a route. (See Compound Lines: Method 2 for creating lines that can be globally edited.)

Tip: Create and print a test sheet to determine what attribute combinations look best in the size you will use in the final artwork. In the figure at left, the top line was created with 2-point dashes, the bottom line with 12-point dashes, and the variations between were created with the Blend tool.

See Dotted Lines and Parallel Curves.

PART III: TECHNIQUES

Compound Lines: Method 2

You can use the technique described here to create the same types of compound lines described in the previous technique. However, this technique, unlike Method 1, yields a system of lines that you can edit globally (that is, the paint attributes of the lines can be easily changed). In this example, you will create another roadmap route, as shown in the accompanying figure.

1

Draw the bottom layer of the whole path (such as a train line on a map) in one sweep with the Pen tool, then use the Style command from the Paint menu (Command-I) to set the attributes of the lower line. The bottom layer in this example has the attributes of 100 percent black stroke, no fill, and 8-point weight.

2

Choose Copy (Command-C) to copy the bottom layer and Paste In Front from the Edit menu (Command-F). Set the second line's attributes by selecting Style from the Paint menu (Command-I). In this example we use a 4-point weight line with a white stroke and 12-point dashes and gaps.

LAYERING

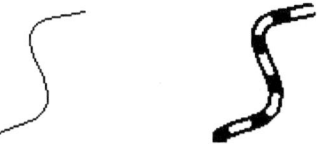

3

To select the two lines (if you need to move them), hold the Option key down as you use the Selection tool to drag a selection marquee across any part of the layered lines (see The Selection Tools in Part I).

Note that you can group the layered lines using Group (Command-G) but you will not be able to change the attributes of the lines globally unless you direct-select layers one by one.

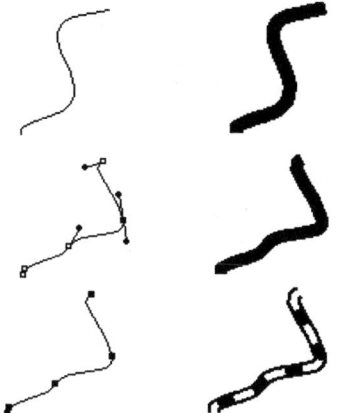

4

If you want to add, delete, or move part of a route, select the route lines and ungroup (Command-U) the two layers (if they are grouped), then Option-click on the top layer to select it and press the Backspace or Delete key to remove it. Then edit the bottom layer.

Copy the bottom layer (Command-C) to the Clipboard and use Paste In Front (Command-F). Use the Style command from the Paint menu (Command-I) to set the attributes to a white dashed line.

Warning: Under this procedure, you cannot very easily add, delete, or move part of a route. This procedure is better for global editing of the stroke attributes. See the previous technique, Compound Lines: Method 1, for creating lines that can be broken up easily.

PART III: TECHNIQUES

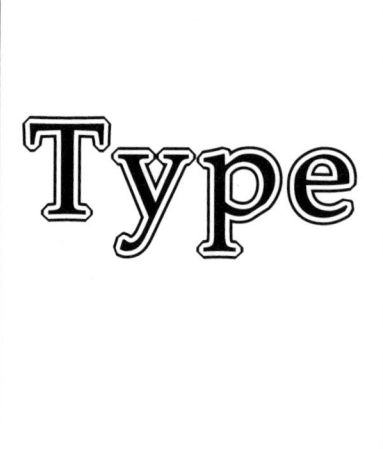

Inline Type

Inline type (as opposed to outline type) is a common decorative treatment for display type. You can use any font to create inline type with the technique described here. The accompanying figure shows an example of the inline type you will create here.

Variations of this technique can be used to create many different decorative variations of a font.

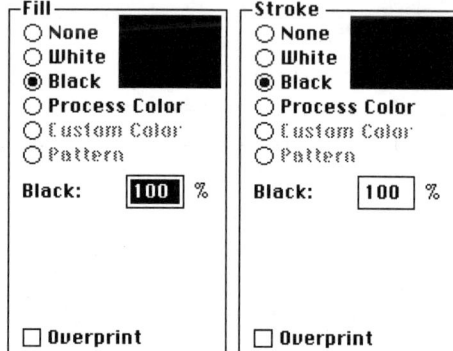

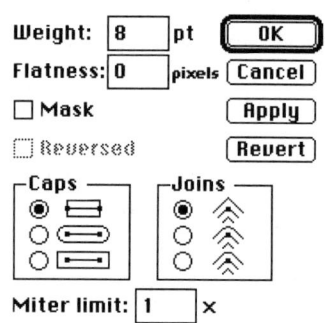

1

Create a type block with the text you wish to use. Select the Type tool and click it in the active window. Type the text you wish to use for the inline type. Then choose Style from the Paint menu (Command-I). Set Fill and Stroke to 100 percent Black, and Weight to 8 points.

The important aspect of this step is that you must set a stroke weight. Variations result by choosing different weights and shades for the stroke.

If you use a wide stroke at a small point size, the type will appear compressed. Add a few points to the desired letter spacing in the Spacing Options dialog box to open up the spaces between the letters. (You can get to this dialog box by clicking the Spacing Options button in the Type dialog box, or by choosing Spacing Options (Command-Shift-O) from the Type menu.)

2

Copy the type block and paste the copy in front of the original, then paint the copy with

LAYERING — Type

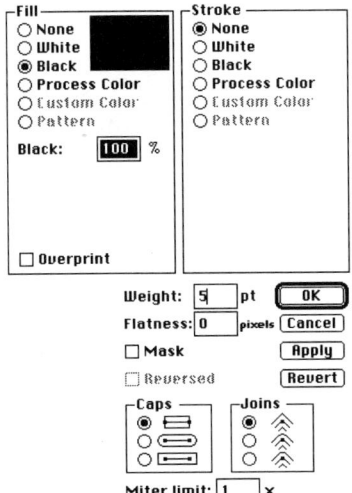

Inline Type

a white fill and a five-point white stroke. To do this quickly, select the type block, then press Command-C to copy, Command-F to Paste In Front, and Command-I to open the Paint dialog box. In the Paint dialog box, set Fill to 100 percent Black, Stroke to White, and Weight to 5 points.

The important aspect of this step is that the stroke weight must be less than that used in step 1. Variations result by choosing different weights and shades for the stroke and different Fill settings.

3

You can use Preview Illustration (Command-Y) to check your results, then choose Artwork Only (Command-W) and make changes. The Preview image of stroked type is not always accurate. Always make a test print.

Tip: Because the two text blocks that compose the inline type overlap precisely, use the following techniques to select and edit the text blocks' fill and stroke attributes. To select the top text block only, click the Selection tool on the top block's anchor point. To select both text blocks, use the Selection tool to drag a marquee over the overlapping anchor points of the text blocks (see The Selection Tools in Part I). To select the bottom text block only, select both blocks, then hold down the Shift key and click on the anchor point of the top block to deselect it.

Warning: This technique may yield unexpected results when it is applied to text blocks with mixed fonts or text on a curved path. It is designed to be used with point type that is set in one font only.

PART III: TECHNIQUES

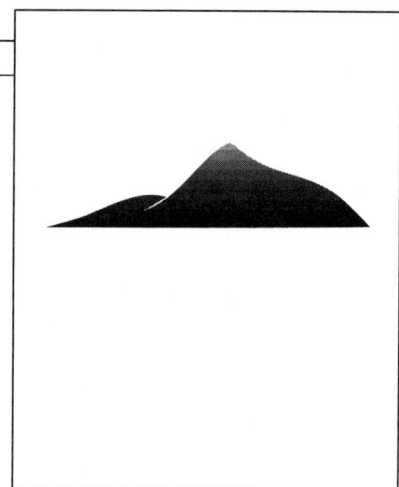

Masking

Masking is a way to crop illustrations, type, or patterns with a specific shape.

Masking can prove useful in many graphic art applications, such as packaging and logo design.

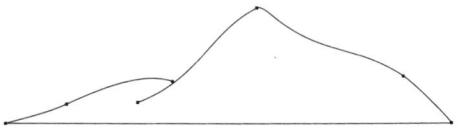

1

For this example use the Pen or Freehand tool to draw the mountain silhouette, which will be the masking path, shown in the figure on the left.

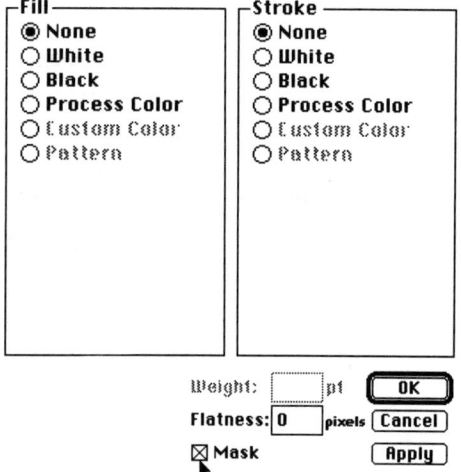

2

With the object selected, choose Style from the Paint menu (Command-I) and select None in the Fill and Stroke boxes. Then click in the box labeled Mask. After clicking OK in the Paint dialog box, choose Lock from the Arrange menu (Command-1).

LAYERING

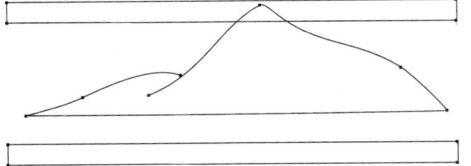

3

In this example, the mountain shape will mask a split fountain background. Draw a long narrow rectangle. Using the Paint dialog box, fill it with 30 percent black, ungroup it with the Ungroup command (Command-U), and—most importantly—delete the center point by selecting it and pressing the Delete or Backspace key. Position the rectangle over the highest peak of the mountain outline.

With the rectangle still selected, drag a copy of the rectangle to the bottom of the mountain outline while holding down the Shift key (constraining your movement vertically) and the Option key (to create a copy of the first rectangle). Use the Style command from the Paint menu (Command-I) to fill this second rectangle 100 percent black.

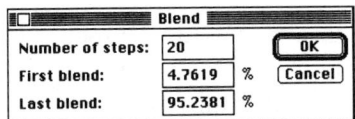
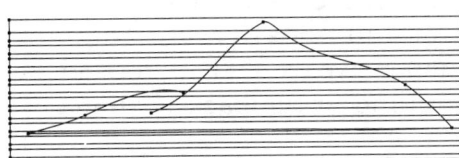

4

Shift-select all points on both rectangles, then select the Blend tool from the toolbox. Click the Blend tool on the left top corner point of each rectangle. The Blend dialog box appears. For this demonstration, type 20 into Number of steps and click OK. Remember, you can type in any number up to 1296 for your custom blends.

PART III: TECHNIQUES

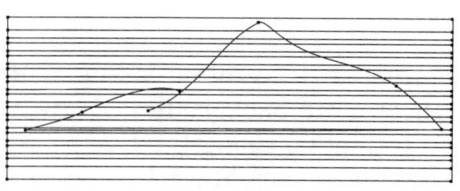

5

Now finish this first mask. If the mountain outline is not already on the lowest layer of the artwork, choose Unlock All from the Arrange menu (Command-2) and send the mountain outline to the back of the illustration using Send To Back from the Edit menu or Command-hyphen.

Select Preview Illustration from the View menu (Command-Y).

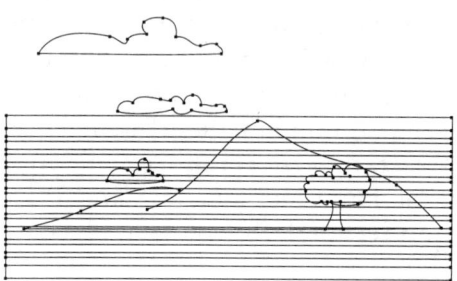

6

Add some additional drawn elements if you like. In this example we will add clouds and a tree using the Freehand tool.

If all is correct, select Artwork Only from the View menu (Command-W), select all of the elements that compose the mask, and then Group from the Arrange menu (Command-G).

In order for the masking effect to work, the mask outline must be on the bottom layer. In this case the mountain was already on the bottom layer because we drew it first. If we drew the mountain after creating the blended fountain, we would have to send the mountain outline to the back (Command-hyphen).

LAYERING

Also, always ungroup rectangles and ovals drawn with the Rectangle and Oval tools if you intend to use them as masks. After ungrouping rectangles and ovals, be sure to delete the center points before masking. If you do not delete the center point, it will become the mask. With a single point as the mask, nothing will show when you preview the illustration.

It's a good idea to group your completed masks. The masking object masks the entire page. By grouping the masked objects along with the mask, the mask will mask only the group, not the rest of the page.

See also Masking a Mask.

PART III: TECHNIQUES

Masking a Mask

Since masking is a way to crop illustrations, type, or patterns into a specific shape, you may find the need to crop or mask a mask. Here's a technique for masking a mask, to fill a shape with an image that is itself a masked view.

This technique is useful in many graphic art applications, such as packaging and logo design.

1

Create the first masked element. For this example use the artwork created in the previous technique, a blend of gray rectangles masked by a mountain outline.

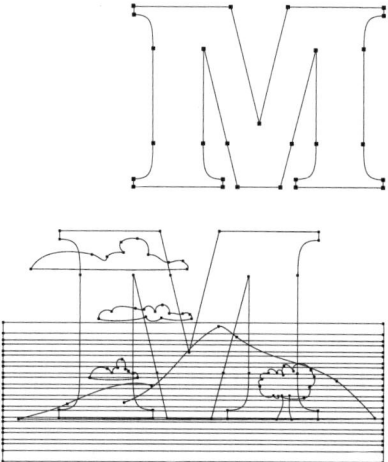

2

Draw a simple block letter M or type a large M with the Type tool and choose Create Outlines from the Type menu. Select the letterform and choose Style from the Paint menu (Command-I) to set Fill to 20 percent Black, and Stroke to None. Click the Mask box, and click OK. Position this new mask over the mountain drawing. After positioning, choose Send To Back from the Edit menu (Command-hyphen).

LAYERING

3

Preview the effect of this second mask masking your first mask by selecting Preview Illustration from the View menu (Command-Y).

4

You can make a copy of the letterform with the Copy command (Command-C) and paste it in front of everything using Paste In Front (Command-F). In the Paint style dialog box, change the attributes of this new object: set Fill to None, 100 percent Black Stroke of 20 points, and, most importantly, unclick the Mask box. Click OK. Preview your drawing (Command-Y), then use Select All (Command-A), and Group from the Edit menu (Command-G).

Continue to add separate elements as you wish and complete your illustration.

Tip: Always group your completed masks if you will be combining masked elements with other masks or unmasked elements in the same illustration.

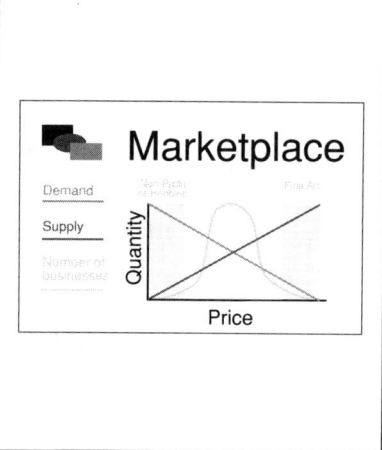

PART III: TECHNIQUES

Overlays: Method 1— Color Separations

The term *overlay* is used to describe any artwork that is designed to be printed or projected on top of another image. This includes the separate overlays used by the offset printer to produce multicolored images and the separate overlays used by a speaker in giving a presentation. Here is the first of three techniques for creating overlays with Adobe Illustrator.

This technique is useful for producing a separate overlay for each color to be used in offset printing the final image, or for creating a series of images that will be projected during a presentation as overlaid transparencies.

 1

Draw the artwork, using the Style command from the Paint menu (Command-I) to assign colors to different parts of the image.

If you wish to use color to separate a series of images that will be projected during a presentation as overlaid transparencies, use the Style command from the Paint menu to assign only one custom color or one of the primary process colors (cyan, magenta, yellow, or black) to all of the elements on each overlay—you can print different overlays for each color using Adobe Separator.

See Overlays: Method 2 if you want each overlay to have multiple colors and print them on a PostScript color printer.

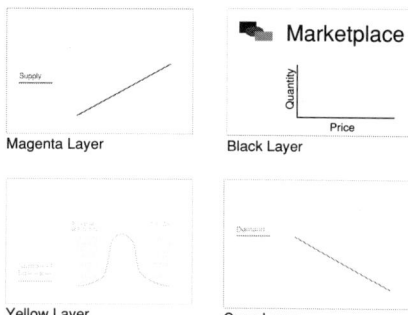

LAYERING

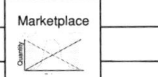

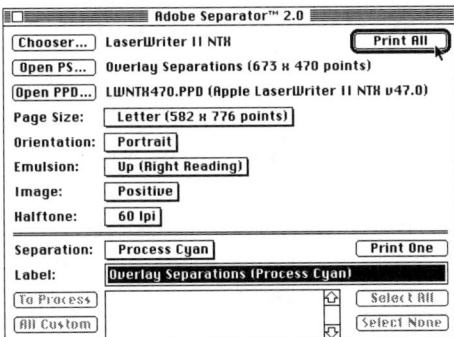

2

Print the image using Adobe Separator (see Appendix B) on a PostScript printer with the Print All option selected in the dialog box. If you are printing to a color printer, the different overlays will each be printed in a different color. Otherwise, on a black printer the overlays will be printed in black and shades of gray.

If you will be offset printing the final image in color, you can use the separated images in black and white to create plates for each color to be used in the printing process.

Tip: The full color image can, of course, be printed in color on a single sheet through a PostScript color printer when separate overlays are not required.

See also Overlays: Methods 2 and 3, and Appendix B: Printing Color Separations with Adobe Separator.

PART III: TECHNIQUES

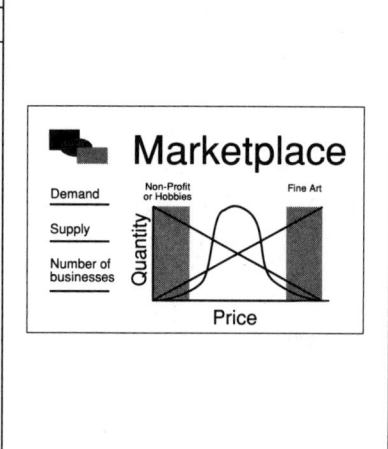

Overlays: Method 2—Layers

This second technique for creating overlays involves grouping the elements that are to appear on each layer. One advantage of this method over Method 1 is that each overlay can include more than one color. Another advantage is that you can print a series of more than four overlays using this technique.

This technique is specifically useful for creating a series of images that will be projected during a presentation as overlaid transparencies.

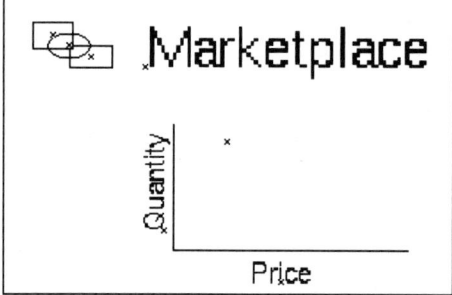

1

Draw the artwork that will compose the first transparency—the bottom layer when additional transparencies are overlaid during a presentation. Use the Style command from the Paint menu (Command-I) to set the Fill and Stroke of each elements, including different colors if you wish. Then, use Select All (Command-A) to select all of the objects that compose the first transparency and use the Group command (Command-G) and the Lock command (Command-1) to group and lock them.

LAYERING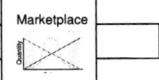

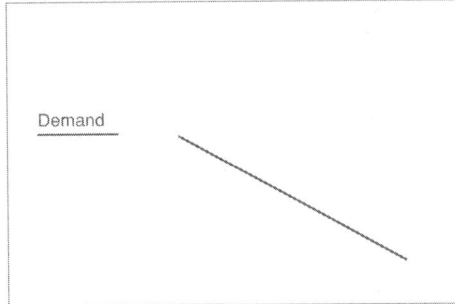

2

Draw the artwork that will compose the second transparency—the second layer when the two transparencies are overlaid during a presentation. Then, use Select All (Command-A) to select all of the objects that compose the second transparency and use the Group command (Command-G) to group them.

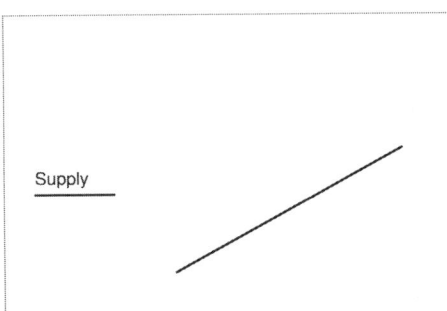

3

If a third overlay is called for, first use the Unlock command (Command-2) to unlock the first layer, then use Select All (Command-A) and Lock (Command-1) to select and lock all of the elements of the first two transparencies.

Then draw the artwork that will compose the third transparency overlay, use Select All (Command-A) to select all of the objects that compose the third transparency, and use the Group command (Command-G) to group them.

Repeat this step for each additional overlay.

4

If you need to make changes to any of the overlays, be sure that only one overlay at a time is unlocked while you are working. Before making edits to the elements on a different overlay, unlock all the layers (Command-2), choose Select All (Command-A), Shift-

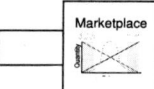

PART III: TECHNIQUES

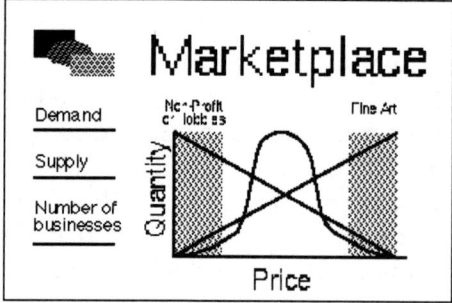

click on the next grouped set you want to edit (to deselect it), and lock the selected layers (Command-1). Then direct-select individual elements in the unlocked overlay you want to edit.

5

When the artwork is complete, preview the whole illustration (Command-Y) to proof the artwork for alignment.

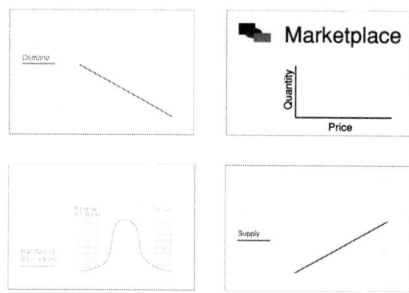

6

Print the artwork for each overlay on a separate sheet, in color or black and white. Do this by first unlocking all locked layers (Command-2), selecting all overlays (Command-A), Shift-clicking on the grouped artwork for the one overlay you want to print (to deselect it), hiding all other artwork using the Hide command (Command-3), then printing the visible overlay (Command-P).

Tip: If you will be printing the separate layers several times, or on different printers, you can save the time it would take to select and hide overlays repeatedly. You save the composite image as a document and then save as many additional documents as there are overlays (grouped layers). Then open each overlay document and delete all elements except those that compose a single overlay.

LAYERING

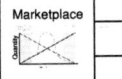

If any changes are required after you separate the composite artwork into different documents, make the changes in the composite document and derive the changed overlays from that document again.

See also Overlays: Methods 1 and 3, and Appendix B: Printing Color Separations with Adobe Separator.

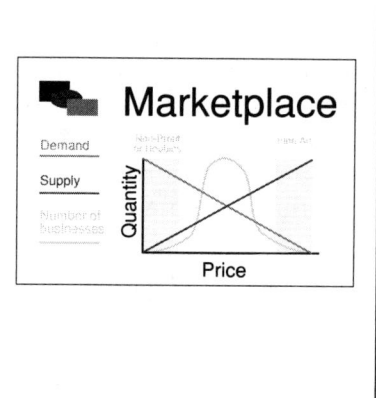

PART III: TECHNIQUES

Overlays: Method 3— Separate Documents

This third technique for creating overlays involves working with the elements that are to appear on each layer in a separate document. This can be a productivity aid when each overlay — or the final composite image — is so complicated or so large that it would tax your system's memory (and slow response rates) if it were all one document.

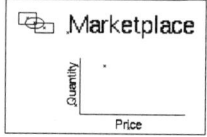

1

Draw the most complicated or detailed overlay first.

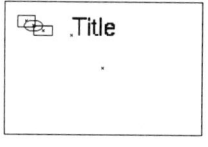

2

Save it as Overlay #1, then delete some of the details, leaving only as much of the artwork as you will need for a grid or guide to create subsequent overlays. Use Select All and choose Make Guide (Command-5) from the Arrange menu, then save the new document as Overlay Boilerplate.

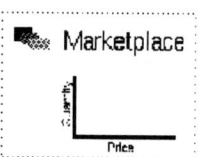

LAYERING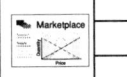

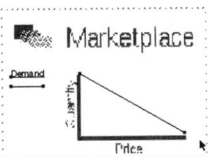

3

To create each subsequent overlay, open the Overlay Boilerplate (from step 2) and add the elements for the next overlay.

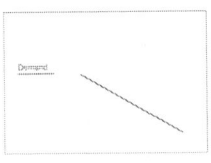 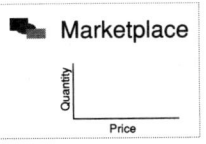

4

Print the overlays on a color or black-and-white printer.

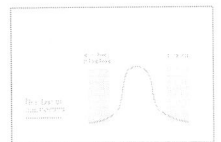 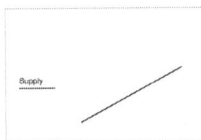

Tip: If all of the overlays but the first are fairly simple and not overlapping, you can build all of the subsequent overlays in a single document and separate them using Method 1 or 2.

Warning: With this method, the image cannot be printed as a single sheet.

See also Overlays: Methods 1 and 2.

233

PART III: TECHNIQUES

Pasting in Layers

When you want to position a selected object on the frontmost or backmost layer of an illustration, you can use the Paste In Front or Paste In Back command (Command-F or Command-B), respectively. Otherwise, when you want to move a selected object to a different layer position, use Illustrator's "smart pasting" ability, described here.

This technique is useful whenever you need to rearrange the layers of an illustration composed of three or more layers, like the three layers of star shapes shown in the accompanying figure.

1

Assuming you have a series of objects layered on top of one another, select the Object-selection tool and click (or use the Selection tool and Option-click) on the object you want to move, as shown in the figure on the left, and choose Cut from the Edit menu (Command-X). The selected object is cut to the Clipboard for pasting later.

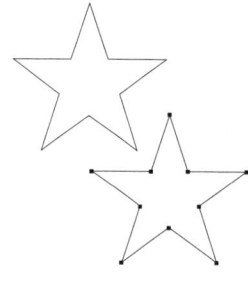

2

Now choose the object you would like to paste behind or in front of and click on it. This selection now acts as a "reference layer" for the pasting function. The bottom star is selected in this example.

LAYERING

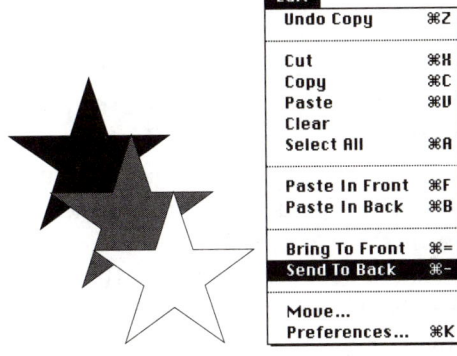

3

Then choose Paste In Front or Paste In Back from the Edit menu (Command-F or Command-B). The cut object is pasted in front or in back of the object you selected as a reference layer in step 2. (If you do not choose a reference layer before pasting, Paste In Front or Paste In Back will simply paste to the frontmost or backmost layer.)

Tip: Use the following two shortcuts when you are layering objects: Use Command- to move a selected object to the layer that is farthest back, and use Command-= to move a selected object to the layer that is topmost.

PART III: TECHNIQUES

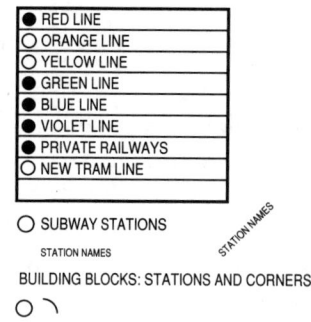

Control Panel

This is a technique for managing artwork composed of several overlapping groups or elements, that share the same attributes (such as Fill, Stroke, Color, or Font). You draw one complete layer or group at a time, and for each group add an element in the Control Panel area that you set up outside the print area required by the final illustration.

The technique can be applied to any complex illustration that is composed of several groups of similar or identical objects, such as a map, floorplan, or diagram, and to any color illustration. The example shown in the next steps is a simple one. The benefits of this technique really come into their own in more complex designs.

1

To draw a two-line subway map, draw the first line as a single, open path and set it as a 5-point black line.

2

In the Control Panel area, type a text label (Line 1) and draw a circle (or a line or a box) next to the text label with the same attributes as Line 1 on the map: a 5-point black line with no fill.

LAYERING

⬥ BLACK LINE

3

Select the artwork that composes Line 1 *and* the circle next to the text label for Line 1 in the Control Panel area and group the objects (Command-G) before starting to build the next layer.

4

Repeat steps 1–3 for each additional group of objects. The following table shows the layering sequence for a two-line subway map.

Layer	Number of Elements	Label
1 (Bottom)	1	Line 1
2	1	Line 2
3	13	Small station markers (not transfer points)
4	2	Large station markers (transfer points)
5	2	Line names
6 (Top)	15	Station names

237

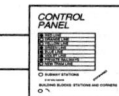

PART III: TECHNIQUES

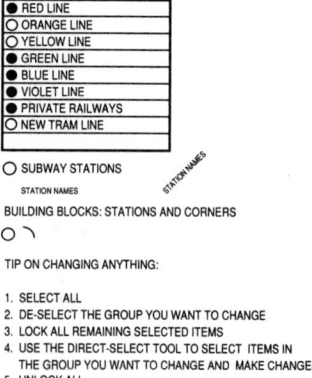

Control Panel in working area

The Control Panel for the groups is positioned beyond the page borders of the artwork, as shown in the figure. When you click on the object left of each rail line name in the Control Panel, you select the whole rail line in the artwork. When you click on the text shown for station names in the Control Panel, you select all station names in the artwork.

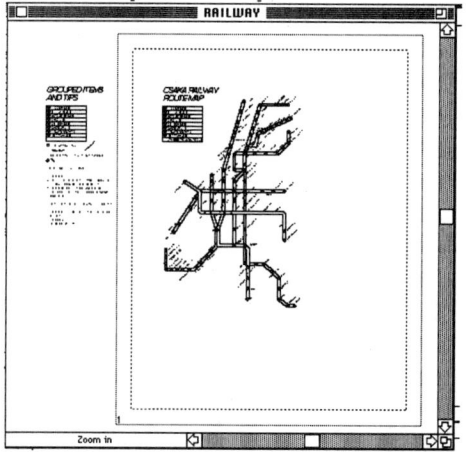

LAYERING

5

In editing the artwork, you can select a whole group by selecting the element that represents the group in the Control Panel and make global changes to attributes shared by the group. To edit or move individual elements within a group, direct-select the element and then make the changes.

Tips: Determine the sequence of layers before you start. A rule of thumb is to start with the bottom layer. You don't have to let this hamper your creative urges—but you need to have a good reason not to start with the bottom layer and build the sequence of the layers upward in developing the illustration.

By having a representative from each group in the control area, you can easily click between groups and change grouped attributes without scrolling around on the screen to find the next group you want to change. This little efficiency is especially useful in large, complex documents, which are slow to scroll and redraw views.

PART III: TECHNIQUES

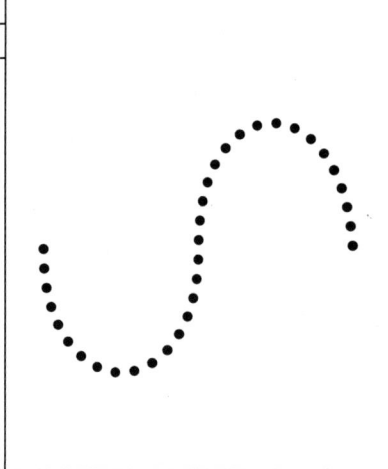

Lines

Dotted Lines

Illustrator allows you to make dashed lines of perfect dots or perfect squares, in any specific size and with any specific spacing you like. This technique will uniformly soften the feeling of your drawings and still allow you to specify them in full black or primary colors.

This style of line is also useful for architectural and schematic drawings. It provides an effective way to indicate movement or sequential steps of a process. It can also be used to add leaders to tabular text formats.

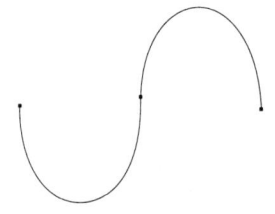

1

Draw a line or shape using one of the drawing tools (the Pen tool, the Freehand tool, or the Autotrace tool). The figure on the left shows a curved line drawn with the Pen tool.

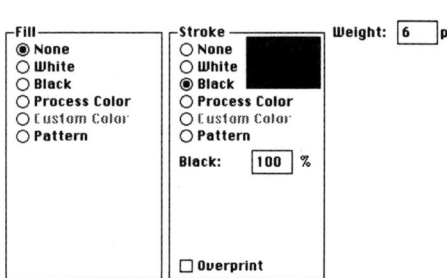

2

With the line still selected, choose Style from the Paint menu (Command-I) to set Fill to None, Stroke to any percentage of black or a color, and Weight to a point size equal to the width measurement of the squares or dots you wish to create. In this example, use a weight of 6 points.

LINES	

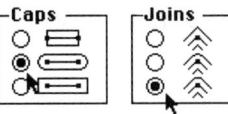

3

Click the second choice under Caps (the round ends) for a line of dots, or the third choice (the extended blunt ends) for a line of squares.

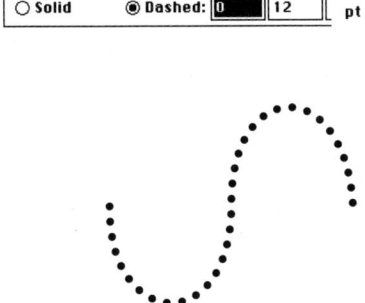

4

Click Dashed in the Dash pattern box located at the bottom of the Paint dialog box. In the first box type the number 0, which creates either perfect circles or squares.

Typing 0 in the first Dash pattern box and clicking None in the Fill box are the only two constants you must remember to enter for this special effect to work. If you type a number of greater value in the first Dash pattern box, you will get ellipses and rectangles instead of circles and squares.

Tab to the second box and type the number of points you want as space between dots. In this case, type 12.

Tips: Try changing the line weight and the gap measurement (the second box under Dash pattern) for different effects. For example, in step 2, you can change the size of the dot or square by specifying a thicker or thinner weight.

In step 4, changing the gap measurement will decrease or increase the distance between the dots or squares. If the gap measurement equals the line weight measurement, the dots or squares will just touch.

PART III: TECHNIQUES

Hand-drawn Look: Method 1

You may want a line that has an uneven, hand-drawn look—one that seems to go from thick to thin, a line you might describe as calligraphic. It is easy to create this effect with Illustrator's layering features. You have complete control of the thickness of the line even after you have drawn it.

You can use this technique to create the effect of a hand-drawn or brush-stroked border around any solid shape (such as a closed path).

In this example, you will draw an uneven black line on a white background.

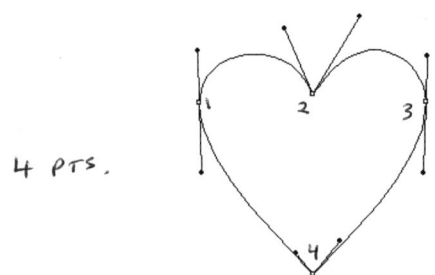

1

Using the Pen tool to draw freehand, or tracing a scanned template, draw a closed shape, such as the heart shape in this figure. The fewer points you click with the Pen tool, the smoother the line will be; the more points you click, the more uneven the line will be.

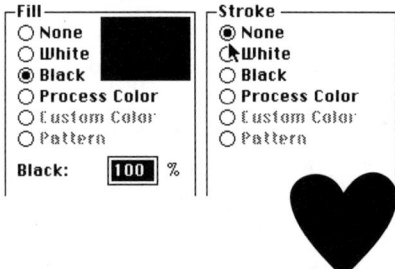

2

Use Style from the Paint menu (Command-I) to set the Fill to the percentage of black or color that you want for the hand-drawn line; set Stroke to None. The figure at left shows the Paint dialog box settings for this example and the resulting heart-shaped path.

LINES

3

Using the Pen tool, draw a similar but slightly different shape that is smaller than the first. If you prefer, use one of the Scale tools from the toolbox and scale a copy. Then adjust the curves and anchor points to change the second shape slightly. Select the second shape and drag it on top of the first shape.

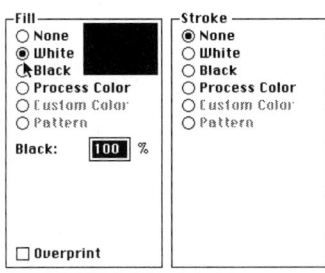

4

With the inside shape still selected, use the Style command from the Paint menu (Command-I) to set Fill to White (to match your paper color or background). For this effect to work, always match the fill color to the desired background color. For this demonstration, assume you are drawing on a white page.

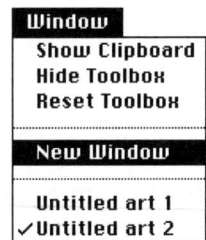

5

Select New Window from the Window menu and arrange your two windows so you can see them both on the screen. Click one of the windows and choose Preview Illustration from the View menu (Command-Y). In the preview window, note that the white-filled shape is covering most of the black-filled shape. The only thing that will print is an uneven black line that is the part of the black-filled heart left uncovered by the slightly smaller white-filled heart. Click on the window that shows the artwork and refine the unevenness of the visible black line by moving the curves or anchor points and direction handles to allow less or more of the black to show.

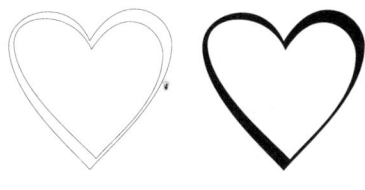

243

PART III: TECHNIQUES

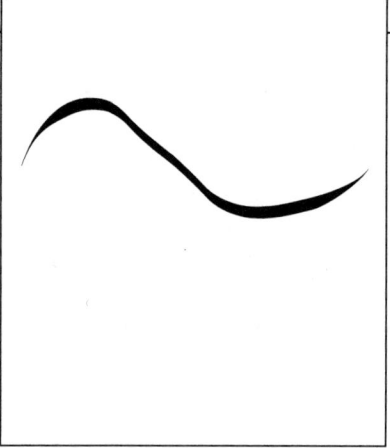

Hand-drawn Look: Method 2

In the preceding technique, you drew lines with a hand-drawn look around a solid shape. In this example, you will use a different technique to create the appearance of hand-drawn lines as open paths.

You can use this technique to add shading effects to solid figures, or to draw complete illustrations such as the Technical Illustration in Part IV.

1

Using the Pen or Freehand tool, draw or trace the line you want to represent as an open path. The fewer points you click with the Pen tool, the smoother the line will be; the more points you click, the more uneven the line will be. This figure shows a hand-drawn curved line drawn with the Freehand tool.

2

Option-click on the line to select the whole path, then choose Copy (Command-C) and Paste In Front (Command-F) to make a duplicate of the line, layered on top of the first.

3

Click away from the pasted line to deselect it, then drag each anchor point, except the two endpoints, a slight distance away from the first position.

244

LINES

4

In turn, select each of the pairs of anchor points at the ends of the shape and choose Join from the Arrange menu (Command-J). You can choose either Corner point or Smooth point in the Join dialog box, which is displayed whenever you join two points that overlap precisely. You now have a solid shape, a closed path.

5

With the shape or some part of it still selected, use the Style command from the Paint menu (Command-I) to set the Fill to the percentage of black or color you wish the line to be. When you have set the attributes, click OK.

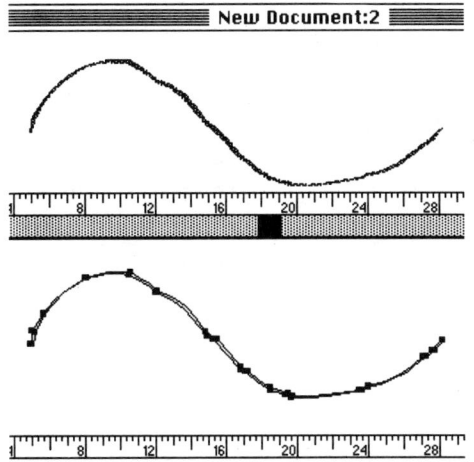

6

Select New Window from the Window menu and size and arrange your two windows so you can see them both, as shown in the figure at left. Click one of the windows and choose Preview Illustration from the View menu (Command-Y).

Click on the window that shows the artwork to make it active and begin to refine the unevenness of the hand-drawn line. Using the Direct-selection tool, move the curves or anchor points and direction handles (see The Pen Tool in Part I) to create a thicker or thinner line. Use the Add-anchor-point tool, or use the Scissors tool while you press down the Option key, to add anchor points if you need them to refine the curves.

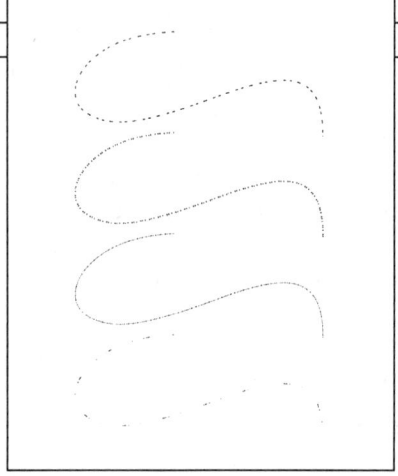

PART III: TECHNIQUES

Hand-drawn Look: Method 3

With the Paint dialog box it is easy to specify perfectly black, inked lines of any weight. But sometimes you may want a softer, more irregular effect, such as a stippled effect or a sketched or brushed ink look.

Here are some tips to help you create these effects in your drawings. There are countless variations on the suggestions listed here. You are encouraged to experiment with them.

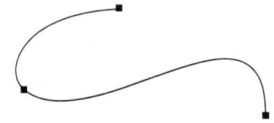

1

Draw a line using one of the drawing tools (the Pen tool, Freehand tool, or Autotrace tool). The figure at left shows a curved line drawn with the Pen tool.

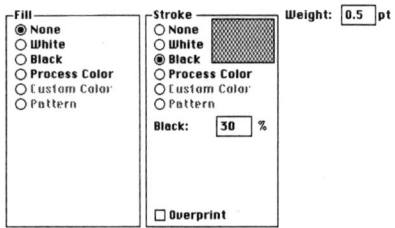

2

With the line selected, choose Style from the Paint menu (Command-I) and set Fill to None. Set Stroke to a percentage of black less than 50 percent (or choose a muted color). Set a fairly thin weight. For this example, enter 30 percent Black and type in .5 points Weight.

LINES

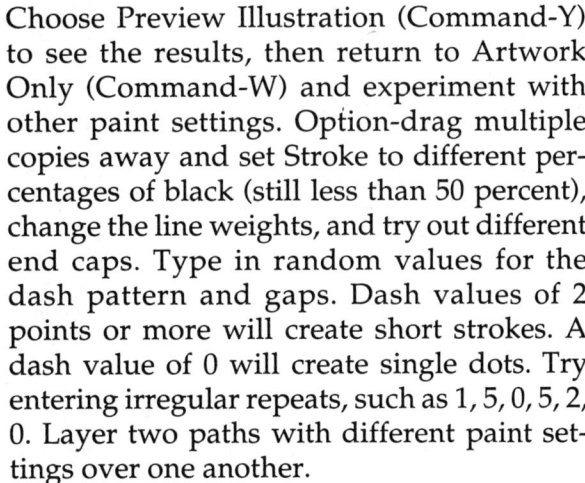

3

Choose Preview Illustration (Command-Y) to see the results, then return to Artwork Only (Command-W) and experiment with other paint settings. Option-drag multiple copies away and set Stroke to different percentages of black (still less than 50 percent), change the line weights, and try out different end caps. Type in random values for the dash pattern and gaps. Dash values of 2 points or more will create short strokes. A dash value of 0 will create single dots. Try entering irregular repeats, such as 1, 5, 0, 5, 2, 0. Layer two paths with different paint settings over one another.

Tips: Using different percentages of black (or muted color) and different random dash patterns can create lines in your final output resembling the etching effect created with a traditional tool called a roulette wheel.

You will find that thinner lines generally create subtler effects. Subtle line effects are difficult to preview on-screen. You probably will want to print a proof on a LaserWriter, or even a Linotronic, to fine-tune the effect. In either case, you can shorten the cycle of experimentation by setting up a variety of lines on one page and printing them all at once. Then decide which one you will use or modify for use in the final artwork.

See also Dotted Lines.

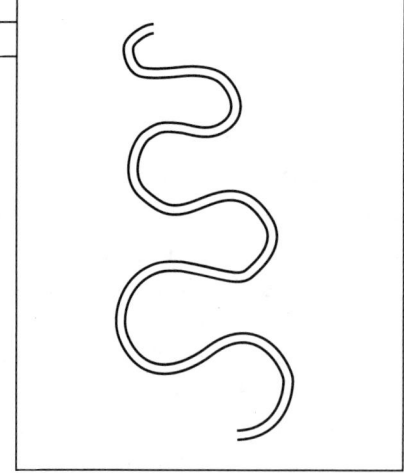

PART III: TECHNIQUES

Parallel Curves

Often you will need two parallel lines separated by a specific distance. If there are no curves in the line, you can draw one line and then drag away a copy. Trying to create curved parallel lines using this method poses a problem; the original line and the copy will not run parallel at the curves. The second figure at left shows the results when a curved line is simply duplicated and moved. Moreover, it is very difficult to place a small, precise distance between each line. This technique provides the solution—and you can make the lines as curved as you like!

Curving parallel lines are often used to represent a highway on a map.

1

Use the Pen or Freehand tool to draw the path you want. The figure at left shows a long, curved path, created for this example.

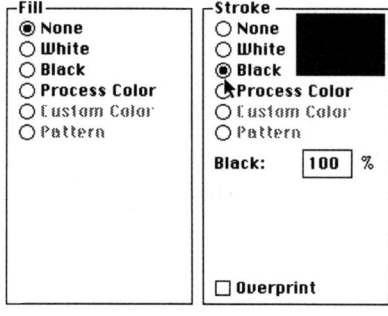

2

Use the Object-selection tool, or Option-click on the path with the Selection tool, to select the entire path (the anchor points turn into filled-in black squares) and use Style from the Paint menu (Command-I) to set Fill to None and Stroke to any percentage of black or color you like. Do not click OK yet.

LINES

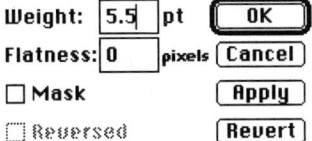

3

To set the line weight for the parallel lines you use a formula, as follows. Decide which line weight you want for each parallel line and how many points of space you want between the parallel lines. Double your desired line weight and add in the number of points you want between the parallel lines. For example:

	2	pts	Line weight for each line
x	2	pts	Times 2
	4	pts	Line weight doubled
+	1.5	pts	Space between lines
	5.5	pts	Total entered as line weight

Type the total into the Weight box—5.5 points in this case—and click OK.

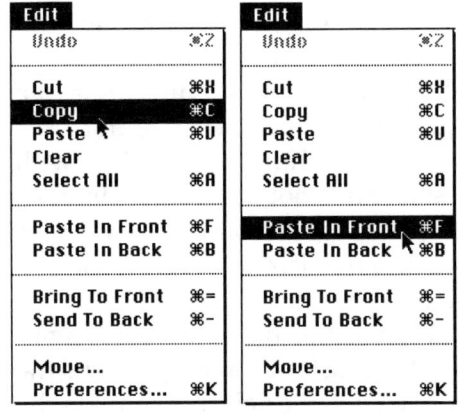

4

Choose the Copy command from the Edit menu (Command-C) to copy the line, then use Paste In Front from the Edit menu (Command-F). A copy of the line is pasted directly on top of your original, so you won't be able to see it immediately.

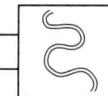

PART III: TECHNIQUES

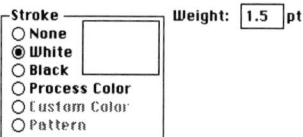

5

With the new copy of the line still selected, choose Style from the Paint menu (Command-I) and set Stroke to White and Weight to the number of points you decided in step 3 would separate the parallel lines—1.5 points in this case.

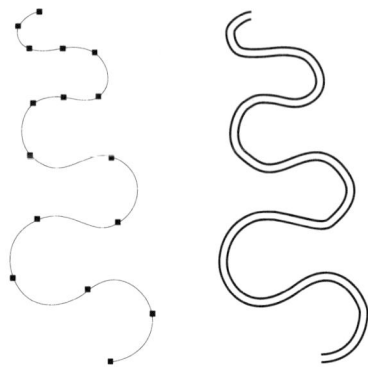

6

Preview your parallel lines by selecting Preview Illustration from the View menu (Command-Y), then return to Artwork Only (Command-W) and make adjustments to the stroke weights if necessary to get the look you want. Because the two paths that compose the curving parallel lines overlap precisely, use the following techniques to select and edit lines:

To select both lines, use the Object-selection tool, or hold down the Option key and use the Selection tool, and drag a marquee over any part of the overlapping lines.

To select the bottom line only, use the technique just described to select both paths, then hold down the Shift key and click with the Object-selection tool on the top line, or hold down both the Option and Shift keys and click with the Selection tool on the top line to deselect it.

To select the top line only, click on it with the Object-selection tool, or hold down the Option key and click the Selection tool on the top line.

250

LINES

7

When you have achieved the results you want, use the Object-selection tool to drag a selection marquee over the curved parallel line path and choose Group from the Arrange menu (Command-G). (See The Selection Tools in Part I.)

See also Compound Lines: Methods 1 and 2.

PART III: TECHNIQUES

Shapes (Closed Paths)

Arrows

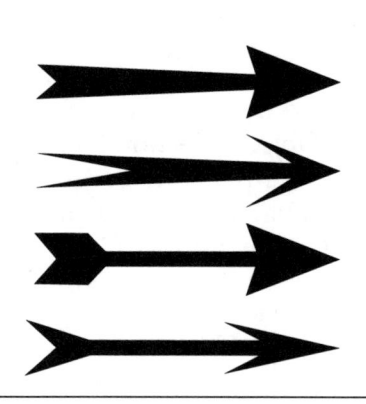

Arrows are common symbols used in many types of illustrations. The accompanying figure shows a variety of arrow shapes. You can use existing arrows from symbol fonts such as Zapf Dingbats and use the Create Outlines command to modify them, or you can create your own arrows using the technique described here.

This technique can be used to create any symmetrical object.

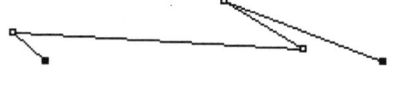

1

Create the top half of the arrow. The figure at left shows the top half of this arrow created with the Pen tool.

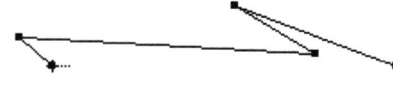

2

With the drawn elements selected, choose the Reflect-dialog tool, or choose the Reflect tool and then hold down the Option key, and click on one of the two endpoints.

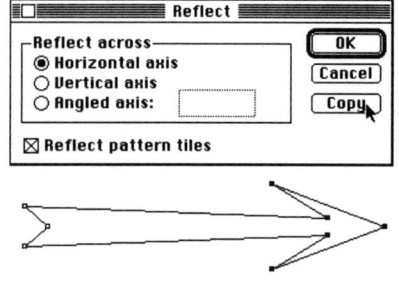

3

When you use the Reflect-dialog tool, or Option-click with the Reflect tool, the Reflect dialog box opens. Select Horizontal axis reflection and close the dialog box by clicking Copy. This creates a horizontal mirror image—in this case, the bottom half of the arrow.

| SHAPES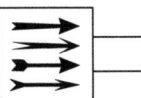

If the arrow you create in this step is not to your liking, delete one half and rework the other half, then go back to step 2.

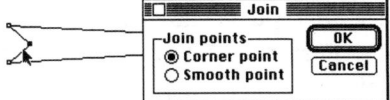

4

With the Selection tool or the Direct-selection tool, drag a selection marquee to select one pair of the common points where the two paths join—in this case, the back end of the arrow. (See The Selection Tools in Part I.) Type Command-J to join the pair. The Join dialog box appears. Click Corner point and click OK to complete the join. Repeat this process with the other pair of common points.

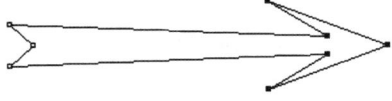

5

To make the arrow longer or shorter, select the point at one end. Press down on the Shift key after starting to drag the point horizontally. The point selected for adjusting in this example is the front tip of the arrow.

Tip: Be sure to select all of the points that compose the tip of the arrow or the base of the arrow when stretching it longer or shorter. Otherwise, you will distort the shape of the arrow.

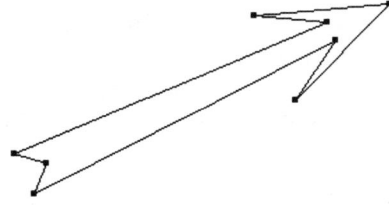

6

To rotate the arrow, click with the Object-selection tool or Option-click the Selection tool anywhere along the path to select it; choose the Rotate tool; put the origin at the tip of the arrow; and, when the pointer becomes an arrowhead, move the pointer in the direction you wish to rotate the arrow.

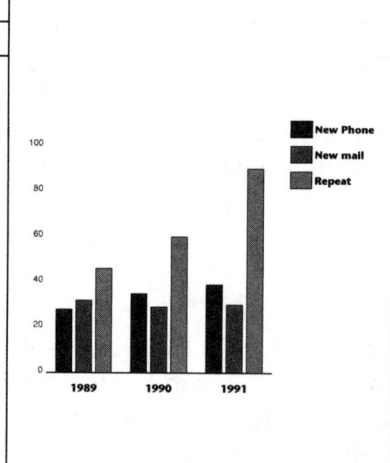

PART III: TECHNIQUES

Charts: Selecting and Modifying

Illustrator's graph tools let you quickly create various types of charts and graphs directly from numeric data. However, the default colors and patterns assigned by the program are often not the ones desired in the final artwork. This technique lets you select related elements of the graph without first ungrouping it. This example refers to grouped-column graphs, but it can be applied to any other graph types generated by the graph tools.

Warning: Unless you have compelling reasons to Ungroup a graph, you should avoid doing so. Once a graph has been ungrouped, you can no longer update it to reflect changes in the underlying numeric data.

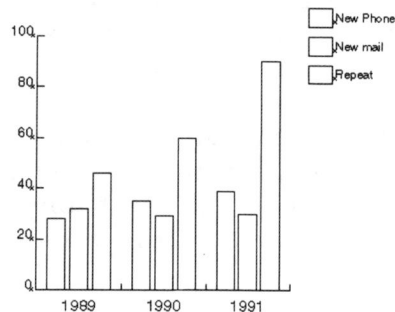

1

Create a grouped-column graph using the Grouped-column graph tool as described in Part I, then either import or type the data into the Graph Data Window, and click OK. The resulting graph is a grouped object, and default fills and strokes are assigned to the various components.

You can use the Direct-selection tool to select individual components of the group. However, you can also use the Direct-selection tool to automatically select related elements, to which you can then assign the desired stroke and fill, or in the case of labels,

SHAPES

type attributes. In each case, the technique involves Option-clicking the Direct-selection tool twice. The first time you click, the object you clicked becomes selected. The second time you click, all the related elements in the graph also become selected. Clicking a third time selects the entire graph.

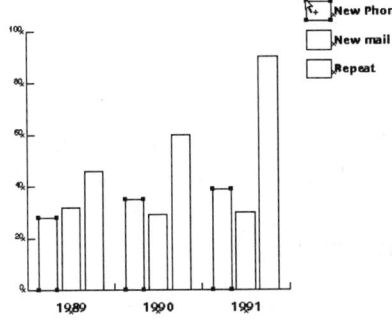

2

To change the paint attributes for the legend and all the columns in a data series, Option-click the Direct-selection tool twice on the legend. The first time you click, the legend is selected. The second time you click, all the columns in the data series are also selected. You can now use the Style command from the Paint menu (Command-I) to change the stroke and fill for the entire data series at once. You can repeat the process for the other data series.

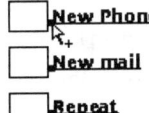

3

To change the paint or type attributes for all the legend labels, Option-click the Direct-selection tool twice on any legend label. The first time you click, the label is selected; the second time you click, all the legend labels are selected. You can now modify the paint and type attributes for all the legend labels.

255

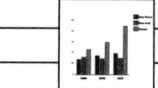 

PART III: TECHNIQUES

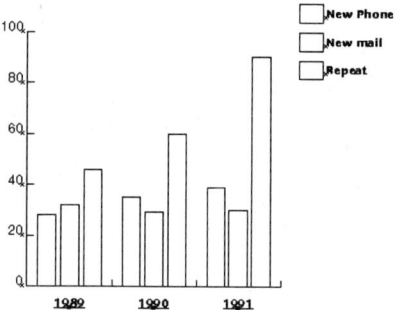

4

To change the paint or type attributes for all the category labels, Option-click the Direct-selection tool twice on any category label. The first time you click, the label is selected; the second time you click, all the category labels are selected. You can now modify the paint and type attributes for all the category labels.

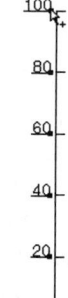

5

To change the paint or type attributes for all the value axis labels, Option-click the Direct-selection tool twice on any value axis label. The first time you click, the label is selected; the second time you click, all the value axis labels are selected. You can now modify the paint and type attributes for all the value axis labels.

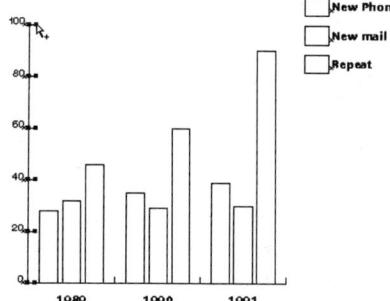

6

To change the paint attributes for all the tick marks on an axis, Option-click the Direct-selection tool twice on any tick mark. The first time you click, the tick mark is selected; the second time you click, all the tick marks are selected. You can now modify the paint attributes for all the tick marks on the axis. You can hide the tick marks by setting their Stroke to None.

SHAPES

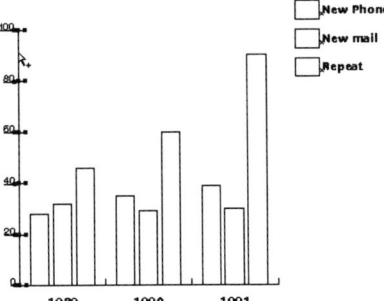

7

To select an entire axis, Option-click the Direct-selection tool twice on the axis. The first time you click, only the axis is selected. The second time you click, both the axis and the tick marks are selected. In the case of the value axis, the axis labels are also selected, but in the case of the category axis, the labels are not selected.

Tip: You can hide an entire axis by setting the Stroke and Fill to None. This solution is better than simply deleting the axis, because to delete the axis you must Ungroup the graph. Ungrouping the graph not only makes it impossible to update the data, but also disables the automatic selection features described here.

See also The Graph Tools in Part I, and the Graph Menu in Part II.

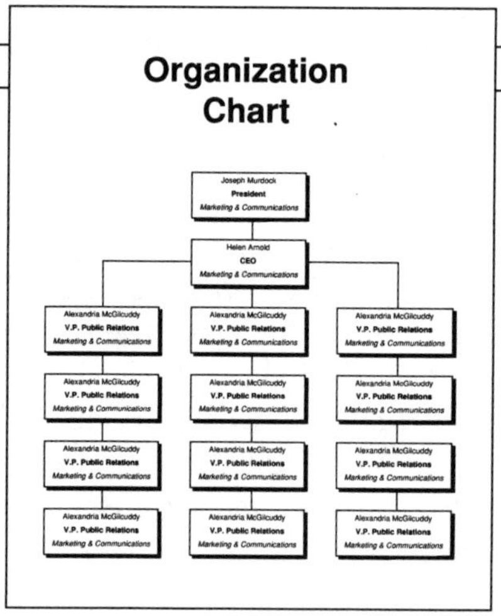

PART III: TECHNIQUES

Organization Chart

Organization Charts

Organization charts, such as the one shown in the accompanying figure, are a very common form of business graphics. Here is a technique for quickly producing an organization chart.

1

Drag the Type tool to create a rectangular text object large enough to accommodate the longest name and title or department that will appear in the organization chart, then type the text and set the font, size, alignment, and leading.

These text elements need not reflect an actual item in the chart—the person's name you type need not hold that title or be in that department—but they do need to have as many characters as the longest entries you will make in the chart.

2

Using the Direct-selection tool, Option-click to select the text rectangle without selecting the text, then use the Style command from the Paint menu (Command-I) to set the Fill to White and the Stroke to the shade and thickness you like.

The fill of the rectangle can be white or any percentage of black or a color, but it cannot be set to None or the lines drawn in step 8 will be visible behind the text.

SHAPES

3

To add a drop shadow, make sure that only the rectangle is selected, not the text, then Option-drag the rectangle using the Direct-selection tool to make a copy. Use the Unlink command (Command-Shift-U) to unlink the copied rectangle. Click anywhere to deselect all objects, then Option-click the Direct-selection tool to select the drop shadow. Use the Style command from the Paint menu (Command-I) to set the drop shadow's Fill and Stroke to Black, and use the Send To Back command (Command-hyphen) to send the drop shadow to the bottom layer.

4

When you have completed the text rectangle and drop shadow, use the Select All command (Command-A) to select all of the elements, then use the Group command (Command-G) to group these elements.

This group will be the basic element used throughout the chart.

5

Working in Fit In Window view (Command-M), make as many copies of this basic unit as you need for the organization chart by selecting the rectangle and all of the text elements and dragging this basic "building block" with the Option key held down (to make a copy) and the Shift key held down (if you want to align copies horizontally or vertically).

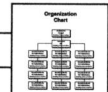 PART III: TECHNIQUES

If you are making several columns of entries, it is a good idea to create one column by dragging a copy of the first box into the second position and then using the Transform Again command (Command-D) to create additional copies spaced equally apart.

Then use the Selection tool to select the whole column and hold down the Option key as you drag copies of the whole column into other positions; hold the Shift key as well if you want to align columns horizontally.

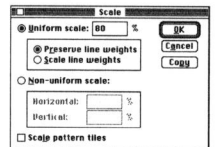

6

If the final layout is too large to fit on one page, you can use Select All (Command-A) and use the Scale tool with the Option key to reduce the size of the chart (including the size of the type).

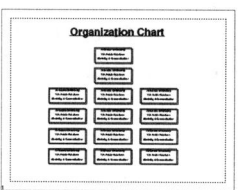

7

Once you have the overall chart arranged on the page, use the Type tool to add a chart title and caption (if appropriate).

8

Use Select All (Command-A) and Lock (Command-1) to select all of the elements and lock them; then use the Pen tool with the Shift key to draw straight lines from the center of each rectangle to the center of adjacent rectangles or to adjoining lines that indicate the structure of the organization.

| **SHAPES** | |

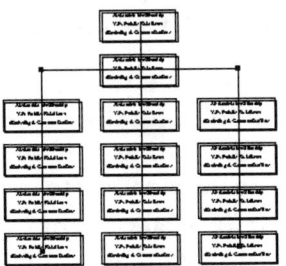

You can start by drawing a long path from the top box down through the longest column and then add other paths to connect the other columns, but remember to click on the Pen tool again each time you want to start with a new endpoint.

9

After drawing all lines, use Unlock (Command-2) to unlock and automatically select all of the boxed elements, then use Bring To Front (Command-+) to bring the boxed elements to the top layer, above the lines you drew in step 8.

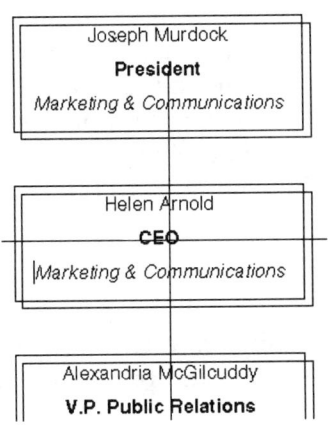

10

Finally, use the Zoom-in tool to change to a magnified view of the top of the chart, then use the Type tool to select each line of text, one by one, and change the boilerplate text to the appropriate name, title, and department in each box on the chart.

Tip: You can select a whole word by double-clicking it with any Type tool, and a whole line by triple-clicking it with any Type tool.

See also Aligning Objects: Methods 1 and 2, Grid: Method 1, Cubes: Methods 1 and 2.

PART III: TECHNIQUES

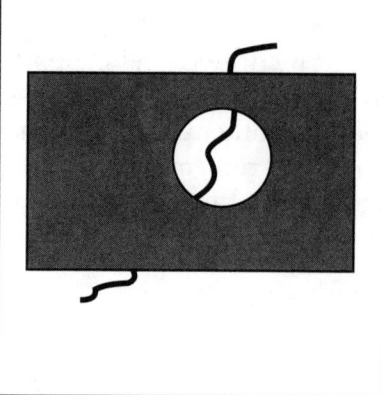

Holes in Solid Objects

You can always make a solid shape appear to have a hole in it by drawing the hole and giving it a fill of white. But what if you want the hole to be transparent to objects below it? You can use the Make Compound command from the Paint menu to create this effect.

This effect is most commonly seen in the holes inside closed letters of the alphabet—something that Illustrator does automatically when you use the Create Outlines command—but you can use the technique described here to combine any two paths.

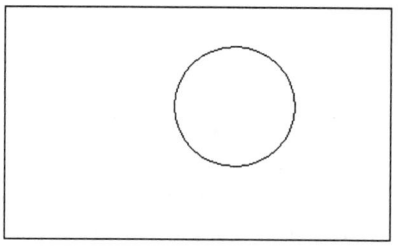

1

Create the whole image as two paths: the outer edge and the shape of the hole. In this example, the outer edge is a rectangle created with the Rectangle tool. The circle just right of center is the shape of the hole, created with the Oval tool and the Shift key.

2

Select both objects and choose the Make Compound command from the Paint menu.

SHAPES

3
To edit either shape, select points using the Direct-selection tool.

See also Masking.

PART III: TECHNIQUES

Polygons

You can use the technique described here to draw any polygon shape with equal-length sides all around—equilateral triangles, pentagons, hexagons, or polygons with seven or more sides. (You can use the Rectangle tool instead of this technique to draw perfect squares.) A five-sided polygon (pentagon) is created in this example.

1

Use the Pen tool with the Shift key to draw a straight vertical line like the one shown in the figure at left.

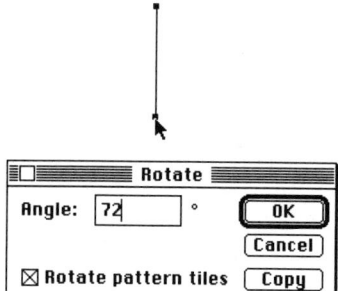

2

Select the entire line, then select the Rotate-dialog tool and click at the bottom point of the line, or select the Rotate tool and Option-click at the bottom point. This opens the Rotate dialog box.

Enter a number of degrees yielded by dividing 360 (degrees) by the number of sides to the polygon, for example, 72 degrees for a five-sided polygon, 60 degrees for a six-sided polygon, and so on.

For a five-sided polygon, type 72 (for 72 degrees) into the Angle field of the Rotate dialog box and click Copy to rotate a copy of the line 72 degrees.

| SHAPES |

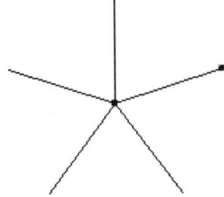

3

With the rotated copy selected, use Transform Again (Command-D) three times. You now have five lines radiating from a common center.

4

Using the Direct-selection tool, drag a marquee over the common center points, then press Delete or Backspace. (See The Selection Tools in Part I.)

You now have five endpoints remaining to use as guides. Each one will be a corner of the polygon.

5

Use the Direct-selection tool to select any adjacent pair of points, then choose Join from the Arrange menu (Command-J) to draw a line connecting them.

Repeat this step until all sides of the polygon are drawn.

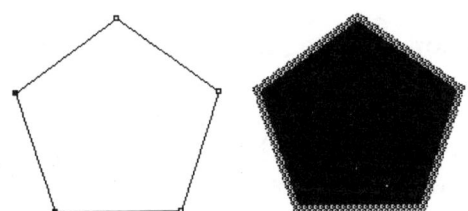

6

Use the Style command from the Paint menu (Command-I), paint the polygon with your desired stroke and fill settings, select the entire object, and group it (Command-G). In this example, the polygon has a 100 percent Black Fill and a 50 percent Black Stroke with a Weight of 5 points.

Radial Symmetry: Method 1

Radial symmetry describes any object composed of a single shape that is repeated in a pattern around a central point. An example of radial symmetry is a flower, such as the one shown in the accompanying figure. In this technique the Rotate tool is used to create simple patterns in which the shapes do not need to meet precisely at the edges—that is, they can overlap, or there can be gaps between them.

You can use this technique to create any radially symmetrical design that allows some gap or overlap between the units of the design.

1

Create an object that will become the basic unit of the radial design, using whatever tool is appropriate. In this example, use the Pen or Freehand tool to create a petal-shaped object, as in the figure at left.

2

Select the Rotate-dialog tool and click (or select the Rotate tool and Option-click) the point you want to use as the center of the design—in this case, the base of the petal. In the Rotate dialog box, enter the number of degrees yielded by dividing 360 (degrees) by the number of repeated units.

SHAPES

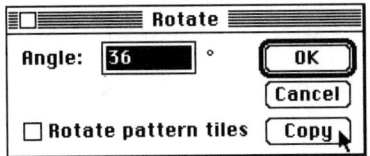

In this example you want ten units, so you type 36 as the number of degrees (360 divided by 10). Some other common values are shown in the following table.

NUMBER OF REPEATED UNITS IN CIRCLE	DEGREES
2	180
3	120
4	90
5	72
6	60
7	51.43
8	45
9	40
10	36

Click Copy to close the Rotate dialog box and make a rotated copy of the first object, then use Transform Again (Command-D) until the circle is complete—eight more copies in this example.

3

Use Select All (Command-A) and Group (Command-G) to group the objects that make up your shape.

Tip: Once you create a design, you can create many variations by scaling, overlaying, and/or shearing the object. The figure on the left shows three copies of the flower petals scaled progressively smaller, with variations in the fill and stroke for each group of petals in the object.

PART III: TECHNIQUES

Radial Symmetry: Method 2

This second technique for creating radially symmetrical designs is more controlled than the first, creating shapes that meet precisely at the edges, such as the one shown in the accompanying figure.

This technique can be used to create any radially symmetrical design.

1

Use the Oval tool with the Shift key to draw a circle (as shown in the figure at left) whose center will be the center of the radial design and whose circumference will cross through the points you want the radial elements to touch or cross.

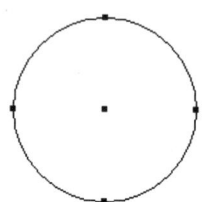

2

Use the Pen tool to set an anchor point anywhere on the circumference of the circle. In this example, the anchor point is just to the right of the top of the circle.

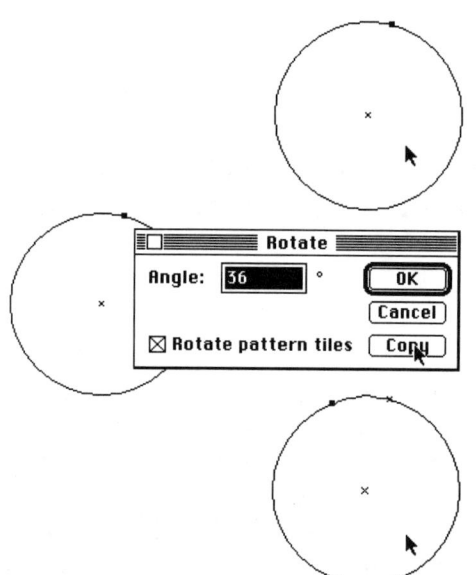

Select the Rotate-dialog tool and click the center of the circle, or use the Rotate tool and hold the Option key as you click on the center of the circle. The Rotate dialog box appears.

In the Angle field of the Rotate dialog box, type the number of degrees yielded by dividing 360 (degrees) by the number of repeated units. See the table in Radial Symmetry: Method 1 for some common values.

Click Copy to close the box and make a rotated copy of the anchor point.

| SHAPES | |

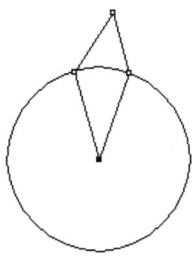

3

Create an object that will become the basic unit of the radial design, using the two anchor points as guides for the edges of the shape. In this example, use the Pen or Freehand tool to draw an irregular polygon.

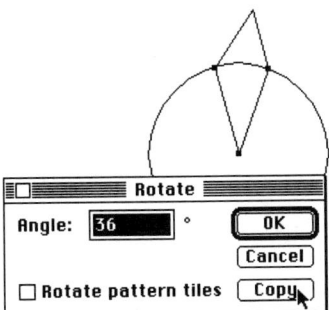

4

With the basic radial element selected, select the Rotate-dialog tool and click the center of the circle, or use the Rotate tool and Option-click the center of the circle, which happens to be the base of the polygon in this example. In the Angle field of the Rotate dialog box, type the number of degrees you used in step 2 (36 degrees in this example), and click Copy to close the box and make a rotated copy of the object. Use Transform Again (Command-D) as many times as needed to complete the design.

5

Select and delete the original circle and the two anchor points you used as guides. Then select the remaining objects and use Group (Command-G).

Tip: If your design does not touch the center of the circle, you can use Ungroup (Command-U) on the circle and delete only the circumference, leaving the center point and grouping it with the rest of the design.

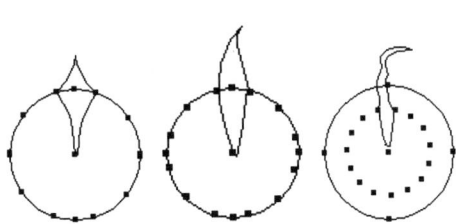

The figure at left shows the correct positioning of the basic radial unit with respect to the circle and anchor points for various other designs that can be created using this technique.

269

PART III: TECHNIQUES

Shared Borders

Separate shapes that share common irregular edges—shapes that must fit together like jigsaw puzzle pieces—are a common drawing situation. Individual countries, states, or counties on a map are a typical example. This simple technique shows the most efficient way for you to handle this drawing situation.

Perfect for map work, this technique also proves useful for illustration styles that simulate dimension by using shapes of various gray fills.

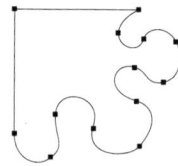

1

Using one of the drawing tools, draw a shape with an irregular path similar to the figure at left. You are going to draw another irregular shape to the right of the first. It will share a common border with the first shape.

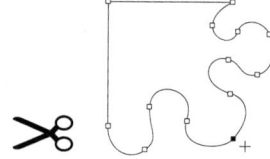

2

Select the Scissors tool and click at two points on the irregular path. The line length between these two cuts will become the new common border. The figure at left shows one point being selected for cutting. The other point to cut is the top point of the curved path.

270

| SHAPES |  |

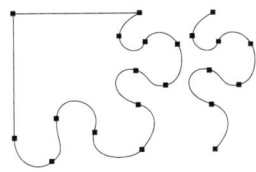

3

Select the Object-selection tool and click (or use the Selection tool and Option-click) on the line segment between the two cut points, selecting that section. Hold the Option key and drag away an exact copy of the selected line segment.

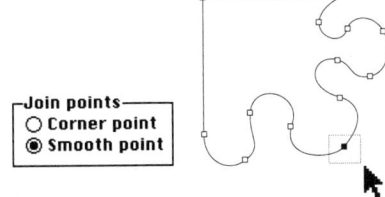

4

Rejoin the cut points on the original path using the selection marquee created by dragging the Selection tool or the Direct-selection tool and Join from the Arrange menu (Command-J). Select the appropriate join from the Join dialog box. Click on Smooth point for this example. Your original path is now closed.

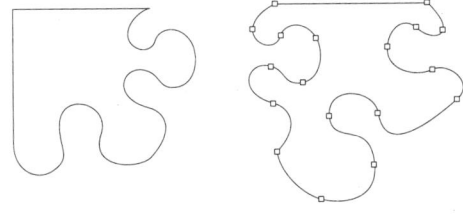

5

Choose the appropriate tool and finish drawing the adjoining shape, beginning with the exact copy of the shared border line segment. When you finish drawing, the two shapes will have identical common borders and will fit together perfectly.

See also The Scissors Tool and The Pen Tool.

PART III: TECHNIQUES

Stars: Method 1

You can use the technique described here to draw any star shape—three-pointed, four-pointed, or more.

1

Use the Pen tool with the Shift key to draw a straight vertical line like the one shown in the figure at left.

2

Select the entire line, then select the Rotate-dialog tool and click at the bottom point of the line. This opens the Rotate dialog box.

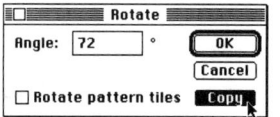

Enter a number of degrees yielded by dividing 360 (degrees) by the number of points on the star. This yields 72 degrees for a five-pointed star, 60 degrees for a six-pointed star, and so on.

Type 72 (for 72 degrees) into the Angle field of the Rotate dialog box and click Copy to rotate a copy of the line 72 degrees.

SHAPES

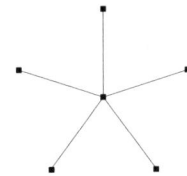

3

With the rotated copy selected, use Transform Again (Command-D) three times. You now have five lines radiating from a common center.

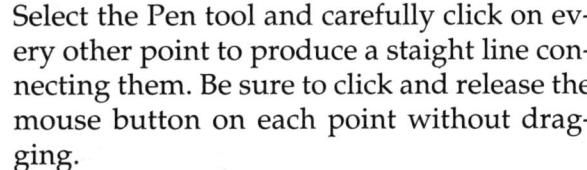

4

Using the Selection tool or the Direct-selection tool, drag a marquee over the common center points, then press Delete or Backspace. (See Selection Tools in Part I.)

You now have five endpoints remaining to use as guides. Each one will be a tip of one of the star points.

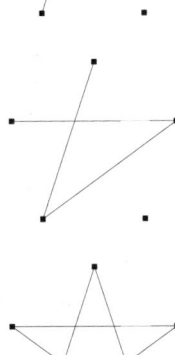

5

Select the Pen tool and carefully click on every other point to produce a staight line connecting them. Be sure to click and release the mouse button on each point without dragging.

For a five-pointed star, start by clicking the top point, then click on the lower left point. Proceed to the upper right point and click, then over to the upper left point and click. Then move to the lower right point and click, and, finally, complete the star and close the path by once again clicking at the top point.

273

PART III: TECHNIQUES

For stars with an odd number of points, clicking every other point will always result in one closed path, such as the seven- and nine-pointed stars shown in the figure at left.

For stars with an even number of points, clicking every other point will yield two paths. For a six-pointed star, click on every other point to draw two triangles. For an eight-pointed star, click on every other point to draw two squares. These and other variations are shown in the figure at left.

6

If you want a solid shaded star with no stroke (or stroke the same as the fill), you are finished. Use Style from the Paint menu (Command-I) to paint the star with your desired stroke and fill settings, select the entire object, and use Group (Command-G). If you would like to be able to stroke a different color around the outside edge of the star, do not group the elements, and go on to step 7.

| SHAPES | |

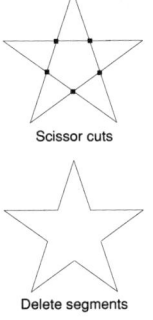

Scissor cuts

Delete segments

Join endpoints

7

In a magnified view, use the Scissors tool to cut lines that cross inside the shape, then use Cut (Command-X), or press Delete or Backspace to delete the inside line segments. Use the Join command (Command-J) to join corresponding inside points.

8

You can now use Style from the Paint menu (Command-I) to set a different stroke and fill for the star shape. In this example, the star has a 100 percent Black Fill and a 50 percent Black Stroke with a Weight of 5 points.

When you finish, select the entire object and group it using Group (Command-G).

275

PART III: TECHNIQUES

Stars: Method 2

You can use the technique described here to draw any star shape, but here you have more control over the length of the points than you did with the previous technique.

1

Use the Pen tool with the Shift key to draw a straight vertical line.

2

Select the entire line, then select the Rotate-dialog tool and click (or select the Rotate tool and Option-click) at the bottom point of the line. The Rotate dialog box appears.

Enter a number of degrees yielded by dividing 360 (degrees) by the number of points on the star. This yields 72 degrees for a five-pointed star, 60 degrees for a six-pointed star, and so on.

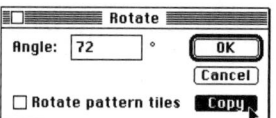

Type 72 (for 72 degrees) into the Angle field of the Rotate dialog box and click Copy to rotate a copy of the line 72 degrees.

276

SHAPES

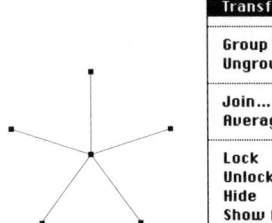

3

Select Transform Again from the Arrange menu (Command-D) three times (or more if you are creating star shapes with more than five points). You now have five lines radiating from a common center.

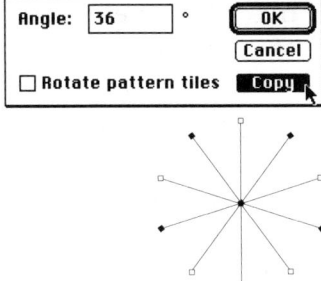

4

Select the entire object, then select the Rotate-dialog tool and click (or select the Rotate tool and Option-click) on the common center points. Type half the number of degrees you typed in step 2—36 for a five-pointed star—in the Rotate dialog box. Click Copy to close the box and rotate a copy of the lines. This yields ten lines radiating from a common center.

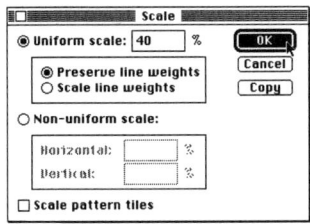

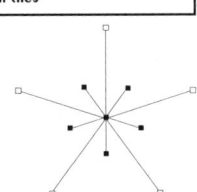

5

With the copied lines still selected, select the Scale-dialog tool and click (or select the Scale tool and Option-click) on the common center points.

With the Uniform scale option selected, type 40 into the percentage box of the Scale dialog box.

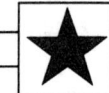 PART III: TECHNIQUES

6

Using the Selection tool or the Direct-selection tool, drag a marquee over the common center points, then press Delete, Backspace, or use Cut (Command-X) to delete them. (See The Selection Tools in Part I.) Be sure that only the center points are selected before you remove them.

You now have ten endpoints remaining to use as guides. Five will be tips of the star points, and five will correspond to the inner angle point of your star's arms.

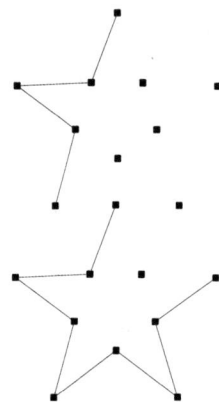

7

Select the Pen tool and connect these points sequentially with careful clicks of the mouse in a clockwise or counterclockwise sequence. Be sure to click and release the mouse button on each point without dragging. Complete the star by clicking at the point where you started.

8

Use Style from the Paint menu (Command-I) to set the fill and stroke of the star as you wish.

SHAPES

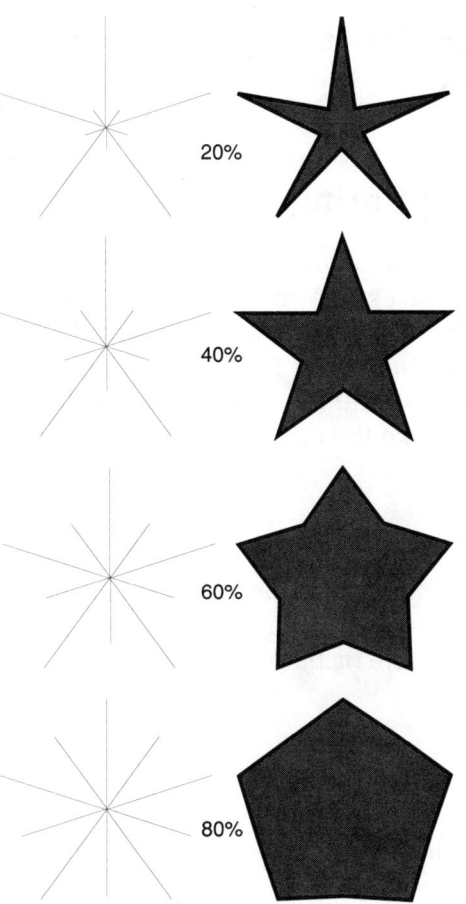

Tip: The percentage reduction you enter in step 5 determines the sharpness of the points. The greater the percentage reduction, the sharper the points. The figure on the left shows the results of different reduction settings.

PART III: TECHNIQUES

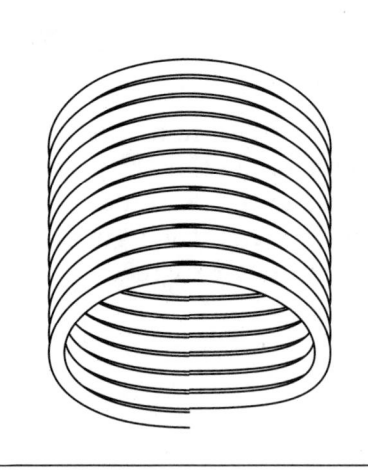

Three-Dimensional Effects

Coils and Springs

Coils and springs are common parts of mechanical devices and appear in many technical drawings, but they can be difficult to create unless you know the right techniques. Using the technique described here, you will draw a coil like the one pictured at left.

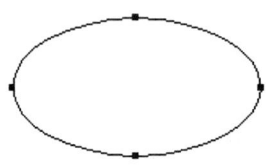

1

Use one of the Oval tools to draw an ellipse. Direct-select and delete the center point using the Delete or Backspace key.

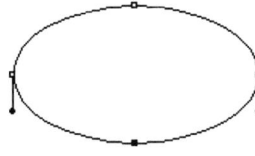

2

Use the Scissors tool to cut the ellipse at its lowest anchor point.

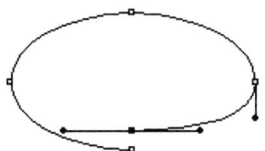

3

With the Selection tool or the Direct-selection tool, select one of the two anchor points created by the cut, and drag it slightly up or down, holding the Shift key as you release the mouse button to constrain the movement to precisely vertical.

You can refine the shape by dragging the next anchor point (along the line from the lower of the two severed points) down about half the distance of the first movement.

THREE-DIMENSIONAL EFFECTS

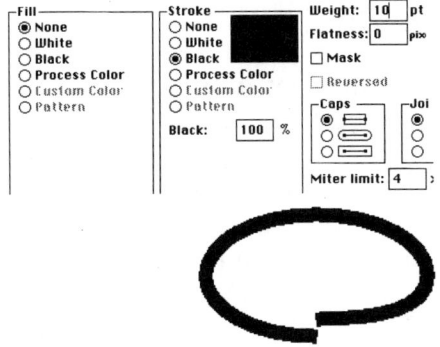

4

Use Style from the Paint menu (Command-I) to set the Stroke of the ellipse to 100 percent Black with a Weight of 10 points (or any thickness you desire) for the coil. In this example, Fill is set to None.

Choose Preview Illustration from the View menu (Command-Y) to check the thickness of the stroke you just set.

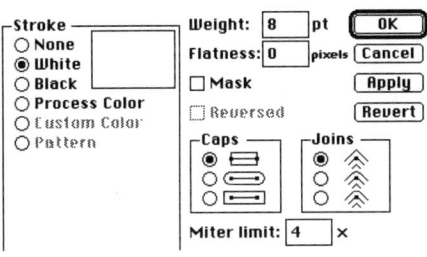

5

With the figure selected, use Copy (Command-C) and Paste In Front (Command-F). With the copy selected, use Style from the Paint menu (Command-I) to change the copy to a Stroke of White with a Weight of 8 points (or two points less than the weight selected in step 4).

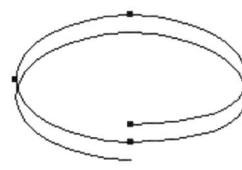

6

Select the composite figure, then use Group (Command-G). With the Object-selection tool, Shift-Option-drag a copy of the figure up (if you want the viewing perspective to be from the top of the coil) or down (if you want the viewing perspective to be from the bottom) to meet the first coil. Be sure to hold down the Shift key and the Option key as you release the mouse button. Select Transform Again from the Arrange menu (Command-D) to create as many additional loops of the coil as you wish.

Select Preview Illustration from the View menu (Command-Y) to see what your coil looks like.

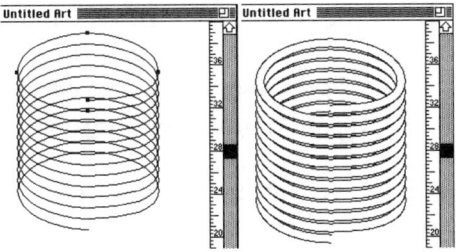

Cubes: Method 1

You can use the simple, visual approach shown here to build a six-sided wire-frame cube.

You can also use this approach to create three-dimensional objects with rectangular sides, like the drawing in the accompanying figure.

Use the Rectangle tool or the Centered-rectangle tool with the Shift key to draw a square like the one in the figure at left. (Recall that holding down the Shift key with a Rectangle tool forces a perfect square.) Direct-select and delete the center point with the Delete or Backspace key.

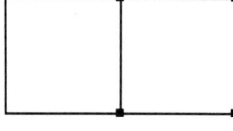

Click with the Object-selection tool (or Option-click with the Selection tool) to select the square, and Shift-Option-drag a copy of it away from the original. Position the copy against the first square so they share a border.

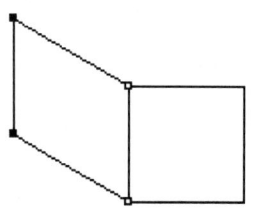

In this step, you can simply use the Object-selection tool with the Shift and Option keys to drag a copy of the first square into the new position, or you can use the Rotate-dialog tool with the pivot point set at the lower left corner of the first square and the rotation set at 90 degrees.

Then select the two leftmost anchor points on the left square and move them up slightly at a diagonal, holding down the Shift key or using the Arrow key if you want to maintain isometric dimensions.

THREE-DIMENSIONAL EFFECTS

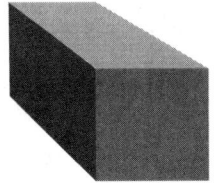

3

Use the Object-selection tool to select the object you just changed into a parallelogram. Holding the Option key to make a copy, drag the copy into position to meet the opposite edge of the first square.

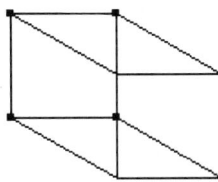

4

Select the first square with the Object-selection tool. Holding the Option key to make a copy, drag the copy into position as the fourth side (the rear).

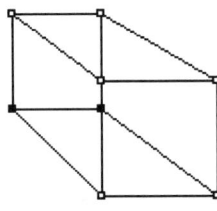

5

To create true perspective, use the Selection tool or the Direct-selection tool to select the two anchor points at the upper, backmost edges of the cube and hold down the Shift key as you drag them down slightly. Then select the two leftmost anchor points of the cube and drag them right slightly.

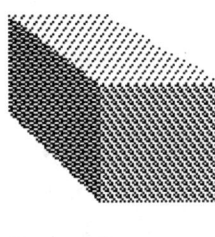

6

To add to the sense of depth, you will need to use the Pen tool to draw a polygon that matches the top side of the cube, then you can shade each of the three "visible" sides (since only three sides would be visible if the object were solid) with a different percentage of black.

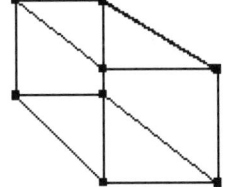

When the cube is complete, drag the Object-selection tool to select the entire object, and use the Group command from the Arrange menu to make it a single object.

283

PART III: TECHNIQUES

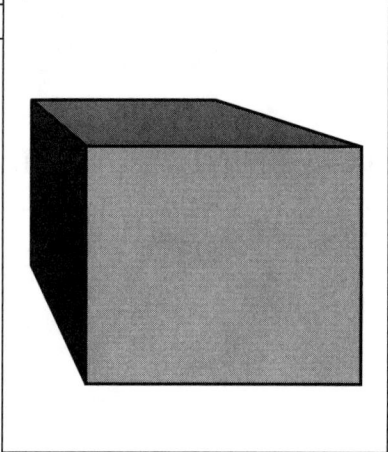

Cubes: Method 2

You can use this technique to create three-dimensional objects with irregular sides.

1

Use the Rectangle tool or the Centered-rectangle tool to draw a rectangle. Direct-select and delete the center point using the Delete or Backspace key.

2

To make one smaller copy of the rectangle, click with the Object-selection tool (or Option-click the Selection tool) on the rectangle to select the whole path, then select the Scale-dialog tool. Click on the rectangle to open the Scale dialog box. Click on Uniform scale and enter 75 percent. Click Copy when you are done.

With the copy selected, position it so it overlaps the first rectangle.

The positioning of the smaller rectangle will determine the apparent length of the box as well as the viewer's perspective. For example, if you position the smaller rectangle above the larger one, the cube will appear deep and will be viewed from an overhead

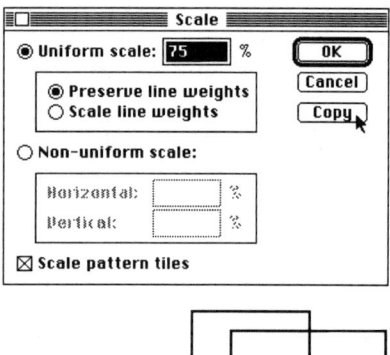

THREE-DIMENSIONAL EFFECTS

perspective; if you position the smaller rectangle to overlap the larger rectangle, as in this example, the perspective will be nearly head-on.

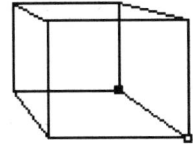

3

Select the Pen tool and draw polygons that match the two new "visible" sides of the cube (since the front of the cube is already a closed path, you need not recreate it).

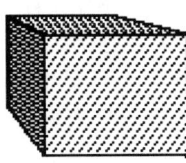

4

To add to the sense of depth, you can use the Style command from the Paint menu (Command-I) to set a gray fill (that is, some percentage of black) to shade each side.

5

When the cube is complete, use the marquee and Option key to select the entire object, and use the Group command from the Arrange menu (Command-G) to make it a single object.

See also Cubes: Method 1, Highlights, and Grid: Method 2.

PART III: TECHNIQUES

Cubes: Method 3

Packaging design often calls for accurate three-dimensional, perspective views of rectangular-sided objects such as boxes. This technique lets you create accurate 3-D perspectives for several common engineering views by creating the sides of the box as rectangular objects, then scaling, shearing, and rotating them into place around a common point.

Warning: For this technique to work correctly, it is essential that the scaling, shearing, and rotating transformations are applied in precisely the order given below. It is also important that all the elements comprising a face of the cube are grouped before starting the transformation.

Create the side, front, and bottom faces of the package as rectangular objects with their long sides touching, as if the package were flattened, then use the Group command (Command-G) to group all the elements on each face, so that you have three grouped objects, one for each face. Use rounded caps and joins for the stroke of each rectangle to avoid "spikes" at the corners of the finished package.

286

THREE-DIMENSIONAL EFFECTS

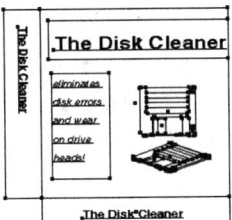

2

Use Select All (Command-A), then Option-click with the Scale tool at the point where all three faces touch. This point of mutual intersection is the origin point for all the transformations used in this technique. In the Scale dialog box, click Non-uniform scale, then enter scaling values of 100 percent horizontal and 86.602 percent vertical and click OK.

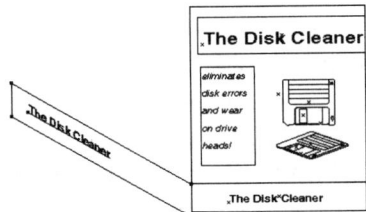

3

Select the group that comprises the side of the package, then Option-click the Shear tool at the point of mutual intersection, and enter a shear value of 30 degrees along the horizontal axis. Then Option-click the Rotate tool at the same point and rotate the side surface 90 degrees.

You will repeat the process of shearing and rotating the two remaining surfaces, using the values in the table on page 289.

4

Select the group that comprises the front of the box, then Option-click the Shear tool at the point of mutual intersection, enter a shear value of −30 degrees along the horizontal axis, and click OK. Then Option-click the Rotate tool at the point of mutual intersection, enter a rotation value of 30 degrees, and click OK.

PART III: TECHNIQUES

5

Select the group that comprises the bottom of the box, then Option-click the Shear tool at the point of mutual intersection, enter a shear value of 30 degrees along the horizontal axis, and click OK. Finally, Option-click the Rotate tool at the point of mutual intersection, enter a rotation value of 30 degrees, and click OK.

6

If the final illustration is too large to fit on one page, you can use Select All (Command-A) and either Scale tool to reduce the size of the package (including the size of the type). Similarly, you can use Select All and any Selection tool to move the package to the center of the page.

The transformation values given here produce an isometric view. The values for some other common views are listed in the table on the facing page. Note that, while an isometric view uses the same vertical scaling percentage for each face, some of the other views require different scaling percentages for the

THREE-DIMENSIONAL EFFECTS

Transformation values for common engineering views

View	Face	Vertical Scale	Shear	Rotate
Axonometric	Side	70.711%	45°	90°
	Front	100%	0°	45°
	Bottom	70.711%	45°	45°
Isometric	Side	86.602%	30°	90°
	Front	86.602%	-30°	30°
	Bottom	86.602%	30°	30°
Dimetric	Side	96.592%	15°	90°
	Front	96.592%	-15°	60°
	Bottom	50%	60°	60°
Trimetric	Side	96.592%	15°	90°
	Front	86.602%	-30°	45°
	Bottom	70.711%	45°	45°
Trimetric	Side	96.592%	15°	90°
	Front	70.711%	-45°	30°
	Bottom	86.602%	30°	30°

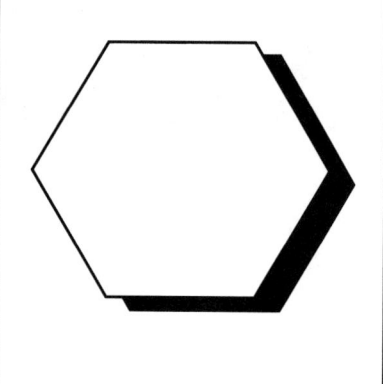

PART III: TECHNIQUES

Drop Shadows: Method 1

The simplest method of creating a three-dimensional effect is to create a "shadow" of a shape. That is, a copy of the shape is placed behind the shape, offset slightly, and given a dark fill. This effect is commonly referred to as a drop shadow in graphic design.

This technique is frequently used to add dimension or visual interest to conceptual illustrations such as bar charts and organization charts. You can add special effects to any illustration by using this three-dimensional technique on text, borders, and other two-dimensional objects.

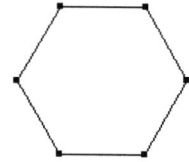

1

Create an object using whatever tool is appropriate. In this example, use the Pen tool to draw a polygon.

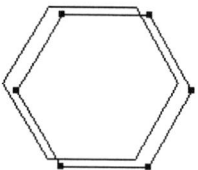

2

Use the Object-selection tool to select the object, or use the Selection tool while holding down the Option key to select all points, then drag the object diagonally a short distance, still holding the Option key to create a copy of it.

3

With the copy still selected, choose Send To Back from the Edit menu (Command-hyphen).

| THREE-DIMENSIONAL EFFECTS | |

4

Use Style from the Paint menu (Command-I) to add shading to the shadow.

Warning: Before you Option-drag a text object rectangle to create a copy for the shadow, use the Unlink command (Command-Shift-U) to unlink the rectangle from the text.

See also Pasting in Layers, Charts: Selecting and Modifying, Cubes: Methods 1 and 2, and Drop Shadows: Method 2.

PART III: TECHNIQUES

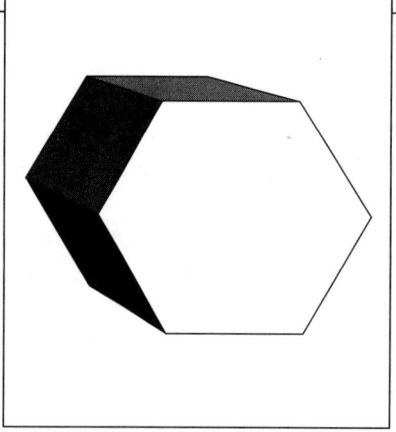

Drop Shadows: Method 2

The three-dimensional objects you can create with Adobe Illustrator are not truly three-dimensional; you cannot rotate a drawing of a house to see a front view and a back view. But you can create a third dimension visually using the technique described here.

Besides adding dimensions to create representation of solid objects such as boxes, buildings, and books, you can add special effects to any illustration by using this three-dimensional technique on text, borders, and other two-dimensional objects.

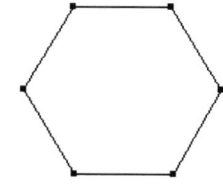

1

Create an object using whatever tool is appropriate. In this example, use the Pen tool to draw a polygon.

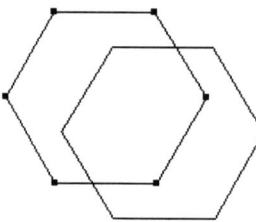

2

Use the Object-selection tool to select the object. Holding down the Option key, drag the object diagonally a short distance to create a copy of it.

3

With the copied object still selected, choose Send To Back (Command-hyphen).

| THREE-DIMENSIONAL EFFECTS

4
With the copied object still selected, select the Scale tool from the toolbox and scale the object slightly smaller than the original object (see of The Scale Tools in Part I).

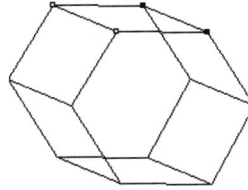

5
Using the Pen tool, draw lines between each set of corresponding anchor points to connect the two objects at the edges, as shown in the figure at left.

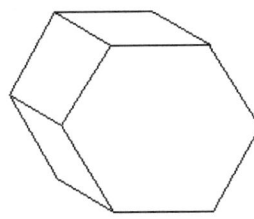

6
Working in a magnified view (using the Zoom-in tool), use the Scissors tool to cut anchor points where the lines drawn in step 2 meet the back face of the three-dimensional object.

Using the Delete or Backspace key, delete the "invisible" lines.

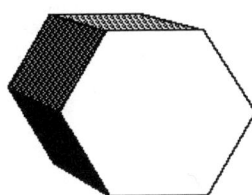

7
If you want to add shading to each face, use the Pen tool to trace the three polygons that form the sides in this example, and use Style from the Paint menu (Command-I) to add shading to the three-dimensional faces of the object.

In the figure at the left, use a fill of 100 percent black for the bottom face, 70 percent black for the middle face, and 40 percent black for the top face.

See also Cubes: Methods 1 and 2, and Grid: Method 2.

PART III: TECHNIQUES

Flower Petals

Flowers are certainly among the most common objects rendered as artwork. Here is a simple technique for creating flowers like the one pictured in the accompanying figure.

You can use variations on this technique to draw other types of flowers, including roses, chrysanthemums, and other more complicated varieties.

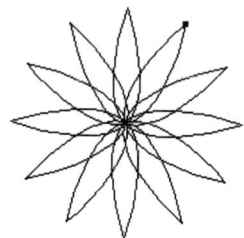

1

Draw one petal that you will use as the basic unit. Click on the petal with the Object-selection tool to select all points, then select the Rotate-dialog tool and click the base of the petal. In the Rotate dialog box, enter the number of degrees yielded by dividing 360 (degrees) by the number of petals in the flower.

In this example, you will want thirty-six units, so you will type 10 as the number of degrees (360 divided by 36). (See also Radial Symmetry: Methods 1 and 2.)

Click Copy to close the Rotate dialog box and make a rotated copy of the first object, then use Transform Again (Command-D) until the flower is complete.

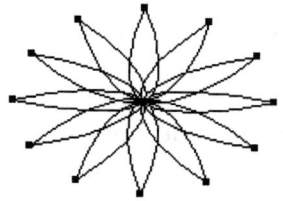

2

Scale the flower nonproportionally. Choose Select All (Command-A) or drag a selection marquee around all the petals to select the flower. Then select the Scale tool and click near the bottom left edge of the petals. Move the pointer to the opposite corner and drag diagonally to achieve an effect similar to the one shown in the figure on the left.

THREE-DIMENSIONAL EFFECTS

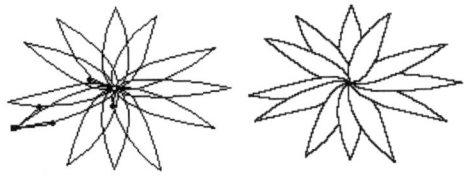

3

With the Selection tool or the Direct-selection tool, select and move the points at the outside tip of each petal, one by one, up or down on random petals to create a more natural, organic look.

4

You can create more complex arrangements of petals by scaling the first set to smaller sizes and overlaying several additional sets. To do this, select the whole flower by dragging a selection marquee around it with the Selection tool. Then select the Scale tool, click the center of the flower as the first point, position the pointer outside of the flower, and drag toward the center until the smaller set of petals is the size you wish. Hold down the Option key as you release the mouse button to create a copy.

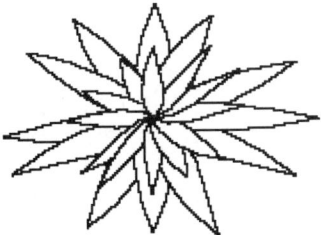

For a more realistic effect, use Group (Command-G) and the Rotate tool to rotate each set slightly.

See also Radial Symmetry: Methods 1 and 2.

PART III: TECHNIQUES

Highlights

You can make highlights easily, quickly, and accurately with Illustrator using the Blend tool. Remember that the Blend tool blends not only different paint attributes (as defined in the Paint Style dialog box from the Paint menu) but different shapes as well. This allows you to blend and highlight gradations between two shapes as diverse as an ellipse and a rectangle, or two colors as different as black and white.

Highlights are usually not the same shape as the object being highlighted. With Illustrator it is possible to blend smoothly disparate shapes to create more realistic three-dimensional shading effects.

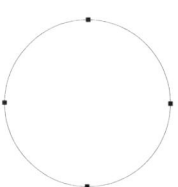

1

The object to be shaded is a perfect circle, shown in the figure at left. To create your circle, choose the Oval tool from the toolbox. In the active window, the pointer becomes a cross. Hold down the Shift key as you draw the object to be highlighted. Recall that using the Oval tool with the Shift key constrains the object to a perfect circle. With the object selected, choose Ungroup from the Arrange menu (Command U).

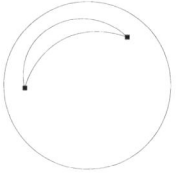

2

Now you will draw the shape of the highlight that would appear if the object were truly three-dimensional and lighted from a single source. Choose the Pen or Freehand

THREE-DIMENSIONAL EFFECTS

tool to draw a crescent shape, which is the natural highlight for a sphere. Position it inside the circle, off center.

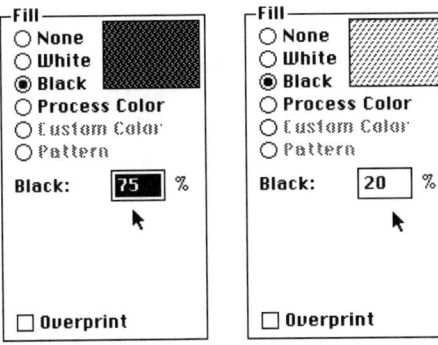

3

With the Selection tool, click on the circle and choose Style from the Paint menu (Command-I). Paint the circle a deep color or a deep gray and click OK. Now, with the Selection tool, select the crescent shape inside the circle, choose Style again (Command-I), and this time set the black or color fill to a lighter shade of the same color, such as 20 percent. This paints the crescent a lighter color or lighter gray. Click OK.

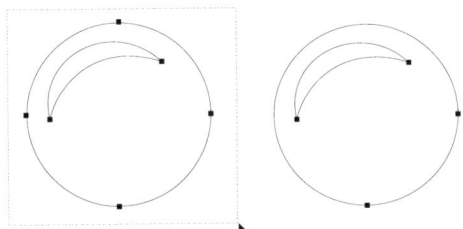

4

Use the Selection tool to drag a selection marquee over the circle and the crescent, and notice where the anchor points are located along the path of each object. (See The Selection Tools in Part I.) Click on an anchor point of the sphere, then Shift-click on a corresponding point of the highlight. These act as reference points for the blend. Continue Shift-clicking alternate points for blending reference. The more paired reference points, the more predictable the blend. (See The Blend Tool in Part I for a detailed explanation of how to determine corresponding points.)

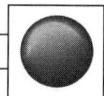

PART III: TECHNIQUES

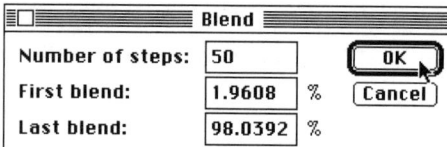

5

Now you are ready to blend. Choose the Blend tool from the toolbox and click once on each object, clicking the larger object (the object to appear on the lowest layer) first. Be sure that the circle is ungrouped, as in step 1.

You must select a point on the larger object first in order to identify this as the lowest layer in the blend sequence. Otherwise, if you select a point on the highlight first, the highlight and all intermediate transformations will fall into layer behind the larger shape and will not appear in Preview or print out.

After you click the second object, the Blend dialog box appears. Type in the number of blend steps you would like the transformation to use. The more steps you request—up to 1296—the smoother the visual illusion. After selecting the number of blend steps, click OK.

The more blend steps you use, the larger and slower the file will be. Usually no more than thirty blends are needed to yield a smooth transition on a laser printer, and fewer blends are needed when the objects are small.

6

Choose Preview Illustration from the View menu (Command-Y) to see the results of the blend on the screen.

You may need to try a couple of different blends to create the most effective visual illusion and highlight. Experiment by choosing

THREE-DIMENSIONAL EFFECTS

different points to blend. Do not forget that blending is affected by the pairs of reference points you choose initially. Successful illusion blending happens when you choose two points that have a smooth and direct transition path.

See also The Blend Tool.

Part IV: Applications

Introduction to Applications

This part of the book presents nine finished works that were created by professional artists using Adobe Illustrator. The descriptions of each of these works include procedures and tips that can be applied to a wide range of applications. They refer to techniques that have already been described in Part III. You can adapt many of the steps described here in creating your own artwork.

The examples in this section are divided into two categories:

CATEGORY	DESCRIPTION
Charts, Maps, and Diagrams	Four examples in this section include bar charts, maps, and floor plans.
Illustrations	Five examples in this section include two illustrations that make use of masks and patterns, a portrait that uses complex shading, a technical illustration that uses lines with a hand-drawn look, and a poster that uses three-dimensional shading and layering.

Within each of these categories, you will find the examples listed alphabetically. A representation of each example is shown at the top outside corner of each page for easy reference.

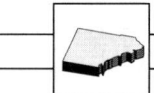

PART IV: APPLICATIONS

Charts, Maps, and Diagrams

Archdiocese of Detroit Map

Overview The artist took only two hours to produce this map of the Detroit area—a task that would have required many hours using conventional techniques (technical pens, Zip-A-Tone screens, and camera-distorted typeset text). He did this map for a magazine, and, since it was reproduced by gravure on a glossy stock rather than the usual offset newsprint, it required finer line quality and cleaner treatment than would have been required for newsprint.

The challenge of this graphic was that no action needed to be indicated graphically. The only information to convey was the location of these counties. So the artist decided to use a three-dimensional approach to make the map more interesting visually—to "punch it up."

Procedure The artist traced an available map of the Detroit area using pencil and tracing paper and scanned the traced outlines using an AST TurboScanner. He used the scanned image as the template in Illustrator for a simple tracing—no curves, all straight lines, even for the right side of the map.

The Counties Since the news agency wanted to be able to use this artwork at other times, the artist made each county a separate object. Where the borders met, he copied individual line segments and Option-dragged them into place, using the Snap to point feature (set in the Preferences dialog box) to align borders. All except the Monroe/Wayne border were straight lines that he created using the Pen tool. He set the counties with 100 percent Black Stroke, 10 percent Black Fill, and the outline of Detroit with Stroke of None and 30 percent Black Fill. Then he traced the lakes and Canada border, and added the box surrounding the map.

After completing the outlines from the template, the artist used Select All (Command-A), and then the Rotate tool to rotate the image approximately 10 degrees. Then he rescaled with the Scale

CHARTS, MAPS, AND DIAGRAMS

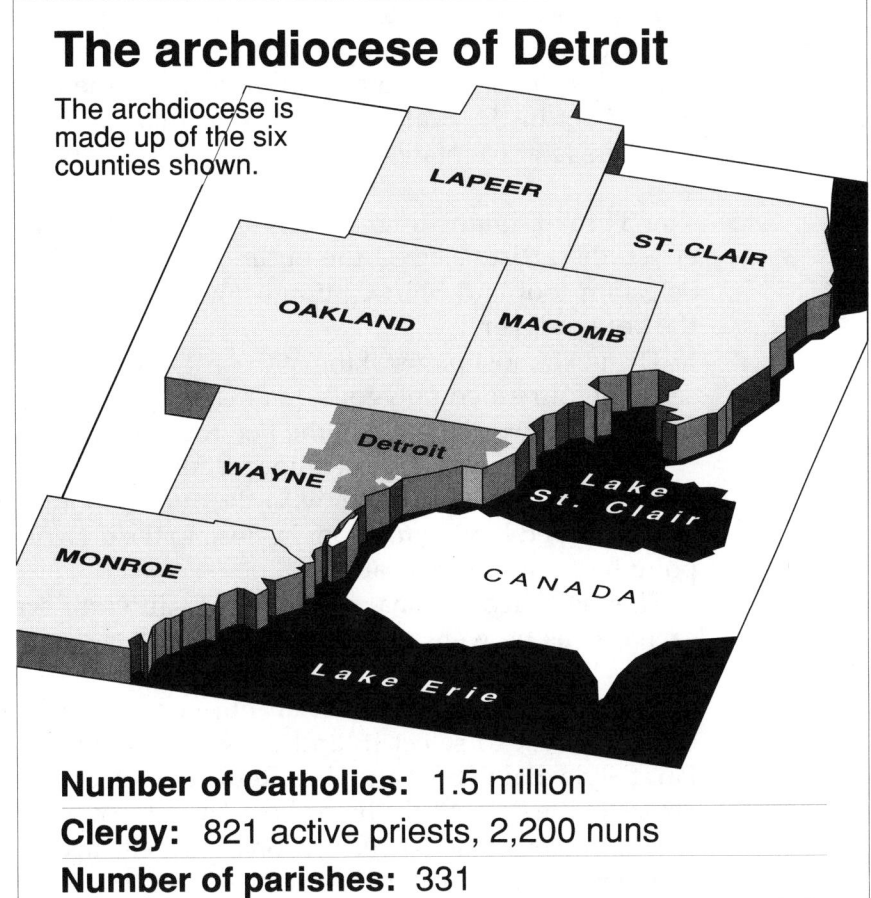

Archdiocese of Detroit, created by John Van Pelt, Detroit Free Press

tool—vertically only—to flatten the artwork slightly. During these steps he made a note on paper of the degrees of rotation he had entered earlier in the Rotate dialog box and the percentage scaling he had set in the Scale dialog box so that he could use the same numbers later to rotate and scale the text (county names).

The Three-Dimensional Effect   To create the three-dimensional effect, the artist selected the outlines of all six counties using the Selection tool and Shift-Option-dragged upward ten points from the bottom layer.

The next, most painstaking, part of the work was completing the series of four-sided polygons that make up the side of the map. The artist connected them using the Pen tool to create straight lines between anchor points on each border, using Snap to point to align the corners of the polygons with the anchor points on the border. (This avoided having to zoom in close to the artwork, since Snap to point has a two-pixel grab.)

Then he filled the shapes with three different screens. He filled each one as he went along, rather than after drawing all the segments. When he knew the next shape would be, for example, 40 percent Black, he clicked on an object previously filled with 40 percent Black to select it, and pressed Command-I (to open the Paint Style dialog box) and then Return to select the default Fill and Stroke in the Paint Style dialog box. Thus, the next shape drawn has the 40 percent Black screen. If one segment needed to be behind another, he cut it (using Command-X) and pasted it in back (using Command-B).

The left part of the figure on the facing page shows the illustration up to this point in Artwork Only view (Command W). When the artist changed to Preview mode (Command-Y), the three-dimensional effect became more obvious.

CHARTS, MAPS, AND DIAGRAMS

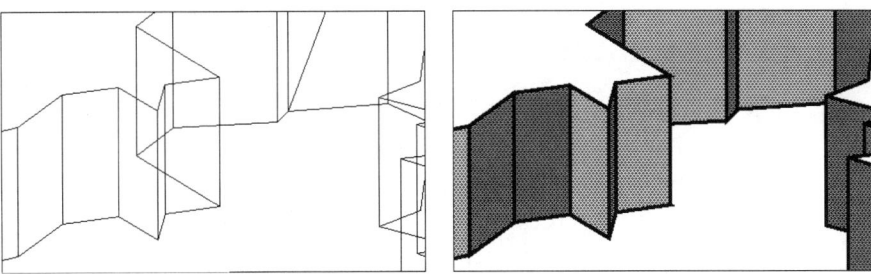

Close-up of three-dimensional border: Artwork Only and Preview

Text Labels First, using the Type tool, the artist typed one county name, Monroe, with center alignment, in the font specified. Then he rotated it with the Rotate tool and scaled it with the Scale tool using the same numbers he used in rotating and scaling the county outlines. With the text block selected, he Option-dragged to position copies inside each county. Then he went back, selected the text in each copy with the Type tool, and typed in the new county name.

Finishing Touches The artist chopped off the corner of the map on the right by doing the following: he used the Add-anchor-point tool to add a new point, then used the new point to bring the side down to the bottom point to close the corner.

He added the title and subtitle to the top of the map and drew a white line with no fill under the subtitle of the chart to eliminate the border of the rectangle that framed the counties.

Tip Although the artist waited until the last step before adding the text, he could have added it before rotating and scaling the counties. A trade-off is involved: By waiting, he could tell exactly what size the text had to be to fit. If, on the other hand, he had added the text before rotating and scaling the counties, he would not have had to note the rotating and scaling percentages, since he would have rotated and scaled the text along with the county outlines. He might, however, have had to adjust some of the text blocks as a finishing touch.

See also Aligning Text: Methods 1 and 2, Shared Borders, and Drop Shadows: Method 2 in Part III.

PART IV: APPLICATIONS

The Pacific Century Chart-Map

Overview The artist combined maps with four variations of bar charts to produce this visual representation of economic trends in Asia. He made the illustration easier to understand by using different kinds of charts (cubes, cylinders, and bars) for the different types of data.

You can apply the techniques used here to any bar charts. Adding a three-dimensional look can help to enliven a chart and create more visual interest, drawing your audience in and adding meaning to your charts.

Procedure The artist began with a pencil sketch of the visual concept and researched the statistical data that appears in the charts. In other words, he developed a clear idea of his goal before starting to use Illustrator.

The Maps He used a scanned map as a template to trace one outline, then selected the outline and set it to 40 percent Black Fill with No Stroke, using the Style command from the Paint menu. He added borders between countries as open paths (curves with two endpoints that are not joined). These borders were set No Fill and Black Stroke with a Weight of 1 point, using the Style command. The artist framed the map area in a rectangular shape with curved sides that matched the curve of longitude, using Style from the Paint menu (Command-I) with a White Fill and No Stroke, and added dashed lines over the map with a 50 percent Black Stroke to indicate latitude and longitude.

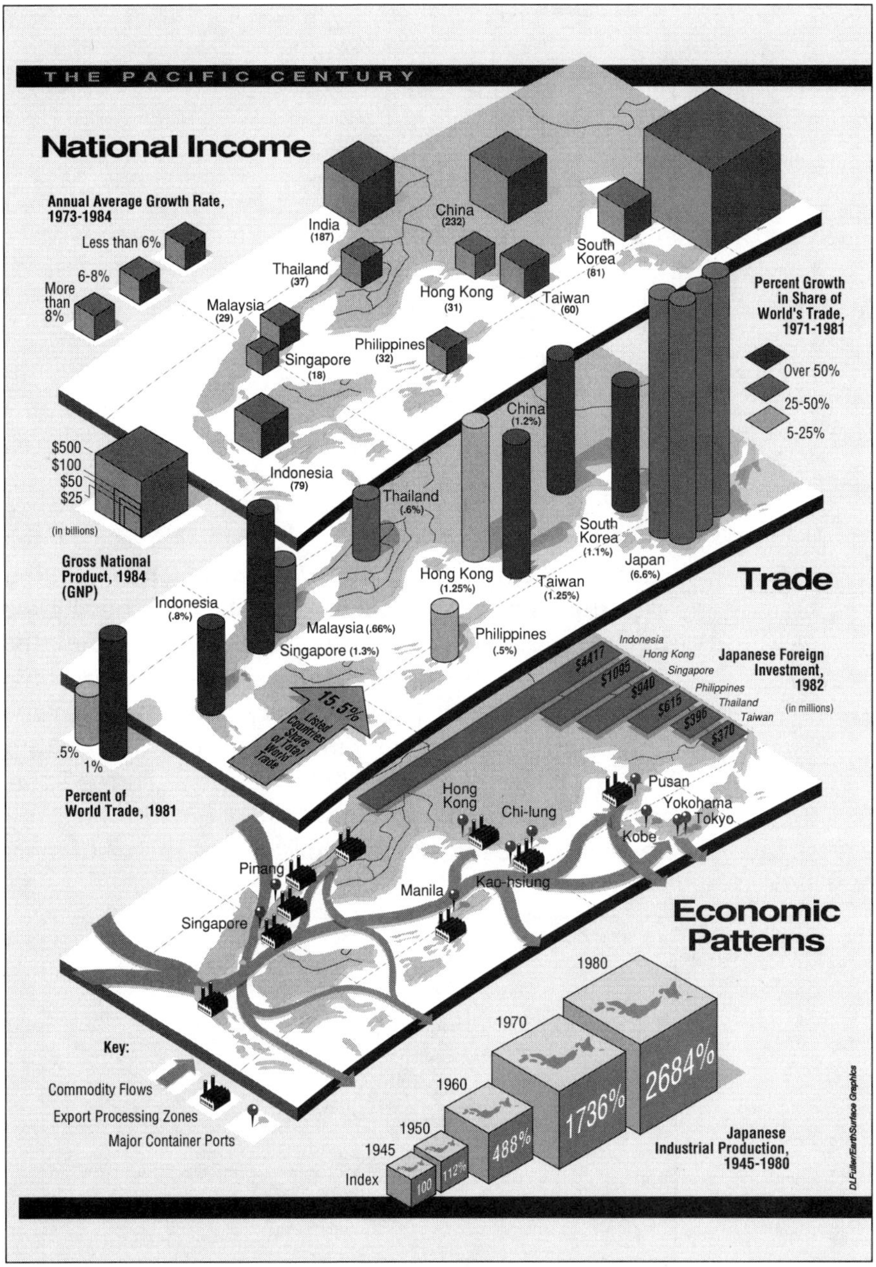

CHARTS, MAPS, AND DIAGRAMS

The Pacific Century, created by D.L. Fuller, Earth Surface Graphics

 **PART IV: APPLICATIONS**

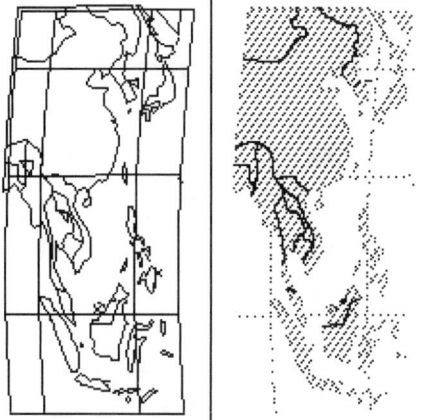

The map was traced from a scanned image, shown here in Artwork Only and Preview

He skewed the whole map visually using the Shear tool. Then, to make a mental note of the angle of the shear for later use with other elements, he held down the Option key and clicked the Shear tool to open the Shear dialog box, which showed the angle of the shear and the axis along which the angle is sheared. Finally, he added the drop shadow to the entire illustration by drawing two polygons along two edges, and used the Style command from the Paint menu to assign the longer edge a 100 percent Black Fill and the shorter edge an 80 percent Black Fill. He then grouped the entire illustration using the Group command from the Arrange menu (Command-G). The following figure shows the results of these steps.

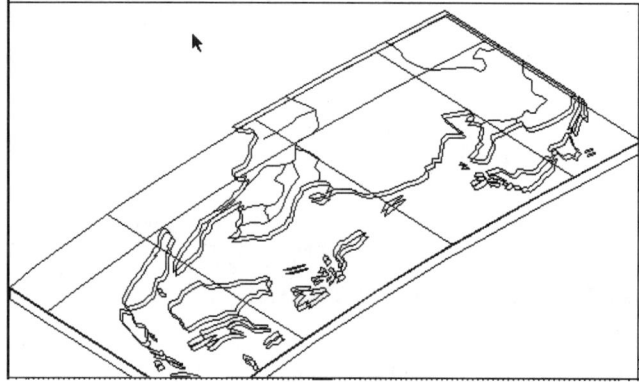

The skewed map with drop shadow border

CHARTS, MAPS, AND DIAGRAMS

Next the artist made two copies of the map and arranged them in three layers. To make the first copy, he selected the entire map and rectangle, then dragged the selection upward while holding down the Shift key (to ensure precise vertical movement) and the Option key (to make a copy) as he released the mouse button. He used the Transform Again command (Command-D) to create the next copy. He added different country or city names to each layer using the Type tool. He typed the first name and set the type specifications to 12 point Helvetica Condensed, then Option-dragged copies into position on the three maps and edited the copies to produce the different city names with the same type specifications, as the following figure shows.

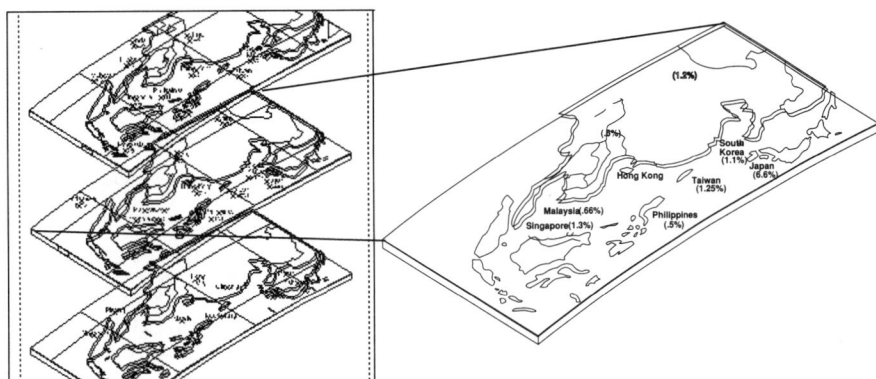

Three maps with cities or countries labeled

Bar Charts The artist then created the three different bar-type objects: cubes for the top map, cylinders for the middle map, and flat bars for the bottom map. In a new untitled window, the artist created one cube and one cylinder and then made scaled duplicates to create a total of three cubes and three cylinders, each with different fill attributes on the faces.

The artist could have used the charting feature of Illustrator 3.0 to create bars as a starting point for each chart, but this map was originally created using Illustrator 88—before the charting feature was available. Whether the Rectangle tool or the commands under the Graph menu are used, he would still have to modify the rectangles or bars as described here to create the custom look of the charts in this map.

He created the left face of the cube by using the Rectangle tool and the Shift key to draw a square. Then he used the Shear tool while pressing the Option key to open the Shear dialog box. In the Angle space of the dialog box, he entered the same value he used to skew the map.

He created the right face using the Reflect tool with the left face selected to mirror a copy of the left face, and the top face by reflecting a copy of one of the other faces. He gave each face a different percentage Black Fill, using the Style command from the Paint menu (Command-I). Then he grouped the entire object with the Group command (Command-G).

To compose the cylinders, the artist drew an ellipse with the Oval tool, then ungrouped it using the Ungroup command from the Arrange menu (Command-U). He copied the ellipse (by Option-Shift-dragging) and moved the copy vertically so it was directly below the original. (See The Selection Tools in Part I for a description of two methods available for this step, Option-Shift-dragging or using the Move dialog box.)

Next he selected and deleted the top anchor point of the copy, leaving the bottom half of the ellipse. Then he used the Pen tool to draw two straight lines up from the bottom ellipse to the top ellipse. He selected the anchor points at each bottom corner of the cylinder and joined them using the Join command (Command-J). Then he brought the top ellipse to the front using the Bring To Front command in the Edit menu (Command-=). He used the Style command from the Paint menu (Command-I) to set the Fill of the top ellipse to 70 percent Black and the Fill of the length of the cylinder to 80 percent Black. He then selected the entire cylinder and Option-dragged to make two copies. He used the Style command again to set one cylinder's Fill to 50 percent Black (ellipse) and 60 percent Black (length) and the other to 30 percent Black (ellipse) and 40 percent Black (length). He finally grouped each cylinder individually using the Group command from the Arrange menu (Command-G).

CHARTS, MAPS, AND DIAGRAMS

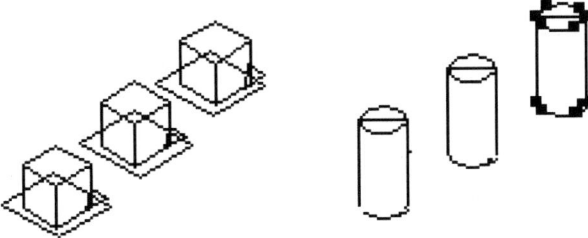

Copied sets of cubes and cylinders, all the same size

To produce scaled copies of the original cubes and cylinders to match various data values, the artist used the Scale tool and Option key to open the Scale dialog box. He numerically scaled each cube, using Uniform scale. Then he numerically scaled each cylinder along the vertical axis only using Non-uniform scale, and clicked the Copy button for each.

The following figure shows the resulting scaled cubes and cylinders.

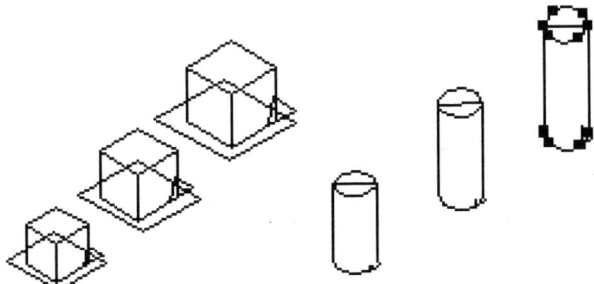

Sets of cubes and cylinders scaled to represent different data values

For the flat bars in the third map, the artist drew one bar with the Rectangle tool and duplicated it five times so there were six flat bars, arranged as shown in the figure on the following page.

PART IV: APPLICATIONS

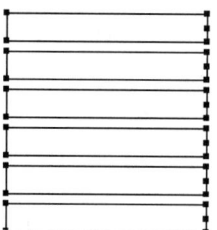

Copied set of bars

He numerically scaled each bar to match the data values by using the Scale tool and the Option key to open the Scale dialog box. In the dialog box, he selected Horizontal scale at a percentage proportional to the data and clicked OK when he was finished with each one. Then he skewed the whole set of bars with the Shear tool and Option key. The following figure shows the flat bars skewed at the appropriate angle.

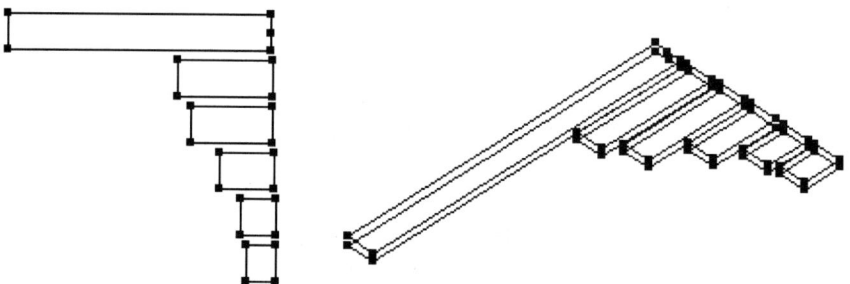

Scaled and skewed set of bars

Finishing Touches With the two documents (the maps and the bar objects) open in different windows on the screen, the artist copied (using Command-C to copy to the Clipboard) the cubes, cylinders, and bars from one document, and pasted (using Command-V) them on the map in the other document.

| CHARTS, MAPS, AND DIAGRAMS |  |

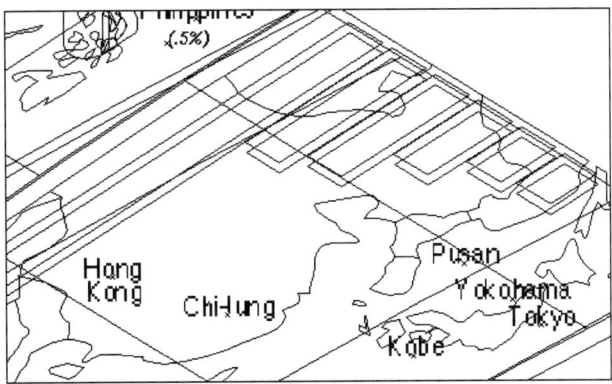

Bars copied from one document onto the maps

The artist repositioned country and city names to make room for the cubes, cylinders, and bars. He then added text labels, icons, and commodity flow arrows. He traced the outline of Japan that appears on the cubes at the bottom of the illustration, then skewed and positioned the outline on one cube, which he then scaled to five sizes.

Warning   This complex drawing is a large document in its finished form, and a Macintosh II is recommended for maximum efficiency in working. The final artwork requires nearly 200K of disk space and is very slow in changing views.

Tips   When you draw maps, lay out the lines for latitude and longitude first as precise guides in tracing the map and labeling cities.

Type one example of a text label and set it to the appropriate type specifications, then copy that label to create additional labels.

The drop shadows were colored in the final version (see color plate). In Illustrator 1.1, a special screen was required where the color touched the land. But in Illustrator 88 and 3.0 you can use the Overprint option in the Paint Style dialog box to create a trap for the color.

See also Cubes: Methods 1 and 2, and Drop Shadows: Methods 1 and 2 in Part III.

PART IV: APPLICATIONS

Pontiac Silverdome Chart

Overview   This example shows the floor plan of the Pontiac Silverdome set up for the pope's mass in 1987. Although the artist worked from a scanned template in this drawing, he used it as the basis for a grid, rather than as the basis for the drawing itself. He drew most of the shapes freehand, using the grid, rather than the template, as a guide.

You can apply the techniques used here to any aerial view.

Procedure   The artist began with detailed research of blueprints, sketches, and some photographs of an architect's three-dimensional model of the Pontiac Silverdome, then developed a fairly careful drawing in pencil.

Using a scanned image of the pencil drawing as a template, the artist started with the outer edge of the processional track that surrounds the floor plan. Then the artist proceeded from the bottom layer of the drawing upward to the top layers, which is a typical technique in most three-dimensional aerial view drawings. The artist left text blocks and captions for last.

He used the Oval tool to draw a grid of ellipses (with Fill and Stroke of None) to match the edges of the concentric rings of seats, rather than precisely tracing the template. The template was necessarily a bit rough, so the ellipses in the sketch were not smooth, and the Oval tool helped make the final drawing more accurate.

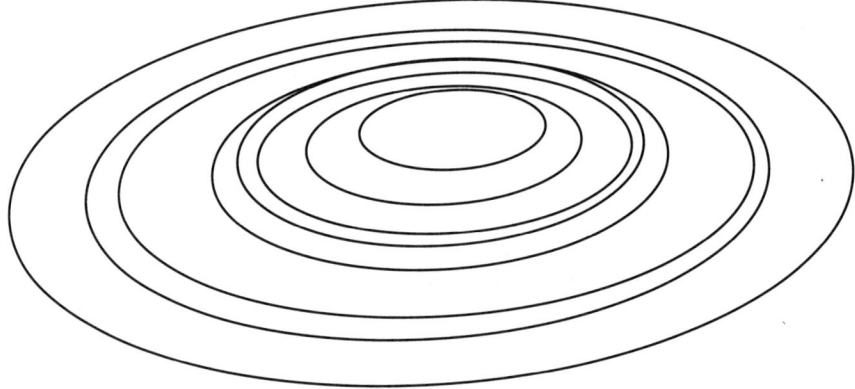

Ellipses traced from scanned template were used as grid

| CHARTS, MAPS, AND DIAGRAMS | 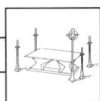 |

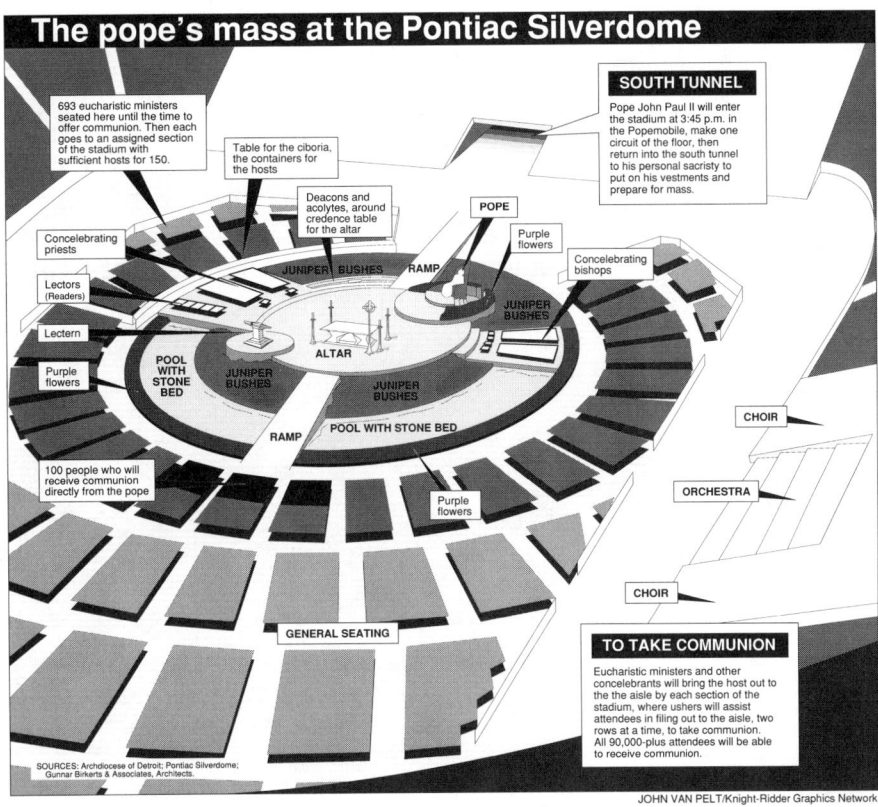

The pope's mass at the Pontiac Silverdome, created by John Van Pelt, Detroit Free Press, ©1987 Knight-Ridder Graphics Network

With the Pen tool, the artist drew four-sided polygons for each seating block, making the edges of each block, which radiated from the center, follow the scanned template. The edges conformed to the Illustrator grid of ellipses in the background. All edges of the seating blocks are straight lines.

Then the artist used Select All (Command-A) and Shift-Option-dragged down to form a copy directly below the original. He copied the copy to the Clipboard (Command-C), selected the originals, then pasted the Clipboard contents behind the originals using the Paste In Back command from the Edit menu (Command-B). Using Style from the Paint menu (Command-I), he painted the copies with 100 percent Black Fill to create the drop shadow effect.

PART IV: APPLICATIONS

He drew the ramps as three-sided open paths, with the same fill as that of the main floor, thus blending the open edge with the floor.

Within the altar area, he ungrouped (Command-U) and copied (Command-C) ellipses. Then he pasted them in front (Command-F) and clipped them with the Scissors tool so that parts of the path could be deleted to form matching segments where needed. These steps allowed him to construct the step levels up to the concelebrating priests, down to the concelebrating bishops, up to the papal chair, and up to the lectern. In each case, he used the copied segment to form the beginning of a new path, with the vertical drops constrained by use of the Shift key.

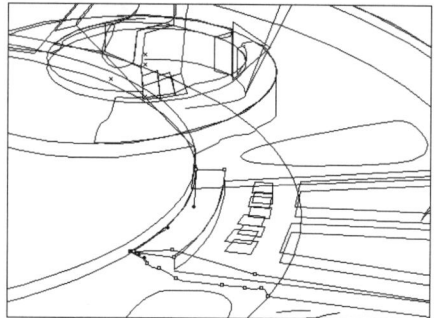 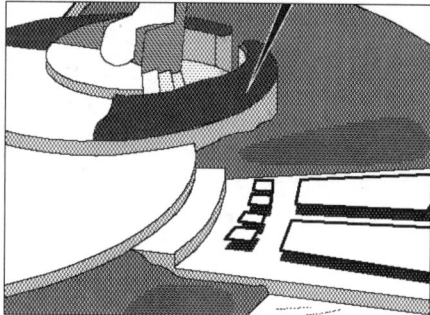

Steps formed by adding vertical lines to copied, clipped ellipses

The artist gave the areas of juniper bushes (surrounding the altar) a darker tone, using the Freehand tool to sketch an amorphous shape and then designating a Stroke of intermediate percentage to give the plants dimension.

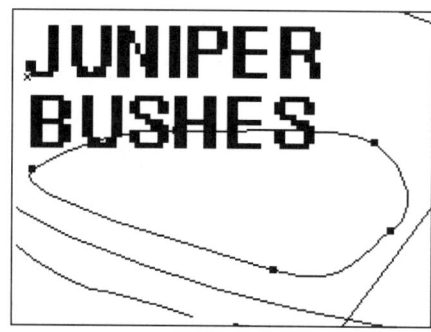 

Juniper bushes drawn as shaded areas, shown here as Artwork Only and in Preview

CHARTS, MAPS, AND DIAGRAMS

Finishing Touches The artist added many details, such as the altar and lectern. The left part of the following figure shows a close-up of the altar area, with surrounding juniper bushes and ramps in the Artwork Only view, selected from the View menu (Command-W). The right side shows the same area of the illustration in Preview Illustration mode, selected from the View menu (Command-Y). Here you can see the results of the Fill and Stroke settings.

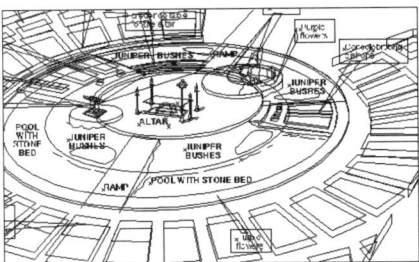 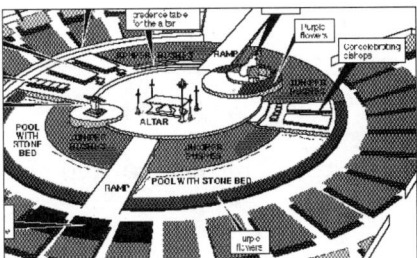

Close-up of center part of the drawing: Artwork Only and Preview

The artist created the text blocks in the illustration by dragging the Type tool to create text rectangles, then typing the text. He used the Direct-selection tool to select the rectangles without selecting the text, and gave them a Black Stroke and White Fill. Lastly, he added the arrows pointing from the text to the objects to which the text refers. Using the Style command from the Paint menu, he painted the pointers with a Black Fill, White Stroke, and .1 Weight, so that they would show up against both light and dark areas.

Tips

You should spend the greatest amount of time in producing pieces like this in the initial research and planning—this project required about ten hours over several days—and in rendering some of the detailed objects, such as the papal chair, lectern, and so on. The basic form of the concentric seating areas in the stadium, the landscaped podium, and the ramps are fairly quick and simple to create.

When the drawing is complete, it is a good idea to delete the grid of ellipses to minimize the size of the saved document. Do this even though the grid will not print (since it has a Fill and Stroke of None).

See also Grid: Methods 2 and 3, Pasting in Layers, and Drop Shadows: Methods 1 and 2 in Part III.

319

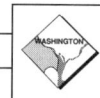

PART IV: APPLICATIONS

Washington, D.C., Street Map

Overview The artist designed this street map to show the geographical relationship between four buildings in Washington, D.C., and simplified it by eliminating superfluous street labels and other geographical markers that are part of the area covered by the map.

You can apply the techniques used here in creating any map.

Procedure The artist first drew the map in perspective with paper and pencil, sketching streets in simple, rough single-line style. Next he determined the rectangular frame needed to incorporate the major points of the illustration, working with the newspaper's layout editor to determine final size and dimensions. He scanned the sketched drawing, using the scanner's features to set the final size, and saved it in MacPaint format, then used it as the template for the Illustrator image.

Water With Illustrator's rulers showing (Command-R) as a guide, the artist used the Rectangle tool to draw a rectangle over the scanned image, capturing the desired area in the size and dimensions determined for the final artwork. He used the Pen tool to trace the boundaries between the land and water, tracing the water as a closed path and using Style from the Paint menu (Command-I) to set the Fill to 30 percent Black, the Stroke to 100 percent Black, and the Weight to 1 point.

Streets The artist traced streets with the Pen tool, extending oblique roads past the edge of the rectangular frame (to be masked later). He used the Style command from the Paint menu (Command-I) to set Fill to None, Stroke to 100 percent Black, and Weight to 5 points. This step created wide black street lines, as the figure at the top of page 322 shows.

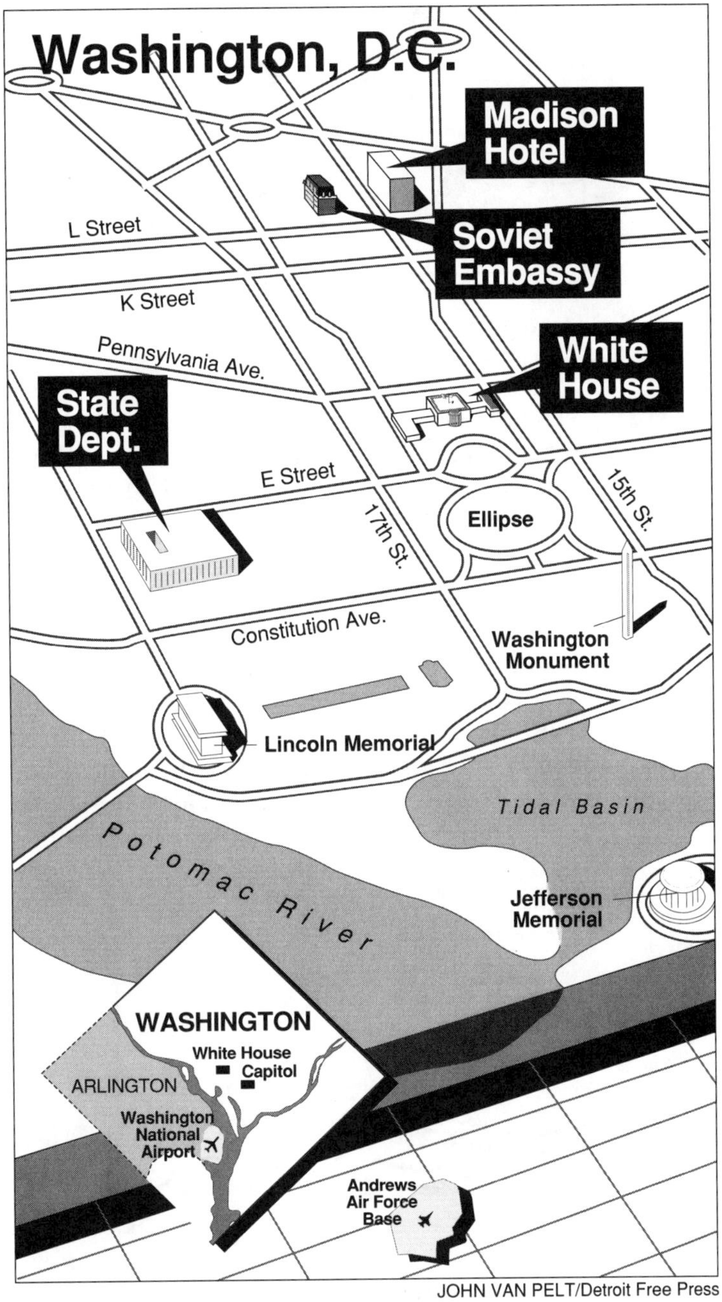

CHARTS, MAPS, AND DIAGRAMS

Washington, D.C., created by John Van Pelt, Detroit Free Press

PART IV: APPLICATIONS

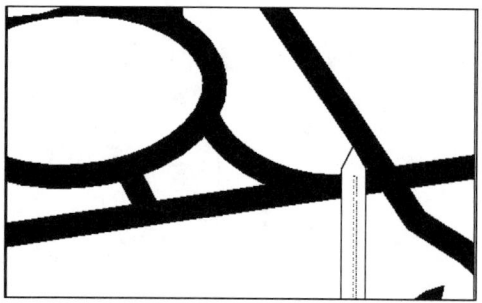

Streets drawn as wide black lines

To yield the final effect of white streets with black edges, the artist selected (with the Selection tool), grouped (using Command-G), and copied (using Command-C) all of the street lines, then pasted them in front (using Command-F) of the wide black street lines. With the Style command from the Paint menu (Command-I), he painted the copied set of street lines with a Fill of None, a Stroke of White, and a Weight of 4 points. This step created the effect of five-point-wide streets with half-point borders. By pasting *all* the white lines in front of *all* the black lines, the artist made sure that the intersections were free of cross lines.

Next the artist held the Option key and clicked on the Selection tool in the toolbox to get the Move dialog box, and moved the white street lines down .2 (–.2 Vertical move) and right .2 (+.2 Horizontal move) to give roads a touch of dimension, as shown in the following figure. This step gave left and top sides of roads .7 thickness, bottom and right sides .3.

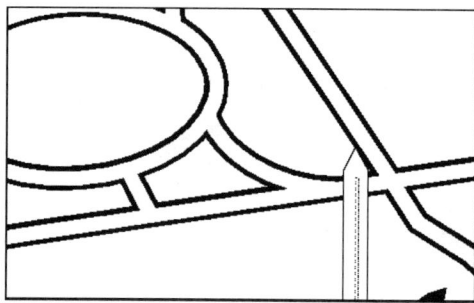

Streets composed of white lines on top of black lines, offset diagonally .2 points from each other

CHARTS, MAPS, AND DIAGRAMS

Finally, the artist used narrow, white-filled, unstroked rectangles along each edge of the outer frame to hide the tips of streets where they fell outside the rectangular border. (This illustration was created using Adobe Illustrator 1.1. With Illustrator 88 or 3.0, the border rectangle could be set up as a mask—using the Paint Style dialog box—and the white rectangles would not be needed to hide the street extensions. See Masking in Part III.)

Land's Edge Using the Pen tool, the artist drew two polygons (one with 50 percent Black Fill and one with 100 percent Black Fill) to add dimension to the edge of the land at the bottom of the map. He used dashed white lines with a .1-point dash and .2-point gap for the grid lines.

Buildings and Landmarks The artist drew buildings and other landmarks without a template, often in 1600 percent magnified view, to add dimension and detail. He drew the black shadows as polygons with the Pen tool and pasted them behind (Command-B) the building structures.

Inset Map The artist traced the inset map in a second document using a new template—scanned from a larger area map—then grouped (using Command-G) and copied (using Command-C) it from that Illustrator document and pasted it into position in the first document (using Command-V or Command-F). Then he scaled it to size using the Scale tool. He used the Carta font for airfield symbols (planes).

Finishing Touches With the Type tool, the artist added text to label streets and landmarks. He used the Pen tool to draw black boxes with pointers to the four buildings that formed the focus of the illustration, and set the type inside each box as Helvetica Bold with White Fill, using .1-point White Stroke for an extra-bold appearance. As a final step, he copied the outer border rectangle and pasted it in front of all the other artwork for a clean outer border.

See also Compound Lines: Methods 1 and 2, Masking a Mask, and Parallel Curves in Part III.

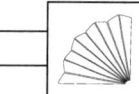

PART IV: APPLICATIONS

Illustrations

Japan Fan

Overview   The artist created the primary feature of this illustration—the wedges of the fan—using two techniques: he filled some with custom patterns, and he used masks over large designs with the others. The final artwork was printed in color (see color plate).

You can apply the techniques used here to any illustration that calls for pattern fills or patterns created by masking.

Procedure   The artist first created one wedge outline with the Pen tool and then mirrored it with the Reflect tool to create the second shape. The following figure shows how the first wedge shape is mirrored by the second. To each of these shapes, he applied a Fill of None and a Black Stroke with a Weight of 1, using Style from the Paint menu (Command-I).

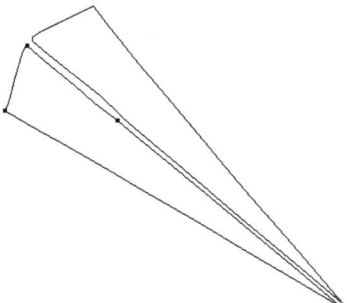

One wedge is a mirror of the other

He then arranged the wedges to form the basic fan shape. He copied the first pair using the Rotate tool, with the point of origin set at the pointed tips of the two fan wedges. He rotated the pair visually to align adjacent borders, holding the Option key as the mouse button was released to create a rotated copy of the wedges. Then the artist used Transform Again (Command-D) to produce the subsequent copies. The figure at the top of page 326 shows the full fan shape after all copies were made.

ILLUSTRATIONS

Japan Fan by David Smith

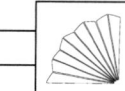 PART IV: APPLICATIONS

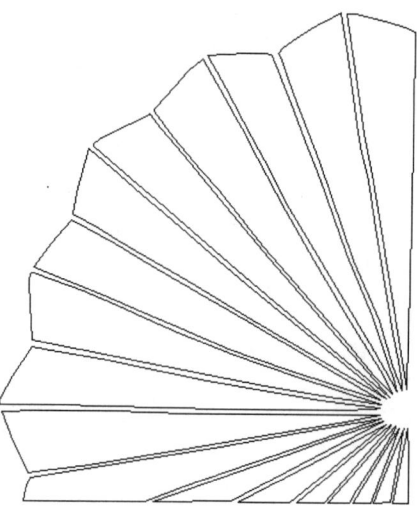

Full fan layout

Pattern Fills   After designing and drawing the patterns, the artist tested each one for repeat frequency, color, and positioning within the wedge. (See Patterns: Methods 1 and 2 in Part III.) He copied (Command-C) a single wedge from the original file and pasted it (Command-V) in a new, separate file to experiment with the patterns. The following figure shows the Pattern dialog box, opened by Pattern from the Paint menu, which displays several pattern names along with a sample of the pattern that is highlighted. The sample appears in the lower right corner of the dialog box.

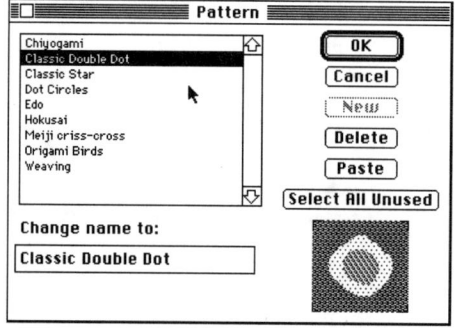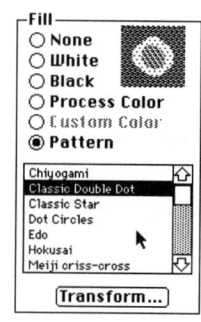

The Pattern dialog box (for adding or deleting patterns) and the pattern palette from the Paint Style dialog box (for applying patterns)

326

ILLUSTRATIONS

Masked Wedges Some of the fills for the wedges were actually large designs masked by the wedges. In these cases, the artist copied the wedge from the Fan file into a separate Illustrator document containing the large pattern and masked it with the wedge. (See Masking in Part III.) He moved the wedge around over the large pattern and previewed it (using Command-Y). In some cases he rotated the large pattern using the Rotate tool, until he achieved the desired effect. Then he grouped (using Command-G) and copied (using Command-C) the masked artwork back into the Fan document.

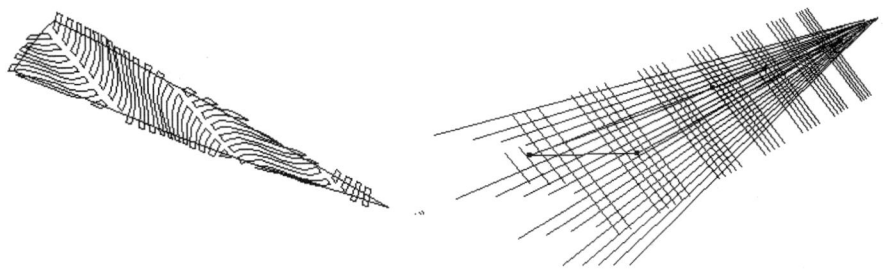

Masked wedges

Finishing Touches The artist filled the dark background around the fan with a pattern of white dashed wavy lines. (See Patterns: Methods 1–3 in Part III.) He had to experiment with the pattern tiling to get the pattern to repeat correctly.

He drew a closed path, following the outline of the fan, about a quarter-inch away from it. Then he set the Fill to Black and sent it behind the fan wedges using the Send To Back command from the Edit menu (Command-hyphen).

Finally, he added the text at the top of the illustration with the Type tool and the Type dialog box by using the command from the menu (Command-T), placing the text behind the fan wedges.

See also Patterns: Methods 1–3, Masking, Masking a Mask, and Radial Symmetry: Method 1 in Part III.

PART IV: APPLICATIONS

Kimono

Overview This kimono is 5 by 8 inches in its original size. The artist printed full-color versions of the document on a QMS ColorScript 100-color PostScript printer, and printed four-color separated negatives on a Linotronic 300 (see color plate).

He composed the kimono using a repeated, rotated, and scaled flower motif on a dark background with blended shading. He created the trim patterns on the sleeves and edges using masking and pattern fills.

You can apply the techniques employed to create the kimono to any illustration that uses a mask, a repeated motif, pattern fills, or blended shading, and to any color illustration.

Procedure The artist derived the design for this kimono from several traditional kimono designs found in historical reference books. He scanned a halftone photomechanical transfer (PMT) of the original color images and used them as templates for the basic shape of the kimono and the positioning of the flowers.

He grouped and arranged the elements of the illustration in the following layers. At the back he used the outline of the kimono as a mask. Immediately in front of this he used the Blend tool to create two hundred rectangular boxes filled with blended shades of purple. He then grouped (using Command-G) and locked (using Command-1) the mask and the blended boxes.

Next the artist constructed the first flower. Then he positioned the other two flowers, which he created by scaling and rotating copies of the first flower. Finally, he pasted the kimono outline as the top object.

The rest of this section describes these basic steps in more detail.

Kimono The artist traced the outline of the kimono from the scanned template. He traced the violet part of the cloth as a closed path and locked it (Command-1). He then created a series of two hundred grouped, narrow rectangles with the Blend tool, using one hundred steps, blending from 100 percent Pantone Violet CV at the top of the kimono to 50 percent Pantone Violet CV at the center.

ILLUSTRATIONS

Kimono created by David Smith

PART IV: APPLICATIONS

To complete the background, he mirrored a copy of the set of one hundred blends with the Reflect tool to shade from 30 percent at the center to 70 percent at the bottom of the kimono.

Next he grouped (Command-G) the blended boxes and positioned them over the outline. He completed the kimono background by using Command-2 to unlock the outline, Command-hyphen to send it to the back of the artwork, and Command-I to open the Paint Style dialog box, where he clicked Mask, to use the outline as a "clipping" path. (See Masking in Part III.) After clicking OK in the Paint Style dialog box, he selected both the outline and the blended boxes, grouped them (Command-G), and locked the group (Command-1).

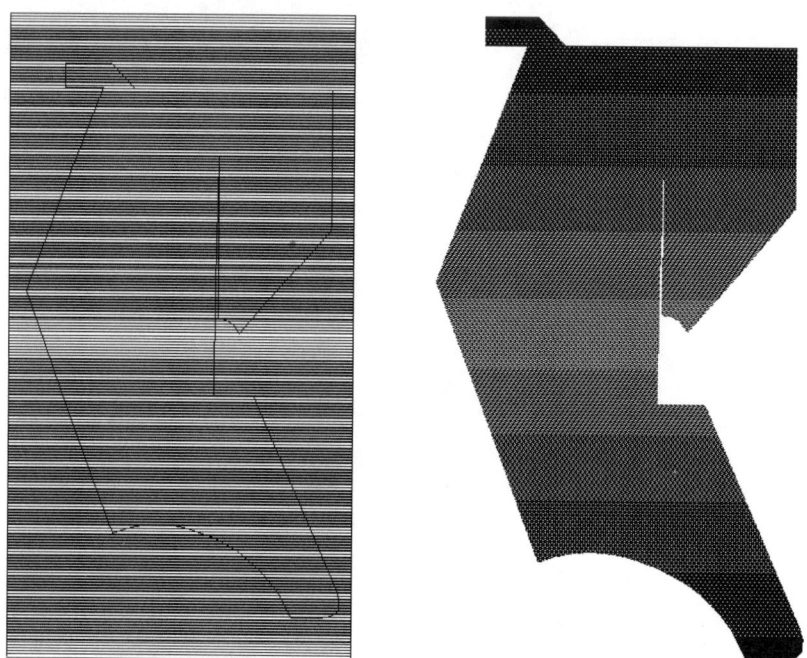

Mask over two hundred narrow boxes: Artwork Only and Preview

In subsequent work, the artist made considerable use of Command-3 and Command-4 to hide and show the background, respectively, for two reasons: first, with so many lines visible, it often became difficult to see the objects he was currently working on;

and second, hiding the background made previewing and screen redrawing much faster.

The figure on the facing page shows the two hundred blended boxes as Artwork Only and in Preview with the kimono masked in the background.

The artist created the solid red areas (which appear black in the final art here; see color plate) that represent the inside lining of the top half of the kimono with the Pen tool, aligned precisely to the kimono outline.

He drew the patterned areas that represent the inside lining of the bottom half of the kimono as closed paths with the Pen tool, then drew a pattern of hexagons slightly larger than the area, starting with a single hexagon and using Option-drag and Transform Again (Command-D) to produce multiple copies. Once he had completed the hexagons, he masked them with the outline paths he had just drawn, then grouped the masked objects with Command-G.

Next he used the Pen tool to draw the sleeve trim and kimono edge as closed paths, filled them with a custom pattern of vertical lines in several weights and colors, and grouped them (Command-G). (See Patterns: Methods 1 and 2 in Part III.)

Flowers First the artist drew one petal shape, then he scaled down a copy with the Scale tool. He set the larger shape with a Fill of White and a Stroke of None, using the Style command from the Paint menu (Command-I). He used the smaller shape to set up two reference points for blending a green color, using lighter shading at the outer edges and darker at the center of the petal. The next figure shows the blended petal shape in Artwork Only and Preview Illustration views. After blending, he drew the innermost shape of the petals with a Red Fill and no stroke. He then copied (Command-C), rotated with the Rotate tool, and scaled with the Scale tool the dimensional-looking petal to form a six- or seven-petal arrangement.

PART IV: APPLICATIONS

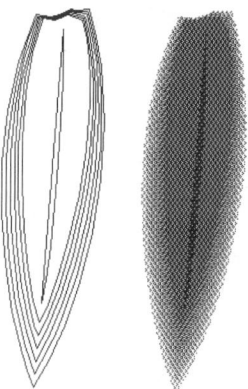

One flower petal as Artwork Only and in Preview

Next the artist composed the central part of the flower using five radially symmetrical half-circles. Once he had drawn the first outer form, he scaled down a copy with the Scale tool. Then he set the larger shape with a White Fill and no stroke, and the inner shape with a shade of Red Fill and no stroke. He rotated a copy of the full-size object using the Rotate tool, then scaled down a copy of the inner portion to create the center. The artist filled each of the layers with a different shade of red, then grouped them all (Command-G).

The following figure shows the center of the flower as Artwork Only and in Preview.

Center of flower as Artwork Only and in Preview

ILLUSTRATIONS

He added the pistils by drawing one, setting it with Green Fill and no stroke, rotating copies around the center point using the Rotate tool, and clicking the Copy button in the Rotate dialog box. He grouped (Command-G) and overlaid the pistils on the flower center, then copied (Command-C), scaled with the Scale tool, and overlaid the set on the flower petals. The following figure shows the pistils as one grouped object prior to overlaying them on the flower petals.

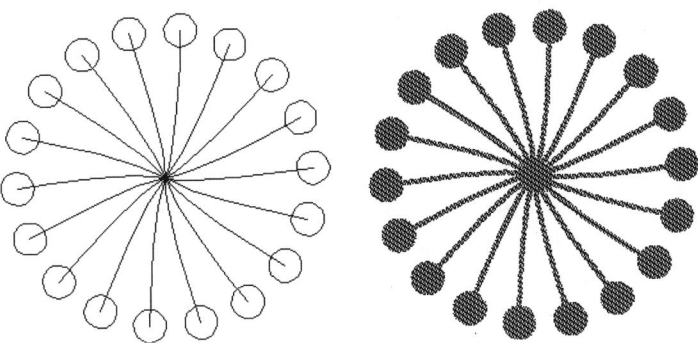

Pistils as Artwork Only and in Preview

Finally, the artist drew the fernlike leaf and the berry branches once, then used all four transformation tools—Rotate, Scale, Shear, and Reflect—to create variety, and arranged them individually for each flower. He also made individual adjustments to the stacking order using the Cut, Paste In Front, and Paste In Back commands. Finally, he used Select All (Command-A) and grouped the leaves, flower centers, pistils, ferns, and berries into a single composite object with Command-G. The figure on the following page shows the finished, composite flower in Artwork & Template view; on the right is the flower in Preview mode (Command-Y).

PART IV: APPLICATIONS

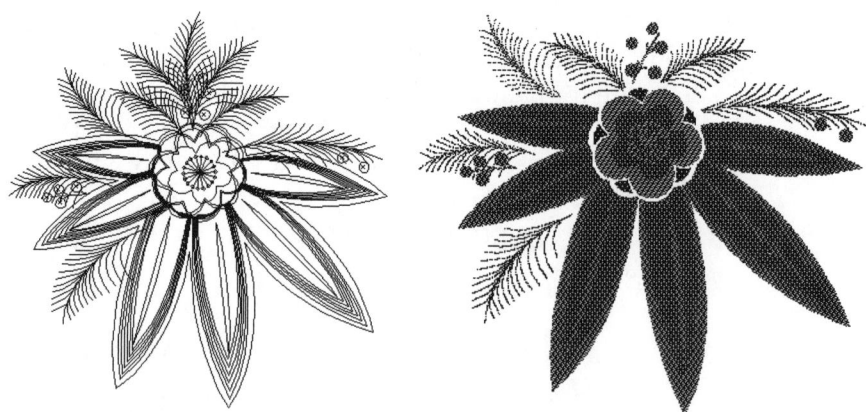

A finished flower in Artwork & Template and in Preview mode

Finishing Touches   Finishing touches included drawing ribbons over the kimono, drawing black and gray lines radiating from the bottom hem of the kimono, and pasting a copy of the kimono outline in front of all other layers (using the Paste In Front command, Command-F), giving it a Fill of None and a Black Stroke of .5 Weight. To accomplish this last step, the artist first chose Select All (Command-A), then Hide (Command-3), which left the locked kimono outline visible. Next he unlocked (Command-2) and ungrouped (Command-U) the outline and blends. Then he selected and copied (Command-C) the outline. Next he regrouped (with Command-G) and locked the outline and the blends (Command-1), chose Show All (Command-4), and, finally, used Paste In Front (Command-F) to paste the copy of the kimono outline on top.

Warning   The grouping of objects and the stacking order of clipping paths is tricky and time-consuming. Complex work of this nature, while theoretically possible on a Mac Plus or SE, realistically requires an accelerated SE or a Mac II for reasonable performance.

ILLUSTRATIONS

Tip   Determine the grouping of composite objects before you start. You can draw different elements in different files and use Copy and Paste In Front or Paste In Back to assemble the parts into one illustration.

See also Blending Colors or Grays, Patterns: Methods 1 and 2, Masking, Masking a Mask, Pasting in Layers, Radial Symmetry: Methods 1 and 2, and Flower Petals in Part III.

PART IV: APPLICATIONS

Portrait

Overview The artist traced this portrait from a scanned photograph. He created areas of different percentage fills for a realistic dimensional effect. He likened the use of progressive layers of lighter and darker tones to portrait drawing with white and black Conté crayon on gray charcoal paper.

You can apply the techniques used here in tracing any scan, but they are especially applicable to images that require shading of irregular surfaces.

Procedure The artist scanned the original photograph, a black and white 2-by-3-inch passport photo, as a halftone (eight gray levels) at 300 dpi on a Microtek 300SF Flatbed scanner. He adjusted contrast and brightness to obtain a template with a full range of density (from deepest shadow to white) and with smooth gradation of density levels. He then used the scanned image as a template for the Illustrator artwork.

The artist layered the face rendering with closed, filled, and stroked paths in this logical fashion: he started with the forehead, then hair, eyes, nose, mouth, chin, and finally the neck, collar, tie, and the background and frame.

He selected a middle tone—about 40 percent Black Fill—as the "ground," or predominant tone, for the face. The basic outline of the face with this midtone gray fill became the foundation for the rest of the art. He built up lighter and darker areas in layers, closely referring to the original photo. He filled each successive layer of shapes (closed paths that outline shaded areas of the face) with an intermediate value to soften the gradations. For example, he drew one of the shadows under the eyes on top of an area already at 45 percent Black Fill. He gave the new darker path a 55 percent Black Fill, but a 50 percent Stroke. Sometimes he thickened the stroke to accentuate the gradation effect. The figure on page 338 shows a close-up of the gradation effect in Artwork Only mode (Command-W) and the same close-up in Preview mode (Command-Y), which shows the gradation effects achieved.

ILLUSTRATIONS

Portrait created by John Van Pelt

PART IV: APPLICATIONS

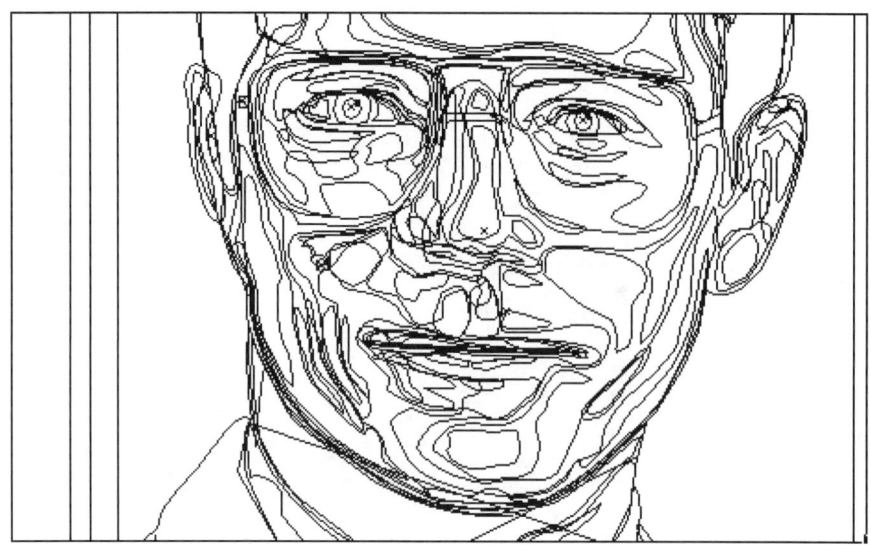

Close-up of graduated shading: Artwork Only and Preview

Warning Setting contrast and brightness for the scan required much trial and error. The artist made about ten scans before he was satisfied with the result.

ILLUSTRATIONS

Tip The artist could have used the Blend tool for some of the gradations of shading, but he achieved a more realistic effect by drawing each layer of shading individually, so the transition from one shape (of shaded area) to another was adjusted by the artist to match his interpretation of the original photo and was not mathematically determined.

See also Blending Colors or Grays and Highlights in Part III.

| PART IV: APPLICATIONS |

Technical Illustration

Overview The artist saw this assignment for a newspaper feature page as an opportunity to do something in a more creative, less rigid graphic style, even though the subject matter was technical. The illustration is a good example of the techniques described in Hand-drawn Look: Methods 1–3 in Part III. The final art was in color, using manually cut amberlith overlays.

This example demonstrates how Illustrator can be used to save time over conventional techniques. The artist comments: "This was done when I had been working with Illustrator for about a week. I debated over how to render the design, as I had in mind a rather loose brush-and-ink style. But in the tight deadline I couldn't see how I would work in the text drop-ins if I had to build the whole thing by conventional (paste-up) methods. The Macintosh was clearly the answer, and what I knew of Illustrator up to then convinced me it was capable of the flexibility I needed."

Procedure The artist made several rough sketches with soft pencil on tracing tissue, and came up with a plan he liked. Then he scanned the rough sketch, with no further refinements. "I wanted to capture the impromptu character even though I knew I would painstakingly trace each line."

Using the scanned image as a template for the Illustrator artwork, he traced each line quickly as a closed path, with a Fill of Black and Stroke of None, working at maximum magnification. Some shapes, such as the droplets of sweat, he drew as closed paths with Black Fill with a smaller, white-filled shape superimposed in White Fill. To maintain the hand-drawn look for the sweat drops, the artist drew the smaller inside shapes with the Pen tool rather than using the Scale tool to produce a copy of the outer shape.

The figure on page 342 shows the magnified view of the lower left part of the drawing in Artwork Only view. The artist then chose Preview Illustration from the View menu (Command-Y) to view the art.

| ILLUSTRATIONS | |

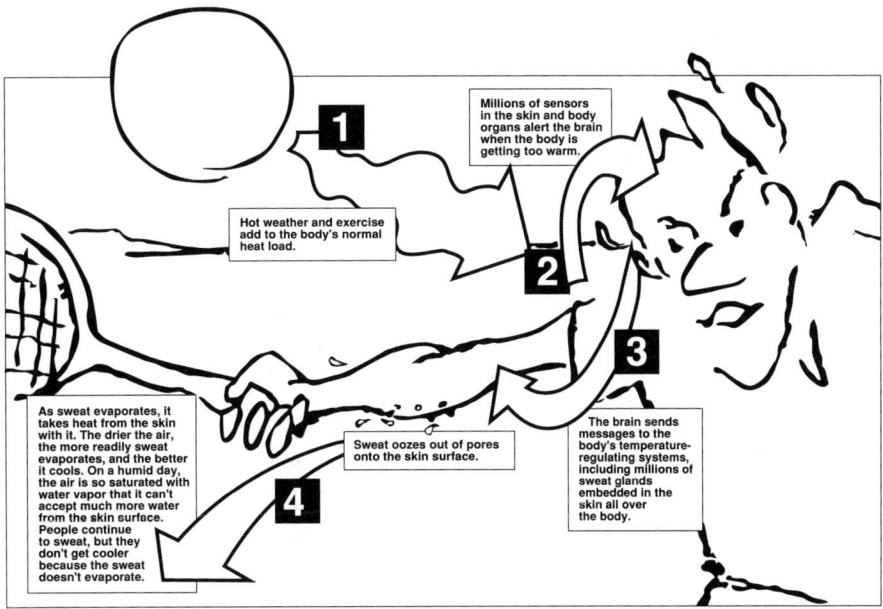

Technical Illustration created by John Van Pelt

The artist drew the sun in the drawing, which juts over the bounding rectangle, as a closed path representing the outline only; the inside area of the sun was not part of the path. To eliminate the part of the rectangular border that crossed the sun, the artist ungrouped the rectangle (using Command-U) and clipped it with the Scissors tool.

For a cleaner look, the artist made the arrows single paths, with a thick 2.5-point Black Stroke and a White Fill. Finally, he added the text blocks using the Type tool and the black blocks with white-filled numerals.

 PART IV: APPLICATIONS

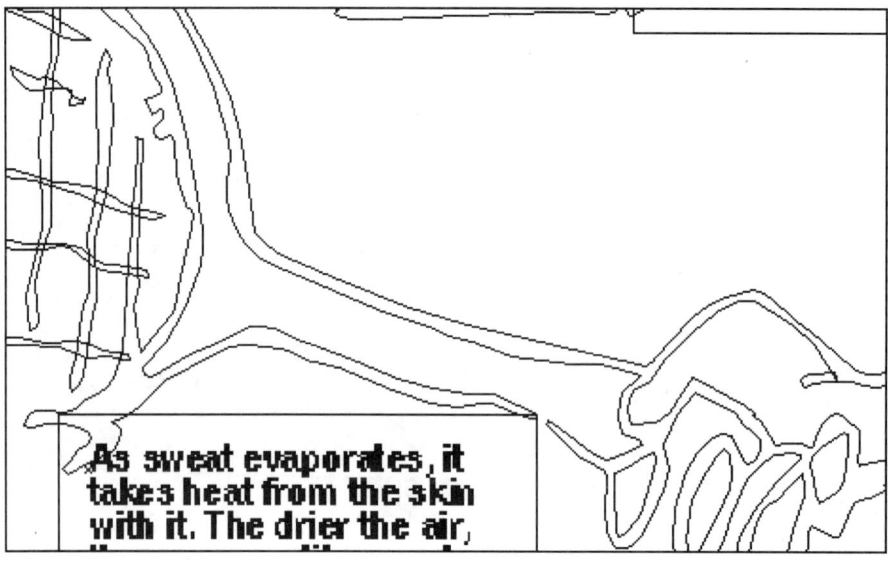

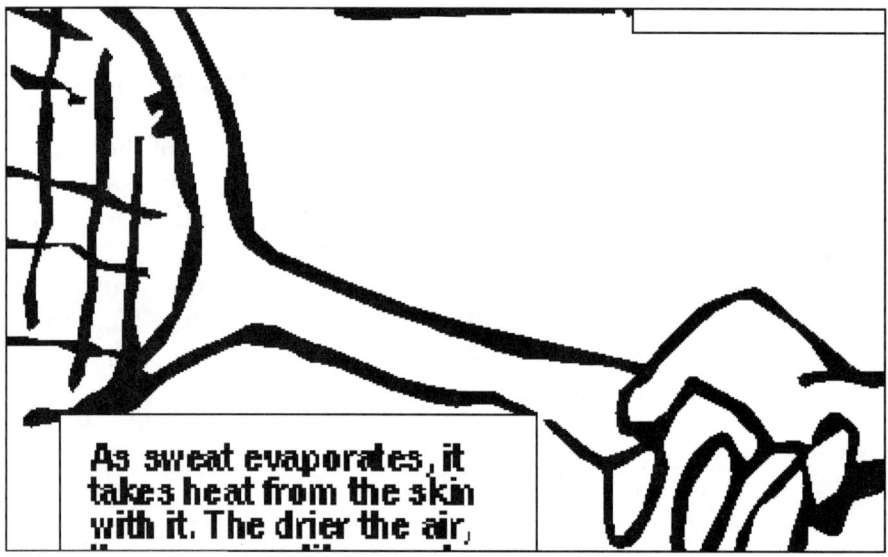

Close-up of part of the drawing: Artwork Only and Preview

The artist derived the design for this kimono from several traditional kimono designs found in historical reference books. He composed the kimono using a repeated, rotated, and scaled flower motif on a purple background with blended shading. The trim patterns on the sleeves and edges were created using masking and pattern fills.

David Smith • Sausalito, CA • Courtesy of Apple Computer Japan

The artist created the primary feature of this illustration—the wedges of the fan—using two techniques: he filled some with custom patterns, and he used masks over large designs for others.

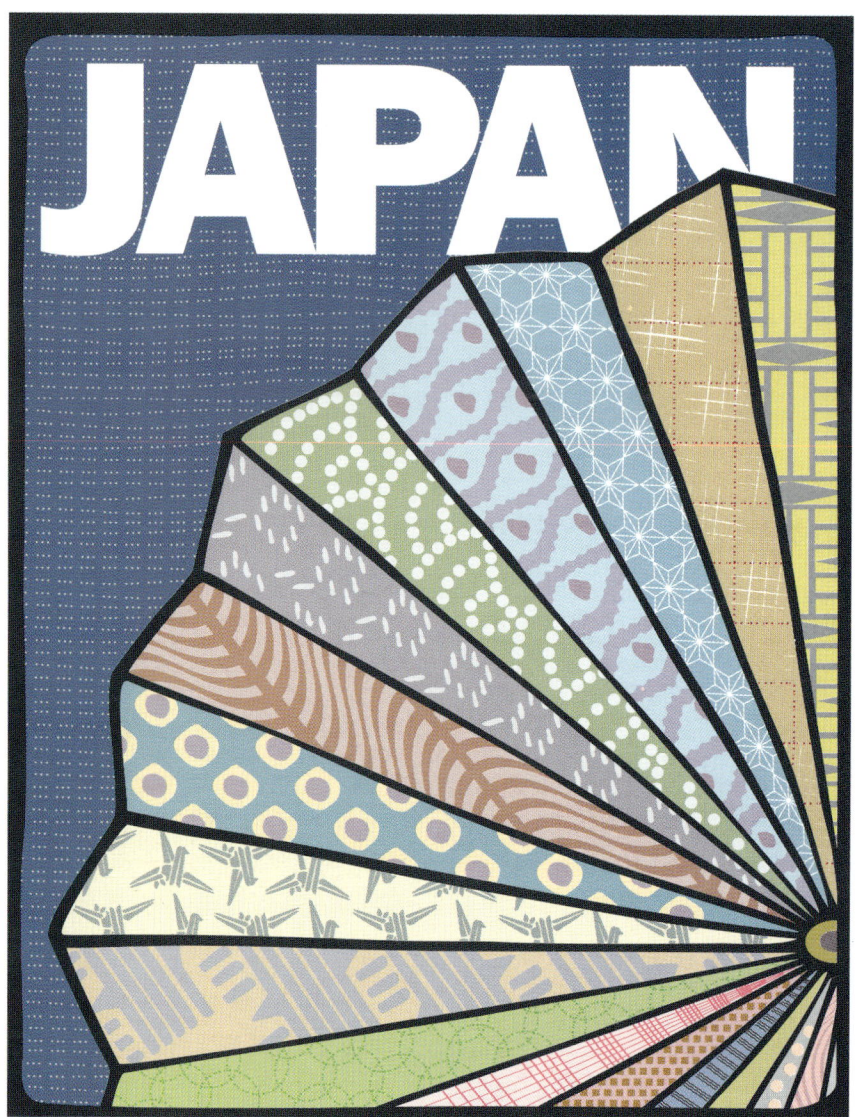

David Smith • Sausalito, CA • Courtesy of Adobe Systems Incorporated. All rights reserved.

The artist combined maps with four variations of bar charts to produce this visual representation of economic trends in Asia. He made the illustration easier to understand by using different shapes (cubes, cylinders, and bars) for the different types of data.

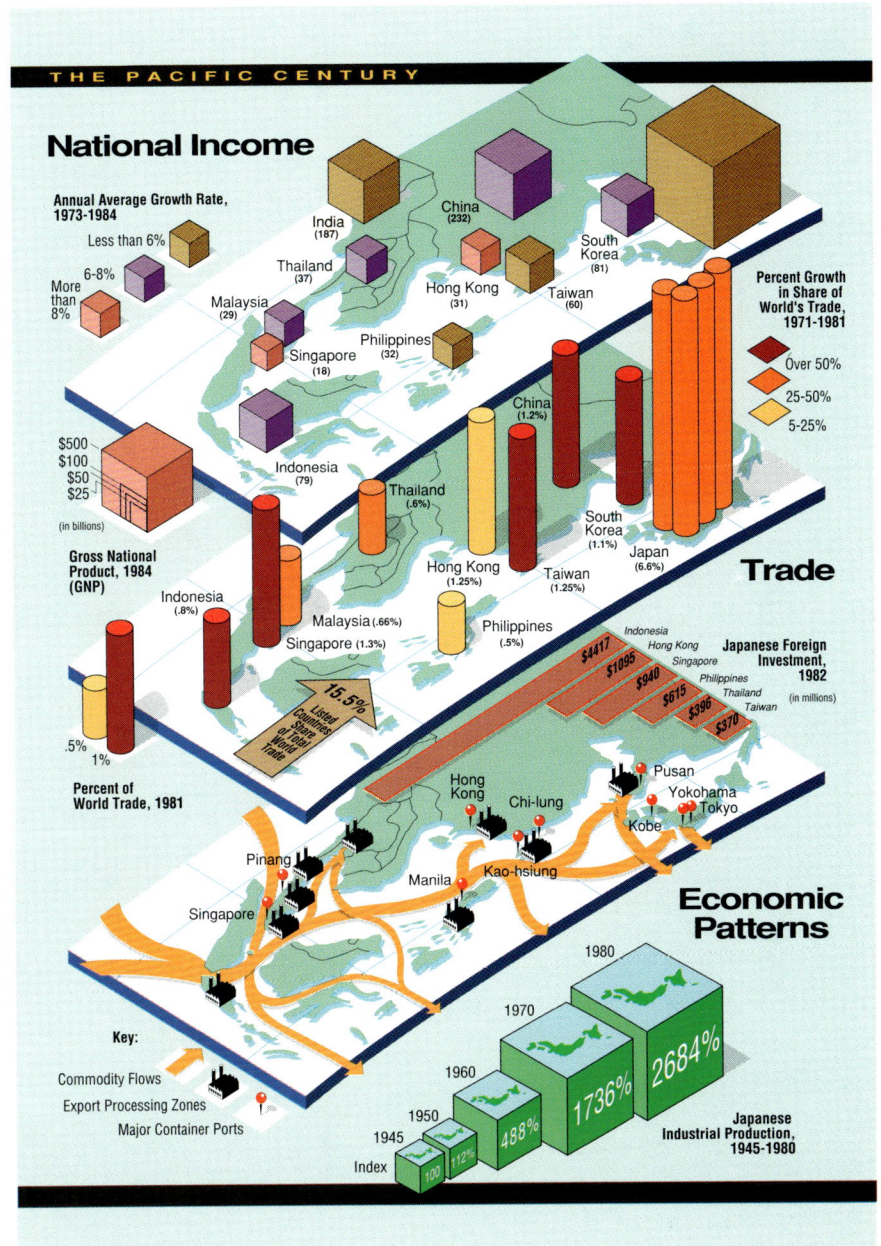

D.L. Fuller • Courtesy of EarthSurface Graphics

The artist composed this poster almost entirely on the computer screen, experimenting freely with placement of the different elements. The hand was the only element that was traced from a scanned template. The artist specified PANTONE® colors and let Illustrator convert them to process colors.

David Smith • Sausalito, CA • Courtesy of Adobe Systems Incorporated. All rights reserved.

ILLUSTRATIONS

Tip In this case the artist chose to cut amberlith overlays for the color separations rather than use Illustrator's separation feature. In the final version, the amberlith was deliberately cut roughly to yield imprecise registration, adding to the sketchy look of the hand-drawn lines.

See also Aligning Text: Methods 1 and 2 and Hand-drawn Look: Methods 1 and 2 in Part III.

PART IV: APPLICATIONS

Collage Poster

Overview The artist composed this poster almost entirely on the computer screen, experimenting freely with placement of the different elements. The only element for which he used a template was the hand, which was scanned from a print, then drawn with the Pen tool. All other elements were created from scratch. The whole process took 12 to 15 hours, most of which were spent experimenting with the placement of different objects. To speed up work on this complex illustration, the artist made frequent use of the Hide, Lock, and Preview Selection commands, and often used separate files when creating the various elements.

The four-color separations for the final artwork were printed on a Linotronic 300 imagesetter. Although the artwork was designed for four-color process, the artist specified most as Pantone colors and let Illustrator convert them to process colors. (See color plate.)

You can apply the techniques used here to create three-dimensional shading and to layer objects.

Procedure The artist first scanned the hand as a template, then drew it with the Pen tool and saved it as a separate file. Then he created the large characters, converted them to paths using the Create Outlines command in the Type menu, and saved these in a second file.

Next, he created the spheres, ellipses, and cylinders, duplicating them as required. He added the squares, the pyramid, and a hexagon. The hexagon was obtained from the Adobe Collectors Edition.

The next step was to assemble the elements created so far into a single file. At this point he also sheared, scaled, and rotated the large letters, then added the wire-frame box for a false-perspective effect. The final elements were the ribbons, which also were created in a separate file.

The illustration was completed by layering the various elements, using the Scissors tool to split paths where necessary, and pasting elements in front or in back of others.

The rest of this section describes these basic steps in detail.

ILLUSTRATIONS

Collage Poster created by David Smith

PART IV: APPLICATIONS

Hand The artist scanned a template of the hand from a Michaelangelo print, then drew over the template using the Pen tool. He applied a .5-point Black Stroke and White Fill, then grouped the entire hand (Command-G) and saved it.

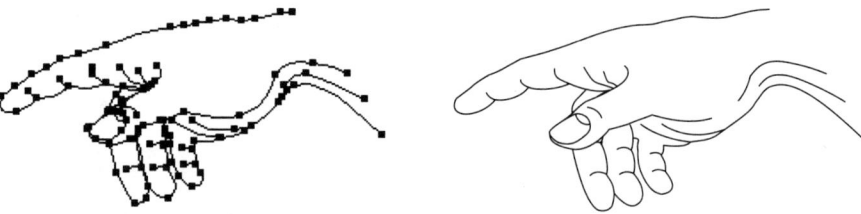

Hand: Artwork Only and Preview

Characters The artist created the characters in a new file as separate point text objects, then converted them to outlines using the Create Outlines command. He painted the resulting outlines with a Stroke of None and Fills of various solid Pantone colors, then saved the result.

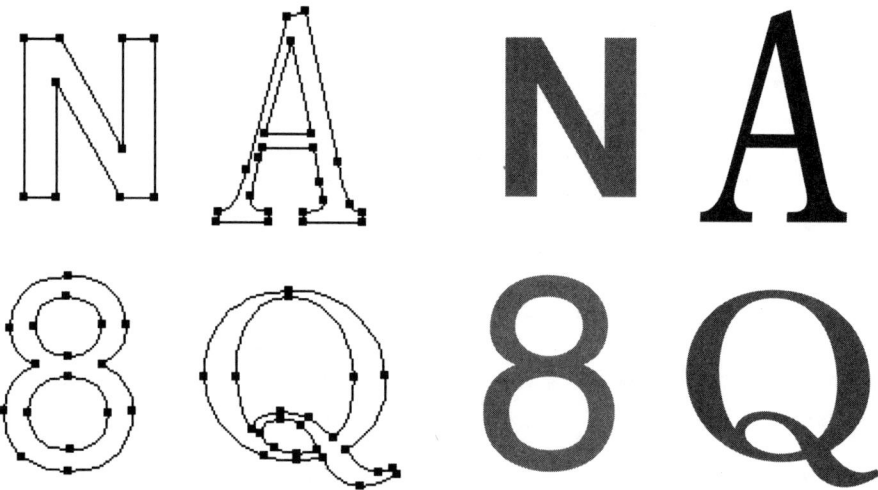

Characters: Artwork Only and Preview

Spheres A third file was used for the spheres. To create a sphere, the artist drew a circle to form the outline of the sphere, then added a second shape, in the form of either a second circle or a crescent, as a highlight. Next, he applied a dark-colored fill to the outline of the sphere and a light-colored fill to the highlight. To complete the sphere, he used the Blend tool to create a 105-step blend between the outline and the highlight for a three-dimensional shading effect. Finally, he grouped the completed sphere (Command-G).

Additional spheres were created by Option-dragging, rotating, and scaling the original. To change the color of some of the duplicates, the artist deleted the blend, recolored the sphere outline and highlight, and blended them once more with the Blend tool. In some cases, he also moved the highlight before blending, to add variation.

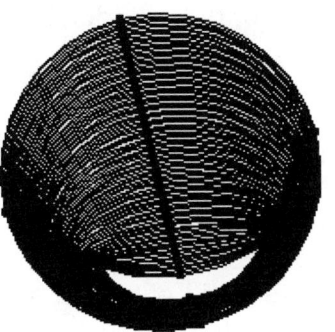 

Sphere: Artwork Only and Preview

Cylinders The cylinders are the most complex of the shapes used here. The front face of the cylinder is a simple ellipse filled with solid color, while the shaft consists of a blend from dark to light which was then copied, reflected, and masked.

PART IV: APPLICATIONS

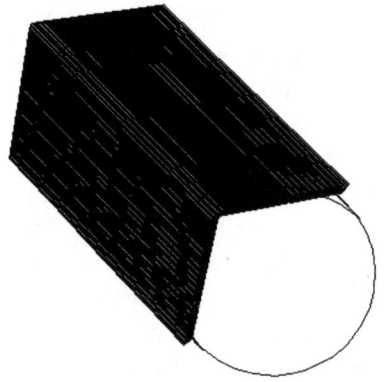 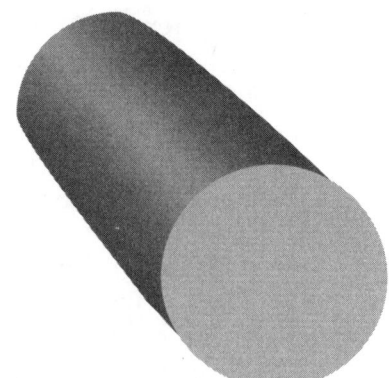

Cylinder: Artwork Only and Preview

First the artist drew the shape of the shaft using the Pen tool. He applied a Stroke and Fill of None and made it a mask. Next, to create the highlight on the shaft of the cylinder, the artist drew two rectangles, rotated them to the angle of the shaft, then placed one at the edge and one at the center of the mask. Next, he used the Blend tool to create a 102-step blend between the rectangles, and grouped the blend with the rectangles (Command-G).

Using the Reflect tool, the artist created a reflected copy of the blend to complete the shading of the shaft. Then he selected both blends and the masking shape, and grouped them to complete the shaft. Finally, he positioned the solid ellipse and grouped it with the elements comprising the shaft to complete the cylinder.

ILLUSTRATIONS

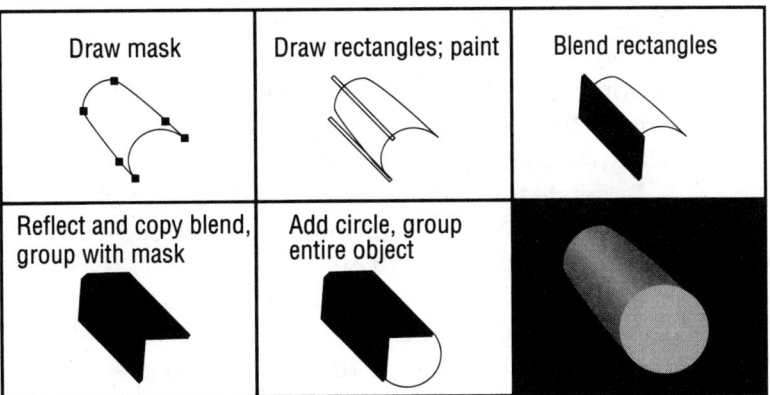

Cylinder: step by step

Other Geometric Shapes The remaining geometric shapes were either drawn using the Rectangle and Oval tools, then transformed by rotating and shearing, or were taken from Adobe Collectors Edition.

Assembly At this point, the artist assembled the various elements, bringing in the hand and the large characters by copying them from the original files and pasting them into the poster artwork. He scaled, sheared, and rotated the large characters, using transformed copies of the Q and the 8 as drop shadows. Then, to add a sense of depth, he drew the wire-frame box using the Rectangle and Pen tools.

Ribbons Working in a separate file, the artist created the two ribbons using a different technique for each. For the narrow blue ribbon, he drew a line using the Pen tool, gave it a 5-point Blue Stroke, then Option-dragged it to produce a slightly offset copy, which he colored a lighter blue to provide a drop-shadow effect.

To create the wide purple ribbon, the artist first drew a line using the Pen tool. Next, he created an offset copy of the line by Option-dragging, and joined the endpoints of the two lines using the Join command (Command-J). He then adjusted individual anchor points to produce the desired shape. The final step in creating the ribbon was to create the illusion of a twisted ribbon by applying a different fill to different sections of the ribbon. To do so, the artist used the Scissors tool to split the path at the points where it overlapped, then used the Join command (Command-J) to join the new endpoints, resulting in five closed paths. He used a Stroke of None and used two different shades of purple for the fill, alternating the fill so that adjacent sections of the ribbon were always filled differently, then grouped the five paths (Command-G).

Finishing Touches To finish the poster, the artist layered the different elements to strengthen the perspective effect. In most cases, he used either the Bring To Front (Command-=) and Send To Back (Command-minus) commands, or the Paste In Front (Command-F) and Paste In Back (Command-B) commands. In some cases, he used the Scissors tool to split paths, then deleted segments. He also used the Scissors tool and the Pen tool to split the drop shadow on the Q into two separate compound objects so that he could apply a darker fill to the portion that overlapped the large circle.

ILLUSTRATIONS

Tips When you are working with composite elements such as the cylinders and spheres used in this illustration, it is always a good idea to group them for easy handling.

You can speed up work on complex illustrations like this by creating elements in separate files, by hiding objects when you aren't working on them, and by using the Preview Selection command (Command-Option-Y) rather than previewing the whole illustration.

Appendices

APPENDIXES — Introduction

Introduction to Appendixes

This part of the book presents descriptions of two programs that come with Adobe Illustrator—DrawOver™ and Adobe Separator—and presents three other topics of interest to advanced users. Appendixes include:

APPENDIX	TITLE
A	Converting PICT Files with DrawOver
B	Printing Color Separations with Adobe Separator
C	Calculating Color Blends in Adobe Illustrator 3.0
D	Color Trapping
E	Using the EPSF Riders file

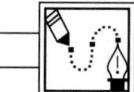

APPENDIX A

Appendix A: Converting PICT Files with DrawOver

Overview You can use DrawOver, an application that Adobe packages with Adobe Illustrator, to convert drawings that have been created or saved in PICT format (created in MacDraw, MacDraw II, or other drawing applications that support PICT formats) into PostScript documents that can be edited in Illustrator. DrawOver is specifically designed to handle drawings created by MacDraw (versions 1.9 and higher or MacDraw II) and converts straight lines, rectangles, ovals, line weights, and fill patterns that are shades of gray. Lines drawn with MacDraw's Freehand tool are converted into vectors with many anchor points along the path. Text is also converted. Converted drawings can be edited using any of the features offered by Adobe Illustrator.

Procedure First create a drawing, using an application that allows you to save it in PICT format. Then, from the Macintosh desktop, double-click on the DrawOver application icon to start it.

In the dialog box that appears next, find and double-click the name of the document you wish to convert.

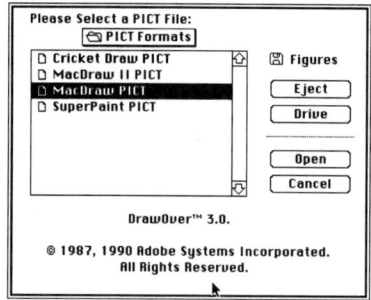

DrawOver dialog box showing PICT documents

356

CONVERTING PICT FILES WITH DRAWOVER

When a window displaying a Preview image of the PICT document opens, click OK (or press Return) if this is the document you wish to convert or click Cancel if you want to end the DrawOver process or choose a different document name.

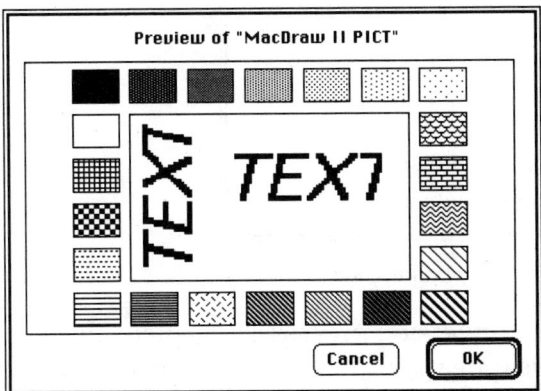

DrawOver displays a Preview of the document you wish to convert

When you click Cancel, the original DrawOver dialog box appears. When you click OK, a new dialog box appears, in which you choose the location for the converted document and type a name for the new document (or accept DrawOver's naming convention that adds .ART to the PICT file name).

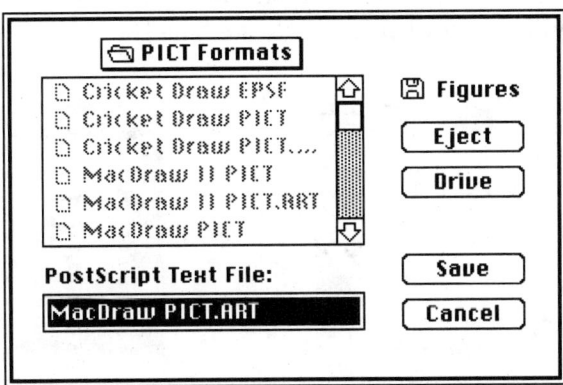

Dialog box for entry of name of new file and its location

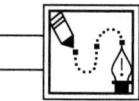

APPENDIX A

After you enter a name and click Save, DrawOver displays a message giving the status of the conversion as it goes through two passes.

```
Pict To PostScript Conversion

Input:   "MacDraw PICT"
Output:  "MacDraw PICT.ART"

Pass 1 Total KiloBytes:   0
Pass 2 Total KiloBytes:
```

Message shows status of conversion

When the conversion process is complete, the original DrawOver dialog box reappears, and you can convert another document or quit the DrawOver application. Converted documents can be opened and edited using Illustrator.

Warning Some elements of the original PICT drawing might not be converted into PostScript. For example, many of the fill patterns that are available in MacDraw and similar applications will not be converted. Colors applied in MacDraw II are converted to black. Bitmaps saved in PICT format, such as elements on the bitmapped layer in Super-Paint, are not converted. You should test conversions of PICT files created with other applications, such as the test files shown below.

PICT format from MacDraw 1.9.5 and resulting PostScript artwork; all fill patterns are converted as shades of gray

CONVERTING PICT FILES WITH DRAWOVER

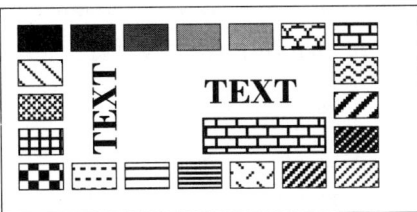 

PICT format from MacDraw II and resulting PostScript artwork; black rectangle was color in MacDraw II file

PICT format from SuperPaint and resulting PostScript artwork; bitmapped layer is not converted

APPENDIX B

Appendix B: Printing Color Separations with Adobe Separator 3.0

Overview   You can print four-color process separations or custom (spot) color separations using Adobe Separator 3.0, an application that Adobe packages with Adobe Illustrator 3.0. This appendix describes how to use Adobe Separator to print color separations. For a description of how to create colors and assign them to artwork, see the Style (Paint Menu) command (for assigning colors) and the Preferences command (for adjusting the color display on the monitor with the Change Progressive Colors option) in Part II, and see Blending Colors or Grays and Overlays: Methods 1 and 2 in Part III.

Procedure   First use Adobe Illustrator 3.0 to create an illustration and apply one or more colors (in addition to black and white). Then, from the Macintosh desktop, double-click on the Adobe Separator 3.0 application icon to start it.

Adobe Separator 3.0

In the dialog box that appears next, find and double-click the name of the document you wish to print.

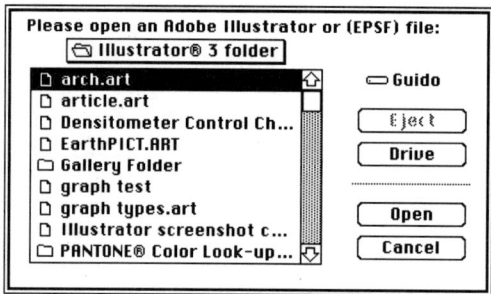

Dialog box for selecting a document to print

PRINTING COLOR SEPARATIONS WITH ADOBE SEPARATOR

After you select a file, Adobe Separator displays a second dialog box that asks you to specify the PostScript Printer Description (PPD) file for the printer you are using. These files are stored in the PPD Folder, which is created when you run the PPD Installer program found on the Adobe Illustrator 3.0 Gallery disk. PPD files contain information about the printer's dot resolution, the available page sizes, whether the printer supports color output, and the acceptable screen settings. Once you have chosen a PPD file, Adobe Separator continues to use that PPD file unless you specify a new one.

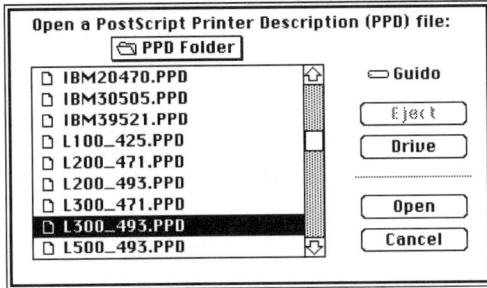

Dialog box asking for a printer description file

Find the PPD Folder and double-click on that name in the dialog box. When the PPD Folder is open, a list of the PPD files is displayed. The name of the printer file is a cryptic abbreviation of the full name and model number of the printer.

After you choose the PPD file that matches the printer you are using, the Adobe Separator window appears. You can accept the default settings to print all four process color separations, or you can choose different options as described on the following pages. The text boxes that show a drop shadow at the right and bottom edges are actually pop-up menus: position the mouse pointer over the text box and hold down the mouse button to view options; drag and release the mouse to choose an option.

361

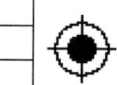

APPENDIX B

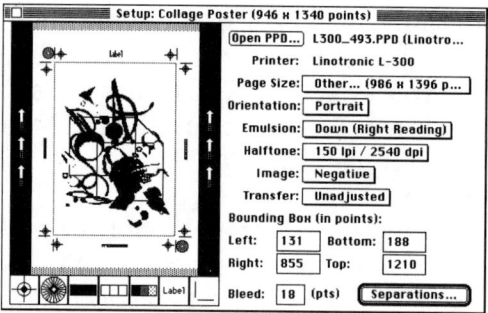

Adobe Separator 3.0 window for setting print options

The following options are available in the Adobe Separator window:

Open PPD... Displays the dialog box that lets you choose a PostScript Printer Description file, described earlier.

Printer This option displays the name of the printer that is currently selected in the Chooser. To change printers, choose Chooser from the Apple menu and select the appropriate printer from the list in the Chooser window.

Page Size Hold down the mouse button on the text box to display and choose from the list of page sizes available for your chosen printer (identified in the PPD file). The dimensions of the printable area are shown next to each page size on the menu; these dimensions include the limits for the registration marks, color labels, and printed crop marks.

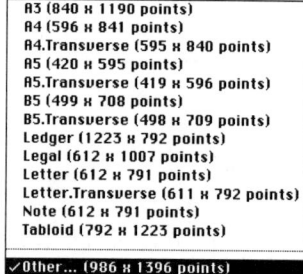

Page Size options are displayed in a pop-up menu

PRINTING COLOR SEPARATIONS WITH ADOBE SEPARATOR

If your printer allows variable page sizes, a custom page size option will be displayed on the page size menu as Other..., where you can enter custom dimensions and offset. You can also print the page transversely (rotated 90 degrees). Using these two options avoids wasting film on phototypesetters.

Orientation Hold down the mouse button on the text box to display and choose from the list of orientations available. In Portrait mode, the top of the image is printed parallel to the short edge of the paper. In Landscape mode, the top of the image is printed parallel to the long edge of the paper.

Orientation options are displayed in a pop-up menu

Note that orientation affects the position of the image on the page (as defined in the Illustrator document by the Page tool), whereas the Transverse available on some printers through the Page Size option affects the orientation of that page (as defined in the Illustrator document) on the printout paper (as defined through the Page Size option).

Emulsion Hold down the mouse button on the text box to display and choose from the list of emulsion settings available. Emulsion Up (Right Reading) means that any text in the image is readable when the printed paper is facing you. Emulsion Down (Right Reading) means that the text is readable when the paper is facing away from you.

Emulsion options are displayed in a pop-up menu

Normally you would print with Emulsion Down (Right Reading) only when printing to a transparent film. When printing to clear film, the emulsion side is dull; the shiny side is the base.

Halftone This option shows the screen ruling of the halftone pattern used to print the separations, in halftone dots per inch, stated as lines per inch (lpi). The available choices vary depending on the PPD file you have opened. If you are printing to a high-resolution device, the screen angles for the four process colors and the custom color are listed in parentheses on the pop-up menu in the following order: cyan, magenta, yellow, black, and custom color.

Note that as the screen rulings increase, the halftone dots are less noticeable, but there is a trade-off between screen ruling and the available number of gray shades. The number of gray shades per screen ruling is determined by the resolution of your printer.

```
  75 lpi / 635 dpi
  90 lpi / 635 dpi
  90 lpi / 1270 dpi
  90 lpi / 2540 dpi
 112 lpi / 1270 dpi
 112 lpi / 2540 dpi
 120 lpi / 2540 dpi
 128 lpi / 1270 dpi
 128 lpi / 2540 dpi
✓150 lpi / 2540 dpi
```

Halftone options are displayed in a pop-up menu

Image Hold down the mouse button on the text box to display and choose from the list of image options available: Positive or Negative. Positive images print exactly as shown in Preview on the screen. Negative images reverse dark and light areas. You can save a step in offset printing by printing negative separations directly to film.

Image options are displayed in a pop-up menu

Transfer This option lets you choose between an Unadjusted transfer function or one that has been customized to your output device. To customize the transfer function for a particular output device, you must first print four separation negatives of the Densitometer Control

PRINTING COLOR SEPARATIONS WITH ADOBE SEPARATOR

Chart, which is included with Adobe Separator 3.0. After printing the negatives, take a densitometer reading of each percentage square on the chart negative and write down the values. Then, choose Adjust Tints from the Transfer pop-up menu to open the Tint Adjustment Chart, and enter the densitometer values in the appropriate places on the Tint Adjustment Chart. You can save the tint adjustment values by clicking the Save button and entering a name for the settings in the Save Tint Adjustments As text box.

```
  Unadjusted
✓ Adjust tints...
```

Transfer options are displayed in a pop-up menu

Unadjusted tint densities:						
Tint	C	M	Y	K	Custom	
0%	0.000	0.000	0.000	0.000	0.000	OK
10	0.046	0.046	0.046	0.046	0.046	Cancel
20	0.097	0.097	0.097	0.097	0.097	Open...
30	0.155	0.155	0.155	0.155	0.155	Save...
40	0.222	0.222	0.222	0.222	0.222	
50	0.301	0.301	0.301	0.301	0.301	
60	0.397	0.397	0.397	0.397	0.397	
70	0.522	0.522	0.522	0.522	0.522	
80	0.697	0.697	0.697	0.697	0.697	
90	0.996	0.996	0.996	0.996	0.996	
100	3.000	3.000	3.000	3.000	3.000	

The Tint Adjustment Chart

Bounding Box This set of options lets you type the positions of the four corners of the bounding box, which is displayed in the image preview area as a dotted rectangle. A fifth text box lets you adjust the size of the bleed area. (You can also adjust the bounding box and bleed area by dragging the sides of the bounding box in the image preview area as described on the next page.)

APPENDIX B

Separations... Clicking this button opens the Separations dialog box, which lets you choose the type of separations to be printed. The Label text box contains the name of the file. When you print individual separations, the color, screen frequency, and angle are appended to the file name on the separation negative. To select individual process color separations, click the check box next to the appropriate process color. To select individual custom color separations, click the check box next to the appropriate custom color in the scrolling list of custom colors. To convert a custom color to process color, click on the custom color name instead of the check box. The custom color name then appears in gray to indicate that it will be converted to process colors.

The Separations dialog box

The preview image area at the left of the Separator window lets you manually position labels, star targets, register marks, black overprint color bars, progressive color bars, gradient tint bars, labels, and trim marks by dragging their respective icons from the icon bar below the preview image into the image area. Trim marks automatically snap to the corners of the bounding box. The other elements can be placed anywhere on the page. Many print shops prefer to control the position of these elements themselves, so you should always check with your commercial printer to ascertain their requirements. You can also adjust the size of the bounding box manually by dragging the dotted rectangle surrounding the image; you can move the image within the bounding box by dragging the image itself.

PRINTING COLOR SEPARATIONS WITH ADOBE SEPARATOR

The File, Edit, and Settings menus offer additional options. The following commands are found on the File menu.

The File menu

Open...   This command opens the dialog box that lets you choose an Illustrator or EPSF document to separate.

Close   This command closes the document that is currently open.

Get Info...   This command opens the Get Info dialog box, which displays information about the currently open document, including the names of any fonts and patterns used and the names of any EPSF files that have been included in the artwork.

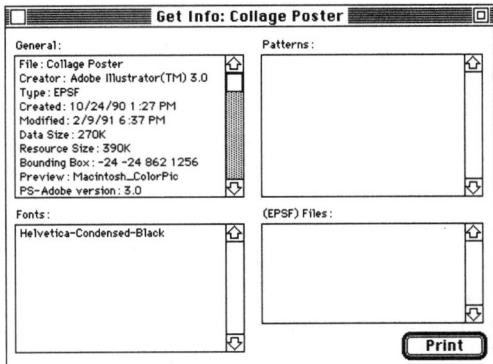

The Get Info dialog box

367

Separations... This command opens the Separations dialog box.

Save Selected Separations... This command lets you save to disk the separations selected in the Separations dialog box. Separator saves these as PostScript files.

Save All Separations... This command lets you save all the separations for the currently open document to disk. Separator saves these as PostScript files.

Print Selected Separations This command prints the separations that are currently selected in the Separations dialog box.

Print All Separations This command prints all separations for the document that is currently open.

Print Composite This command prints a composite of the currently open document. Its function is identical to the Print command in Adobe Illustrator 3.0.

Quit Closes the currently open document and quits the Separator application.

The Cut, Copy, Paste, and Clear commands on the Edit menu operate only on the contents of text boxes within Separator. The Undo command lets you undo most actions that can be performed in Separator.

The Settings menu contains commands that let you apply default settings to your color separations.

Settings	
Use Default Marks	⌘M
Use Default Settings	⌘T
Use Default Bounding Box	⌘B

The Settings menu

PRINTING COLOR SEPARATIONS WITH ADOBE SEPARATOR

Use Default Marks   This command places eight register marks, two star targets, a progressive color bar, a black overprint color bar, a gradient tint bar, a set of trim marks, and a label on each separation, in their default positions.

Use Default Settings   This command applies the output device's default settings to the separation. The actual settings vary depending on the kind of output device used. Adobe Separator uses the defaults contained in the currently active PPD file.

Use Default Bounding Box   This command sets the bounding box to the exact size of the image area of your document.

Appendix C: Calculating Color Blends in Adobe Illustrator 3.0

Overview Color banding is the appearance of distinct bands of different colors or shades, an effect that is usually undesirable. What you usually want is a perfectly smooth graduation from one color or shade to the next. In using the Blend tool to produce smooth gradations of color, two factors influence whether and to what extend color banding will occur: the number of steps in the blend and the screen frequency used in the final output. In some cases, banding is inevitable in color blends, but the techniques explained here will minimize banding in color blends.

Banding is more evident with only 18 blends (left) than with 256 blends (right)

Procedure The first step in preventing banding is to enter the correct number of steps in the blend. The PostScript language allows a maximum of 256 color gradations in a blend. Illustrator will let you use a higher number, which is useful for blending shapes, but using more than 256 steps for blending colors simply complicates the file unnecessarily. To calculate the correct number of steps, you must first look at the percentage of the colors being blended.

A blend across the entire spectrum from 0 percent (white) to 100 percent (black) requires 256 steps. To blend between other shades, you should use the percentage difference between the two shades. For example, a blend from 30 percent to 90 percent should use 60 percent (the difference between 30 percent and 90 percent) of 256, or 154 steps. These rules apply to gray, but are also valid for the dark colors cyan and magenta. To blend from 50 percent cyan to 40 percent magenta should be treated as a blend from 50 percent cyan to 0

CALCULATING COLOR BLENDS IN ADOBE ILLUSTRATOR

percent cyan, plus a blend from 0 percent magenta to 40 percent magenta. Use the color with the greatest percentage difference, in this case cyan (0 percent to 50 percent). This blend requires 50 percent of 256, or 128 steps.

Banding with light colors (yellow) is normally almost imperceptible when these colors are used alone. However, when they are combined with dark colors, the results can be hard to predict. In general, the more colors used in the blend, the more likely banding will result. For this reason, you should use 256 steps when your blend contains several colors.

The second step is to make sure that the imagesetter can produce 256 levels of gray at the screen frequency you specify. You need 256 levels of gray at the imagesetter even if your blend has fewer steps. You can determine the maximum line screen that a given imagesetter can use and still produce 256 levels of gray by dividing the imagesetter resolution (in dots per inch) by 16 (the square root of 256.) For example, an imagesetter with a resolution of 2400 dpi can use a 150-line-per-inch screen and still produce 256 levels of gray, whereas a 1200 dpi imagesetter can do so only with a screen of 75 lines per inch or lower.

Bear in mind that the imagesetter usually substitutes its closest line screen for the one requested—the actual screen frequency can vary from your specification by 10 lines per inch or more. If you use a screen frequency that limits the imagesetter to 240 levels of gray rather than 256, you will not necessarily see banding, but in general you should use a resolution and screen frequency that comes as close as possible to producing 256 levels of gray.

Appendix D: Adobe Illustrator Color Trapping

1 Black Overprint

Printing without a four color black and no knock out creates a bad ink show-through problem.

2 Black Knock out

Producing a knock out of black, instead of defaulting to overprint, creates a bad trapping problem.

3 Four Color Black

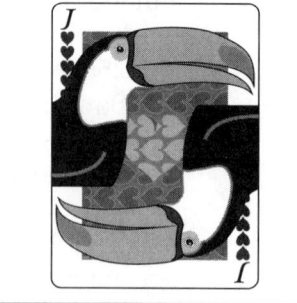

Four color blacks eliminate trapping problems and enhance color quality.
20% C / 10% M / 10% Y / 100% K

4 Line Trap

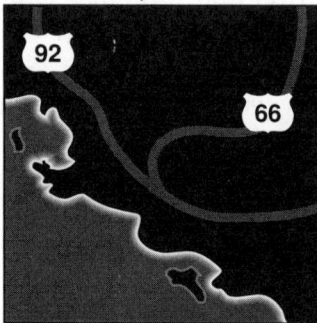

Trapping a solid or dashed line on a solid background using two lines.

5 Text Trap

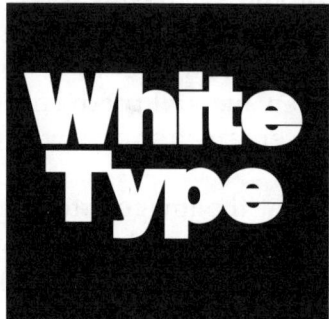

Stroking text with an overprinted line to eliminate color show-through on a four color black background.

6 Shadow Trap

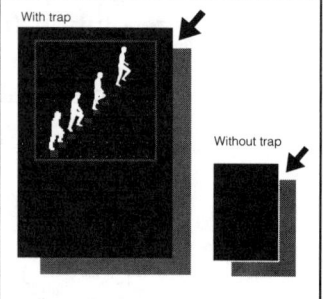

Trapping a drop shadow with an overprinted stroke to eliminate a possible white gap.

7 Overprinting Solids

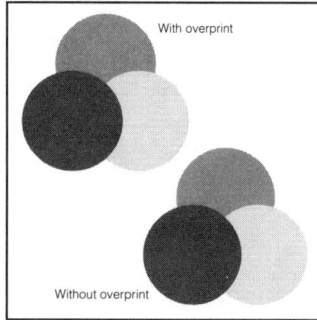

Overprinting with solid shapes makes them transparent to each other.

8 Overprinting Tints

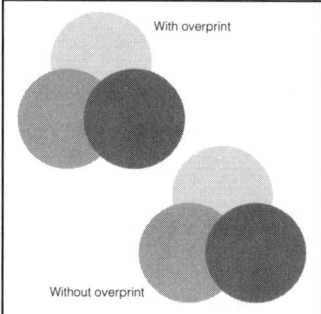

Overprinting with tinted shapes makes them transparent to each other.

9 Custom Color Trap

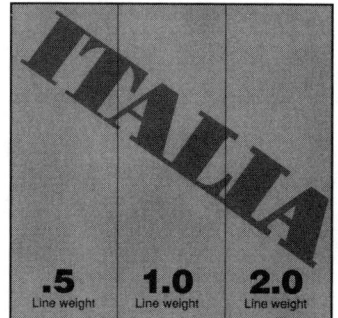

Trapping two custom colors with a stroked line.

© 1989 Adobe Systems Incorporated. All rights reserved. PostScript and Adobe Illustrator 88 are trademarks of Adobe Systems Incorporated. This page was produced using Adobe Illustrator 88 and separated on a PostScript Imagesetter at 2540 dpi using a 133 line screen.

1 Black Overprint

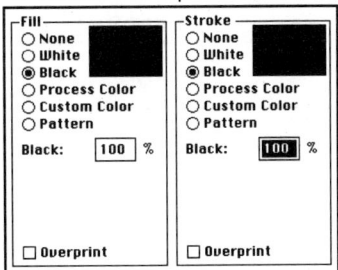

Black overprint is the default setting. When you select Black from the paint dialog box you do not need to select overprint.

2 Black Knock out

To override the default black overprint feature in Adobe Separator™ you must specifiy your black as a process color. Note: The .1% value of Cyan, Magenta & Yellow will not print because the .1% value is too fine to be imaged. This process will affectively turn the overprint feature off.

3 Four Color Black

For best results, a true four-color black should be used as indicated. It eliminates trapping problems and enhances the black. Ask your printer for his recommendation for screen mixture.

4 Line Trap

Bottom line, 3 points   **Top line, 2 pts = 1/2 pt trap**

When trapping lines it is necessary to have two lines on top of each other. The bottom line should be a heavier line weight, set to overprint. The top line should be the desired line weight with no overprint. The trap will be one half of the difference between the line weights, in this case it is 1/2 point.

5 Text Trap

When white text is placed on a four-color black background it is difficult to hold registraton on the press. Stroking and overprinting the text with .1% of Cyan, Magenta, and Yellow will push the color away from the edges, so there will not be any dot show through.

6 Shadow Trap

Drop shadow will often generate a problem of drifting between the foreground color and shadow. Place a stroked line at the intersection of the two shapes or stroke the foreground shape with a line and set to overprint. Beware of show through, see example.

7 Overprinting Solids

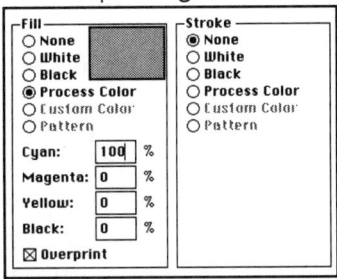

Setting a filled or stroked shape as overprint will make them transparent to each other as shown in this example. Note: The overprint setting will not preview and will only print correctly through Adobe Separator.

8 Overprinting Tints

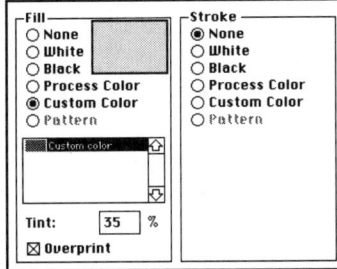

Overprinting tinted shapes (in this case a custom color) works in the same way as solid shapes as you can see in the example they become transparent to each other.

9 Custom Color Trap

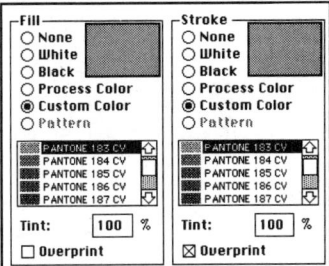

When trapping custom colors be sure to stroke or spread the shade that is lightest in to the darker shape. If the two colors are of similar value an outline will appear as in this example. Reduce the trap when needed.

373

Appendix E: Using the EPSF Riders File

After normal installation of Adobe Illustrator 3.0, you will find *Riders Folder* in the Adobe Illustrator application folder. The contents of this folder is one file called Adobe Illustrator EPSF Riders. The EPSF Riders file is PostScript code that can be used to modify Adobe Illustrator 3.0 documents during the printing process, or whenever you save a document with an EPSF header. The full text of the Adobe Illustrator EPSF Riders file is given at the end of this appendix. You can adjust the code in the EPSF Riders file to do the following:

- Add text or graphics that will appear on all pages you print from Illustrator.
- Set the default flatness for your print job.
- Set the default screen frequency and angle.
- Define your own halftone cell spot function.
- Add code that affects the setup or trailer sections of the PostScript code used in printing the Adobe Illustrator document.

Modifications to the Riders file will not be seen in the onscreen preview of any document but will appear in the printout. There are three steps in using the Riders file:

- Open the file as a TeachText file by double-clicking its icon and then edit the code. (You can also open it using any word processor and modify the code as described in this appendix.)
- Copy or move the file into the main Adobe Illustrator application folder (i.e., out of the folder called Riders Files).
- Use the Print command to print an Illustrator document if you want the effects of the Riders file to apply to this printing only. Otherwise open a document and use the Save as command to save the document with the Preview option set to "None (include EPSF Header)" if you want the effects of the Riders file to apply to future printings when the Riders file is not in the application folder.

APPENDIX E

As long as a Riders file is in the same folder as the application, the changes specified in that file will be applied to the printout. To disable the Riders file, either move it to a different folder or rename it. It is possible to have several Riders files, each with a unique descriptive name, modified to create different effects. When a certain effect is desired, simply rename that Riders file "Adobe Illustrator EPSF Riders" and place it into the application folder.

Warnings: If the EPSF Riders file is not being used, it should not remain in the application folder since it can slow down the program's performance. Line screen frequency and angle setting contained in an active Riders file will override similar settings in Separator.

The Adobe Illustrator User Guide warns that, "this file is intended only for users who are fluent in the PostScript language." We agree that this file is not for everyone, but if you think you can understand how to use the file from the instructions given here, you can experiment with it by printing and saving test files when the Adobe Illustrator EPSF Riders file is in the application folder—and by moving it out of the Adobe Illustrator application folder (or back into the folder called Riders Files) before opening, printing, or saving files that you do not want to affect.

Although the Riders file allows a wide variety of modifications that experienced PostScript programmers will find useful, there are several code fragments included in the file that can easily be modified by anyone to create commonly requested effects such as modifying the flatness, line screen, and screen angles of documents. Another useful effect is the addition of a text line to the bottom of document pages, such as a repeated copyright line, a site identification, or a project identification line.

The EPSF Riders file consists primarily of lines of code that have been made into comments only (i.e., disabled) by the addition of a percent sign (%) at the beginning of the line. Lines that begin with a percent sign and a bullet (%•) are precoded lines that you can activate by deleting both characters from the front of the line. You can then modify the code as desired. Lines in the EPSF Riders file that begin with a percent sign *not* followed by a bullet are permanent comment lines that should not be activated (by deleting the percent sign).

APPENDIX E

Specific examples follow.

Setting a Default Flatness You can create a global flatness setting for all objects in the document that currently have a flatness setting of zero. Increasing the flatness sometimes allows the printing of complex documents that otherwise would exceed the memory of the output device. Find the line in the Riders file that contains the word "setflat." Remove the %• at the beginning of the line and enter in a numeric value or leave the value of 2, which the line currently contains.

These are the lines in the orginal EPSF file:

```
%—
% The following statement can be used to set the default flatness for your print job.  All
% objects that have a Paint Style with flatness set to 0 will use the flatness specified
% here.   If this statement remains commented out, objects painted with flatness
% set to 0 will use the device default.
%•2  setflat
%—
```

The same lines with the setflat line activated by removing the %• characters:

```
%—
% The following statement can be used to set the default flatness for your print job.  All
% objects that have a Paint Style with flatness set to 0 will use the flatness specified
% here.   If this statement remains commented out, objects painted with flatness
% set to 0 will use the device default.

2  setflat
%—
```

Note that the setflat line in the EPSF Riders file affects only those elements in the Illustrator artwork that were originally set to a flatness value of zero—it does not affect the printing of objects with other flatness settings.

Setting the Line Screen Frequency and Angles The following lines in the EPSF Riders file affect line screen frequency and angle:

```
%—
% The following statements can be used to set the default screen
frequency and angle
% for your print job.  If these statements remain commented out,
then all objects will
% use the device default screen frequency and angle.  Note that
color printers have
% multiple screen frequencies and angles.  See the PostScript
Language Reference Manual -
% Second Edition for more information on using halftone screen
operators for color printers.

%— set screen frequency (halftone cells per inch)
%•currentscreen 3 -1 roll pop
%•30 % <- screen frequency
%•3 1 roll setscreen

%— set screen angle (degrees)
%•currentscreen 3 -2 roll pop
%•30 % <- screen angle
%•3 2 roll setscreen
%—
```

When these lines are commented out, Illustrator uses the default settings for line screen and angle of the printer. To set the line screen frequency (lpi), find the line that reads "set screen frequency" and remove the %• from the beginning of the next three lines of code. A default of 30 is already entered; this can be modified to whatever frequency you want. Follow the same procedure to change the screen angle, the code for which appears just below the screen frequency code in the Riders file.

APPENDIX E

Adding a String of Text   A useful method for dating or indicating ownership of documents is an inconspicuous text line on the bottom of document pages. In the EPSF Riders file the lines that are set up to do this include the following:

```
%—
% A simple procedure to print a string at the bottom of a page.
% Can be called by annotatepage (see below) if you wish.
%
%•/PrintX          % string PrintX -
%•{
%•  count 0 gt
%•      {
%•   dup type /stringtype eq
%•              {
%•                  /Helvetica findfont 9 scalefont setfont
%•                  36 36 moveto
%•                  show
%•              } if
%•} if
%•} bind def

%—
% The following procedure is called by the Adobe Illustrator prolog during the print job immediately
% before the showpage operator is executed.  You may use this procedure to perform operations like
% placing a logo or other information on each page.

%•/annotatepage
%•{
%•gsave   initgraphics
% Insert your PostScript language code between the %=== lines below
%=======================================
%•(From the desk of <your name here?>) PrintX
%=======================================
```

APPENDIX E

```
%•grestore
%•} def
%—
```

To add a line of text at the bottom of the page, find the code segment that begins with "PrintX." Remove the %• from the front of this and the next eleven lines of code, as follows:

```
/PrintX              % string PrintX -
{
 count 0 gt
   {
   dup type /stringtype eq
       {
       /Helvetica findfont 9 scalefont setfont
       36 36 moveto
       show
       } if
   } if
} bind def
```

The middle line contains the default font, which is Helvetica 9 pt. You can change this to any font or point size (but be sure to spell the font name correctly). You can change the position of the line on the page from "36 36 moveto" (i.e., 36 points, or one half inch, up from and to the right of the bottom left corner).

Next go down and find the line that contains the word "/annotatepage" and remove the %• from this line and wherever it appears in this section of code, ending with the line "%•} def." The line containing the words "(From the desk of...)" is where you substitute your text string. In the example below, the text that will print at the bottom of the page reads "© 1991, TechArt, Inc."

```
/annotatepage
{
gsave initgraphics
```

APPENDIX E

```
% Insert your PostScript language code between the %===   lines below
%=====================================
(© 1991, TechArt, Inc.) PrintX
%=====================================
grestore
} def
```

Full Text of Adobe Illustrator EPSF Riders

```
%!AI3_Riders        % signature (do not remove this line)

% Modifications to this file should be performed only by those users who are fluent in
% the PostScript® language. If you are not an experienced PostScript language
% user, you should not modify this file. If you use this file, place it in the folder
% with the Adobe Illustrator® application. If you are not using this file, do not place
% it in the folder with the Adobe Illustrator application because the EPSF Riders
% file can slow down the program's performance.

% This file shows how to insert custom PostScript language code into
% four different sections of an Adobe Illustrator document.

% What you put between lines beginning with double comments '%%' will
% be inserted into the file. The inserted lines will be bracketed between
%   %AI3BeginRider and %AI3EndRider comments.  The Adobe Illustrator program will know to
% ignore sections of the file bracketed within these comments when reading
% a file that contains riders.
```

APPENDIX E

```
% This file contains an error handler and several sample
PostScript language
% code fragments to set the default flatness, screen frequency,
and screen
% angle of your print job.  It also contains a simple example
of how
% you can annotate each page of your output.  Except for the error
% handler, all code fragments are commented out to disable them.
% To enable a particular fragment, just remove the %• characters
% from the beginning of the line.  Note that even though these
code
% fragments are disabled by comments, they are still written out
% to all files with headers;therefore, you may wish to remove
everything
% that you don't need from between the lines with double comments
'%%'.

% Everything BETWEEN %%BeginComments and %%EndComments will be
% inserted at the end of the comments section in an Adobe
Illustrator document:
%————————
%%BeginComments         % do not remove this line
%%EndComments           % do not remove this line


% Everything BETWEEN %%BeginProlog and %%EndProlog will be
% inserted at the end of the prolog section in an Adobe
Illustrator document:
%————————
%%BeginProlog           % do not remove this line

%——
% The following statement can be used to set the default flatness
for your print job. All
% objects that have a Paint Style with flatness set to 0 will
use the flatness specified
% here. If this statement remains commented out, objects
painted with flatness
% set to 0 will use the device default.
```

APPENDIX E

```
%·2 setflat
%—


%—
% The following statements can be used to set the default screen frequency and angle
% for your print job.  If these statements remain commented out, then all objects will
% use the device default screen frequency and angle.  Note that color printers have
% multiple screen frequencies and angles.  See the PostScript Language Reference Manual -
% Second Edition for more information on using halftone screen operators for color printers.

%— set screen frequency (halftone cells per inch)
%·currentscreen 3 -1 roll pop
%·30 % <- screen frequency
%·3 1 roll setscreen

%— set screen angle (degrees)
%·currentscreen 3 -2 roll pop
%·30 % <- screen angle
%·3 2 roll setscreen
%—


%—
% The following statements can be used to define your own halftone cell spot function
% for your print job.  If these statements remain commented out, all objects will
% use the device default halftone cell spot function.  Note that a procedure stub
% for defining your own spot function is provided, but you need to provide an implementation
% if you intend to modify the spot function.  You should not define spot functions unless
% you're an experienced PostScript language programmer.
```

APPENDIX E

```
%— set   halftone cell spot function
%•currentscreen   pop
%•{ }   % <- halftone cell spot function must be inserted inside curly braces
%•setscreen
%—

%—
% A simple procedure to print a string at the bottom of a page.
% Can be called by annotatepage (see below) if you wish.
%
%•/PrintX              % string PrintX -
%•{
%•  count 0 gt
%•              {
%•    dup type /stringtype eq
%•      {
%•        /Helvetica findfont 9 scalefont setfont
%•        36 36 moveto
%•        show
%•      } if
%•  } if
%•} bind def

%—
% The following procedure is called by the Adobe Illustrator prolog during the print job immediately
% before the showpage operator is executed.  You may use this procedure to perform operations like
% placing a logo or other information on each page.

%•/annotatepage
%•{
%•gsave initgraphics
% Insert your PostScript language code between the %=== lines below
%=====================================
%•(From the desk of <your name here?>) PrintX
%=====================================
```

APPENDIX E

```
%•grestore
%•} def
%—


%—
% The following statements define an error handler that prints
out   diagnostics
% on the output media if the print job fails due to a PostScript
error.
%

% Standard  Error  Handler

/$brkpage  64  dict  def  $brkpage  begin
/prnt
{dup type/stringtype ne{=string cvs}if dup length 6 mul/tx exch
def/ty 10 def
currentpoint/toy  exch  def/tox  exch  def  1  setgray  newpath
tox toy 2 sub moveto 0 ty rlineto tx 0 rlineto 0 ty neg rlineto
closepath  fill  tox  toy  moveto  0  setgray  show}bind  def
/nl{currentpoint exch pop lmargin exch moveto 0 -10 rmoveto}def
/=={/cp  0  def  typeprint  nl}def
/typeprint{dup  type  exec}readonly  def
/lmargin  72  def
/rmargin  72  def
/tprint
     {dup length cp add rmargin gt{nl/cp 0 def}if
        dup length cp add/cp exch def prnt}readonly def
/cvsprint{=string  cvs  tprint(  )tprint}readonly  def
/integertype{cvsprint}readonly  def
/realtype{cvsprint}readonly  def
/booleantype{cvsprint}readonly  def
/operatortype{(–)tprint  =string  cvs  tprint(–  )tprint}readonly
def
/marktype{pop(-mark-  )tprint}readonly  def
/dicttype{pop(-dictionary-  )tprint}readonly  def
/nulltype{pop(-null-  )tprint}readonly  def
/filetype{pop(-filestream-  )tprint}readonly  def
/savetype{pop(-savelevel-  )tprint}readonly  def
```

APPENDIX E

```
/fonttype{pop(-fontid- )tprint}readonly def
/nametype{dup xcheck not{(/)tprint}if cvsprint}readonly def
/stringtype
     {dup rcheck{(\()tprint tprint(\))tprint}{pop(-string-
)tprint}ifelse
    }readonly def
  /arraytype
  {dup rcheck{dup xcheck
    {({)tprint{typeprint}forall(})tprint}
    {([)tprint{typeprint}forall(])tprint}ifelse}{pop(-array-
)tprint}ifelse
  }readonly def
/packedarraytype
   {dup rcheck{dup xcheck
    {({)tprint{typeprint}forall(})tprint}
    {([)tprint{typeprint}forall(])tprint}ifelse}{pop(-
packedarray- )tprint}ifelse
  }readonly def
/courier/Courier findfont 10 scalefont def
end %$brkpage
errordict/handleerror
   {systemdict begin $error begin $brkpage begin newerror
    {/newerror false store
      vmstatus pop pop 0 ne{grestoreall}if initgraphics courier
setfont
      lmargin 720 moveto(ERROR: )prnt errorname prnt
      nl(OFFENDING COMMAND: )prnt/command load prnt
      $error/ostack
      known{nl nl(STACK:)prnt nl nl $error/ostack get aload
length{==}repeat}if
      systemdict/showpage get exec(%%[ Error: )print
       errorname =print(; OffendingCommand: )print/command
      load =print( ]%%)= flush}if end end end}
dup 0 systemdict put dup 4 $brkpage put bind readonly put
%---

%%EndProlog           % do not remove this line
```

385

```
%----------
% Everything BETWEEN %%BeginSetup and %%EndSetup will be
% inserted at the end of the setup section in an Adobe Illustrator
document:
%%BeginSetup           % do not remove this line
%%EndSetup             % do not remove this line


%----------
% Everything BETWEEN %%Trailer and %%EOF will be
% inserted at the end of the trailer section in an Adobe
Illustrator document:
%%Trailer              % do not remove this line
%%EOF                  % do not remove this line
```

Glossary

actual size A view of a page on the screen, scaled to approximately the same size it will print, depending on the characteristics of your screen display.

additive primary colors Red, green, and blue. The three colors used to create all other colors when direct, or transmitted, light is used (television, for instance).

alignment How type lines up. Illustrator gives you three choices: align left (flush left, ragged right); align center (ragged left, ragged right); align right (ragged left, flush right) and justified. The alignment of a block of type is indicated by the position of its alignment point.

alignment point The point used to align a block of type. The alignment point is also used to select and move the type. Each block of type has one alignment point. The point appears as a solid square when the block of type is selected, and otherwise appears as an *x*.

anchor point The point on a segment that determines where the segment starts or ends. Anchor points are invisible unless any segment of the path they form is selected. Anchor points that end curve segments have direction lines and points associated with them. A single anchor point, with no segments connected to it, appears as an *x* when not selected.

artwork The paths and type created with Illustrator that constitute a single image. Stroke and fill attributes are not visible in an Artwork Only image. Artwork is saved as a PostScript program. Compare with *preview image* and *template*.

autotrace To trace around the shapes or lines in a template automatically.

average To find the average location of selected anchor points and move the selected points to that location. When you average points, the points remain distinct points. Compare with *join*.

baseline A horizontal line that coincides with the bottom of each character in a font, excluding descenders (tails on letters like *p*). In Adobe Illustrator, the baselines of a block of type are visible when the type is selected. You click on a baseline to select type, and drag it to move type.

benday An old printing term for screen tints. Taken from the name of a company that used to produce screens for the printing industry.

bevel join A squared-off corner, created when the notch formed by two perpendicular lines is filled with a triangle. Compare *miter join* and *round join*.

Bezier curve A curve, named after Pierre Bezier, that is defined mathematically by four control points. These control points are the four direction points at the ends of the two direction lines that are tangent to each curve. All curves in Adobe Illustrator are Bezier curves. See *curve*.

bitmap An electronically displayed graphic image made up of a matrix of dots. Templates and Preview images are bitmap images.

blend To create a series of successive shapes or shadings between two selected paths.

blueline A prepress proofing material, used to proof black-and-white art before printing.

boilerplate A document set up with text and graphic elements that will be included routinely in a series of documents based on the boilerplate without the need to recreate the repeated elements each time. See also *template*.

butt cap A square line cap that is perpendicular to the end of a line. It is called a butt cap because the cap butts up against the end of the line. Compare *round cap* and *projecting cap*.

cap See *line cap*

Chromalin An integral proofing system produced by DuPont. See *integral proof*.

click To press and then immediately release the mouse button.

clip art Off-the-shelf art for the Macintosh.

clipping path A mask as defined in Illustrator's Paint dialog box.

closed path A path with no endpoints; a loop. Compare with *open path*.

C

GLOSSARY

coated stock Paper that has a light clay or plastic coating. A glossy or slick paper is coated. The same color of ink will appear different when printed on different types of stock. Compare with *uncoated stock*.

coincident Occupying the same position. In a straight line, an anchor point and its two direction points are coincident.

collinear Occurring along the same straight line. The anchor point and two direction points of a smooth point are collinear.

color keys A color overlay proofing system produced by 3M Company. See *overlay proofs*.

color separations In offset printing, separate plates used to lay different colors of ink on a page printed in multiple colors, to reproduce the proportional amount of cyan, magenta, yellow, and black in the original. Adobe Separator™ prints color separations of documents created in Illustrator 88™.

comp A graphic arts term for comprehensive drafts. In Adobe Illustrator, a paper proof printed on a color printer before you print the final negatives is the equivalent of a comp.

condensed type A narrow typeface having proportionally less character width than a normal face of the same size. Although you can achieve this effect by graphically scaling characters from the normal font, usually condensed characters are individually designed as a separate font. Condensed typefaces are used where large amounts of copy must fit into a relatively small space (tabular composition being the most common area of usage). See also *kerning*.

constrain To restrict drawing, moving, or transforming to an angle that is a multiple of 45 degrees, relative to the angle of constraint you specified in the Preferences dialog box.

continuous tone image A photographic image that contains gradient tones from black to white. When you scan an image, it is converted from a continuous tone image to a halftone.

corner point An anchor point that is not on a straight line with its two direction points. Corner points are used to join two segments traveling in different directions. Compare with *smooth point*.

corner radius The radius of the circle used to form rounded corners in a rectangle.

crop marks Lines printed on a page to indicate where the page will be trimmed when the final document is printed and bound. Adobe Separator™ prints these marks if the bounding box is smaller than the paper size.

current attributes The fill, stroke, and type attributes that are in effect when you create a path or specify type. The current attributes appear in the Paint dialog box when no objects are selected.

cursor key distance The distance that selected objects move each time that you press a cursor (arrow) key. The distance is set in the Preferences dialog box.

curve A smooth path defined by two anchor points and two direction points. The anchor points define where the curve starts and ends. The direction points determine the shape of the curve.

custom color An ink color that you assign to objects in your drawing. With custom color, you can use Adobe Separator™ to produce one negative for each color used in the artwork. Compare with *process color*.

cyan The subtractive primary color that appears blue-green and absorbs red light. Used as one ink in four-color printing. Also known as process blue.

CYMK Shorthand notation for cyan, yellow, magenta, and black.

dash pattern The pattern of lines and gaps between lines that make up a dashed line. You create a dash pattern by specifying the length, in points, of each dash and of each gap between dashes.

default The initial setting of a value or option. Used to describe the value(s) or mode that Illustrator will use in processing information when no other value or mode is specified. A preset response to a question or prompt. Default settings can be changed.

define (pattern) To draw or place artwork inside a rectangle and then give it a name in the Pattern dialog box.

F

dialog box   A window or full-screen display in response to a command that calls for setting options.

digitizer   See *scanner*.

direction line   The straight line connecting an anchor point and its direction point. A curve is tangent to the direction line at the anchor point.

direction point   A point that defines the direction from which a curve enters the curve's anchor points. The position of a curve's two direction points determines the curve's shape.

dots   See *halftone dots* and *pixel*.

drag   To hold down the mouse button while you move the pointer.

DrawOver   An application that converts MacDraw files to Adobe Illustrator documents.

Dylux   A brand name for blueline proofing material.

emulsion   The photosensitive layer on a piece of film or paper.

Encapsulated PostScript (EPS) format   A file format that describes a document written in the PostScript language and that contains all the code necessary to print the file.

endpoint   An anchor point at the beginning or end of an open path. Illustrator displays endpoints as *x*'s.

fill   To paint an area enclosed by a path with black, a gray shade, a color, or a pattern.

film   Photosensitive material, generally on a transparent base, which receives character images, and may be chemically processed to expose those images. In phototypesetting, any photosensitive material, transparent or not, may be called film.

flatness   The maximum distance, in device pixels, of any point on a rendered curve from the corresponding point on the true curve.

folio   Page number.

font   One complete set of characters in the same face, style, and size, including all of the letters of the alphabet, punctuation, and

GLOSSARY

symbols. For example, 12-point Times Roman is a different font from 12-point Times Italic, 14-point Times Roman, or 12-point Helvetica. Screen fonts (bitmapped fonts used to display text accurately on the screen) can differ slightly from the printer fonts (outline fonts used to describe fonts to the laser printer) because of the difference in resolution between screens and printers.

freehand tolerance A value that controls how sensitive the Freehand tool is to variations in your hand movement.

ghosting The shift in ink density that occurs when large, solid areas interfere with one another. Also, a procedure in which two images are combined together electronically. The images are given specific weight in relation to each other to create the effect.

grid The underlying design plan for a page. In Illustrator, the grid can be composed of a series of nonprinting horizontal and vertical lines that intersect to form a "grid."

gripper The top part of a page where the printing press grabs the paper. Nothing can be printed in this area.

group To combine two or more objects so that they act as a single object. You can manipulate groups just as you do individual objects.

hairline The thinnest rule possible—generally 0.25 point.

halftone An image composed of dots of different sizes. Using a scanner, you can convert continuous tone images, such as photographs, into halftones.

halftone dots Dots as they appear on the printed page. The size of the halftone dots depends on the screen ruling used.

hide To remove a path or block of type from the artwork temporarily. Objects that are hidden do not preview or print.

insertion point A blinking vertical line that indicates where characters you type will appear.

integral proof A color proofing system that bonds all four process colors to a single sheet.

interpreter Code built into PostScript-compatible printers and typesetters that converts PostScript commands into a form the printer can use to draw an image, or software that converts PostScript commands before sending them to a printer.

join (noun) See *line join*.

join (verb) To connect the endpoints of an open path. When you join the endpoints of one path, Illustrator closes the path with a straight-line segment. When you join the endpoints of two open paths, Illustrator combines them into one longer path. Compare *average*.

kerning The amount of space, in points, that is added or taken away from between pairs of characters in a type block. Kerning affects the amount of white space displayed in a type block.

knockout A generic term for a positive or overlay that "knocks out" part of an image from another image. The most obvious example of this is white type on a black background. The white type is knocked out of the background.

landscape A horizontal printing orientation in which the top of the artwork is along the larger side of the page. Compare *portrait*.

layer To place objects in layers. See also *painting order*.

leading The amount of vertical spacing, in points, between lines of type in a type block.

line The straight line between two anchor points. In a line, each anchor point and its corresponding direction point occupy the same location.

line cap A cap placed at the end of a solid line or segments of a dashed line. Illustrator provides three kinds of line caps: butt, round, and projecting.

line join The style of connector used when Illustrator strokes a path. The choice of joins becomes important when stroking paths that contain corners. Illustrator provides three kinds of joins: miter, round, and bevel.

line weight The weight or thickness of a line, expressed in points. Line weight is a characteristic of the Stroke, set in the Paint dialog box.

lines per inch (lpi) See *screen ruling*.

magenta The subtractive primary color that appears blue-red and absorbs green light. Used as one ink in four-color printing. Also known as process red.

marquee A dashed rectangular region created when dragging the Selection tool to select objects.

mechanicals Traditionally, the final pages or boards with pasted-up galleys of type and line art, sometimes with acetate or tissue overlays for color separations and notes to the offset printer.

mechanical separations Color separations, usually black-and-white art, that are used to print different colors of ink on offset printing color pages.

memory A hardware component of a computer system that can store information for later retrieval. The area inside the computer where information is stored temporarily while you are working (also called RAM or random access memory). The amount of memory a computer has directly affects its speed and the size of the documents you can create.

menu A list of choices presented in either a drop-down or pop-up window, from which you can select an action.

miter join A corner created by extending the edges of two converging lines until they meet. Compare *bevel join* and *round join*.

miter limit The ratio that determines the angle at which Illustrator switches from a mitered (pointed) line join to a beveled (squared-off) line join. The miter limit is equal to the maximum ratio of the diagonal line through a line to the width of the lines producing the join. The smaller the miter limit, the less sharp the angle at which Illustrator switches from a mitered to a beveled line join.

moiré pattern A grid pattern (usually undesirable) that can result when two or more screen tints are overlaid incorrectly. See also *rosette*.

negative A reverse image of a page, produced photographically on a clear sheet of film as an intermediate step in preparing plates from camera-ready mechanicals for offset printing.

object An anchor point, segment, path, or type block, or a group of anchor points, segments, paths, and type blocks.

offset To move the image away from the right edge of the film or paper on which it is printing.

offset printing A type of printing that uses an intermediate step to transfer a printed image from the plate to the paper. The type of printing done using a printing press to reproduce many copies of the original that is printed out on a laser printer. The press lays ink on a page based on the raised image on a plate that is created by photographing the camera-ready masters.

open path A path with two endpoints; that is, a path that has a beginning and an end. Compare with *closed path*.

orientation The page position: portrait or landscape.

overlay A transparent acetate or tissue covering over a printed page, where color indications and other instructions to the offset printer are written. Also, an overhead transparency that is intended to be projected on top of another projection.

overlay proofs A color proofing system that uses a transparent overlay for each of the four process colors.

overprint To specify that a colored object show through another colored object that overlaps it. Normally the object underneath is hidden by the object in front, and the inks are not overprinted.

paint To fill a region defined by a path with black, a percentage gray shade, or color, or to stroke a line.

painting order The sequence in which the objects in a document are painted. Objects are painted from back to front, meaning that in a series of layered objects, the frontmost object will obscure all or part of the objects that lie behind it.

Pantone Matching System A popular system for choosing colors, based on ink mixes.

path One or more connected segments. You can fill a path, or you can stroke a line that is centered on the path.

pattern One or more objects that has been bounded by a rectangle and defined as a pattern. Once defined, patterns can be used to paint paths.

phototypesetter A device that sets type photographically, using a photochemical process and special film as output.

pica A unit of measure equal to 12 points, or approximately one-sixth of an inch.

PICT format A format used to store MacDraw documents. Before Illustrator can read a MacDraw document, it must be saved in PICT format.

pixel Short for picture element. A point on the graphics screen; the visual representation of a bit on the screen (white if the bit is 0, black if it's 1). A single dot on the Macintosh display. A template is a collection of pixels. Also, the dot a printer uses to create a halftone dot.

place To import a scanned image or an EPS format file into an Adobe Illustrator document.

point Unit of measure, used in Illustrator for specifying type and line attributes. There are approximately 72 points in an inch.

point of origin A fixed spot that you specify in your artwork, from which a transformation begins.

portrait A vertical printing orientation in which the top of the artwork is along the short side of the page.

PostScript A computer language invented by Adobe Systems that is used to define the appearance of type and images on the printed page. When you save an Illustrator document, you are actually saving a PostScript language program.

PPD file PostScript Printer Description file. The document used by the Adobe Separator program to set the default information for the type of printer you are using.

preset attributes The paint, stroke, and type attributes that are in effect if you have not specified any other attributes. Default attributes.

preview image The view of your Illustrator artwork that is displayed on your screen as a bitmap and that approximates the printed output. You can specify whether paint and pattern attributes appear in the preview image. A version of the preview image is saved along with the PostScript language code for the artwork document when you specify one of the preview options before saving your artwork. Compare *artwork*.

primary colors The elemental colors of either pigments or light. Red, green, and blue are additive primaries. White light is produced when red, green, and blue lights are added together. Cyan, magenta, and yellow are subtractive primaries. The inks used to print three-color process or four-color process with black.

process color One of the four colors—cyan, magenta, yellow, and black—blended to produce colors in the four-color process. With process color you produce a maximum of four negatives, regardless of the number of colors used in your artwork. Compare with *custom color*.

process separations Four-color separations made from color artwork.

progressive color bar A bar displaying all the possible combinations of cyan, magenta, and yellow. Progressive color bars are printed on each sheet of a process color printing job to ensure proper ink coverage and color. The bar is usually trimmed off before the job is shipped. Sometimes the progressive color bar will also include black and screen tints of the combinations.

progressive colors The four process colors plus white and the various combinations of cyan, magenta, and yellow. The Change Progressive Colors… option in the Preferences dialog box allows you to adjust the appearance of the progressive colors on your computer display.

projecting cap A square line cap placed at the end of a solid or dashed line. The cap is perpendicular to the end of the line and extends one-half line width beyond the line's endpoint. Compare *butt cap* and *line cap*.

QuickDraw A graphics language built into the read-only memory (ROM) of the Macintosh.

reflect To create a mirror image of an object.

reflected light See *subtractive primary colors*.

registration The accuracy with which images are combined or positioned, particularly in reference to multicolored printing where each color must be precisely aligned for the accurate reproduction of the original.

registration mark One of a number of small reference patterns placed on separations printed by Adobe Seoparator™ to aid in the registration process.

resolution The number of dots per inch displayed on a screen or printer. The Macintosh screen has a resolution of 72 dots per inch. The Apple LaserWriter has a resolution of 300 dots per inch. The resolution of PostScript language image-setting devices (LaserWriter Plus, Linotronic 300, and so on) is measured in pixels per inch. See *pixel*.

RGB Shorthand notation for red, green, and blue. See *additive primary colors*.

rosette The circular dot pattern that occurs when screen tints are overlaid correctly.

rotate To pivot an object about a given point.

round cap A semicircular line cap placed at the end of a solid or dashed line. The diameter of the cap is equal to the width of the line. Compare *butt cap* and *line cap*.

round join A corner created when two lines are connected with a circular arc whose diameter is equal to the width of the line. Compare *bevel join* and *miter join*.

scale To change the size of an object either vertically, horizontally, or both.

S

GLOSSARY

scanned image The image that results when a photograph, illustration, or other flat art is converted into a bitmap. On the Macintosh, scanned images are stored as MacPaint documents.

scanner An electronic device that converts a photo, illustration, or other flat art into a bitmap. A video camera is a scanner that converts three-dimensional objects into bitmaps.

screen ruling The number of lines per inch in a screen tint or halftone.

screen tint A screened percentage of a solid color.

segment A line curve that is defined by an anchor point and its direction point.

select To define an object to be acted upon by the next command or mouse operation. You must select an object before you can change or edit it in any way. You generally select an object by clicking on it with the Selection tool or by dragging the selection marquee around it.

selection marquee A dashed rectangular region created when dragging the Selection tool to select objects.

selection pointer An arrow-shaped pointer used for selecting and moving objects.

shear To slant an object vertically, horizontally, or along an arbitrary line.

shrink A positive image that has been reduced in width to create trap. See *trap*.

smooth point An anchor point connecting two segments in which the anchor point and its two direction points are located on the same straight line.

spacing The amount of space, in points, that is added or removed between pairs of characters in a type block. Spacing affects the amount of white space in a type block.

spec sheet A copy of the drawing showing the various color values.

spot color See *custom color*.

spread A negative image that has been automatically expanded by Illustrator to create trap. See *trap*.

stripper The person who "strips" negatives in the proper position so that they will run correctly on the press. The stripper is also usually the person who cuts the color-separation masks when mechanical separations are made.

stroke To draw a line that is centered on its path.

subtractive primary colors Cyan, yellow, and magenta. The three colors used to create all other colors when reflected light is used (for instance, in printed material).

tangent Touching a line or curve at only one point. The direction line is tangent to the curve at the anchor point.

tangent line See *direction line*.

template The scanned image or the image in MacPaint or MacDraw PICT format that you use as the basis for Illustrator artwork. A bitmap. The template appears on the screen as a gray image behind the artwork; it is not part of the final printed document. Compare with *artwork* and *preview image*.

tile (page) To divide Adobe Illustrator's drawing area into pages for the page size currently specified in the Page Setup dialog box.

tile (pattern) To repeat a pattern in columns and rows across the layer of the document in which that pattern paints a path.

tint A percentage of one of the process or custom colors.

toggle A command that lets you switch between two settings. The Show/Hide Rulers command is an example of a toggle.

toolbox The set of tools displayed (as icons) to the left of the drawing area when a document is open.

transmitted light See *additive primary colors*.

transverse Rotation of the page on the film or paper on which it is printing. Currently, this option is applicable only to Linotronic typesetting machines.

trap   Overlap needed to ensure that a slight misalignment or movement of the separations will not affect the final appearance of the job.

uncoated stock   Paper that is not coated. Uncoated stock is usually less smooth and absorbs ink more readily than coated stock. Compare with *coated stock*.

ungroup   To separate groups into individual objects or into subgroups.

x axis   The horizontal reference line to which objects are constrained.

y axis   The vertical reference line to which objects are constrained.

yellow   The subtractive primary color that appears yellow and absorbs blue light. Used as one ink in four-color printing.

zoom   To magnify or reduce your view of the current document.

Index

INDEX

A
About Adobe Illustrator, 66
actual size, 67
Actual Size command, 67
Actual Size, using hand tool, 16
Add-anchor-point tool, 45
Adobe Collectors Edition, 344, 349
Adobe Illustrator 1.1 compatibility mode, 134
Adobe Illustrator 88 compatibility mode, 134
Adobe Illustrator 3.0 compatibility mode, 133
Adobe Illustrator Startup, 81, 84, 86, 116, 158
Adobe Separator, 360-369
Adobe Type Manager, 76, 78
Aldus Freehand, 117, 134
aligning borders, 304
aligning objects, 164-167
aligning text, 184-187
alignment, 67-68
Alignment command, 67
alignment, paragraph, 68
alignment techniques, 164-189
    aligning objects: method 1, 164
    aligning objects: method 2, 166
    dividing equally, 168
    grid: method 1: quadrille rules, 170
    grid: method 2: perspective, 174
    grid: method 3: page layout, 176
    "hidden" notes, 178
    measuring with a point, 180
    perspective, 174
    spacing guides, 182
    three-dimensional perspective, 174
alignment, text, 68, 152
amorphous pattern design, 206
anchor points, 24, 26
    adding, 45
    converting, 46
    deleting, 46
Apple Color Picker, 122
Apple menu, 60
AppleShare network, 73, 133
AppleTalk network, 73
applications examples, 303-351
Archdiocese of Detroit map, 304
Area graph tool, 48
Area-type tool, 17
Arrange menu, 61
arrows, 252
Artwork & Template command, 69
artwork vs. preview, 108
artwork board, 123
Artwork Only command, 69
ATM, 76, 78
auto kerning, 151
auto leading, 100, 151
autotrace gap distance, 22
autotrace over gap, 121
Autotrace tool, 22-23
Average command, 70, 99, 186
Average dialog box, 187
axis options in graphs, 91
    tick lines and marks, 93
    values, 93

B
banding, 36
    preventing, 370-371
bar charts, 308, 311
bevel joins, 146, 147
bitmapped, 106
Black & White Macintosh preview mode, 132
blend color, 192
Blend tool, 33-36, 169, 175, 193, 221, 296, 348
    blending colors or grays, 192
    calculating blends, 370-371
    scaling with, 38
boilerplate document, 172, 177
borders, 304
    shared, 270
boundaries, 320
bounding box, 365
bounding rectangle, 136
Bring to Front command, 72
brushed ink look, 246
butt caps, 147
buttons, 59

C
cache, 75
caps, 147
categories for graphing, 88
Centered-oval tool, 31
Centered-rectangle tool, 28
Centered-rounded-rectangle tool, 28
charts, 304-323
    selecting and modifying, 254
charts (cubes, cylinders, and bars), 308
check boxes, 58

INDEX

Chooser, 73
Clear command, 73
clipboard, 113, 138
clipboard window, 137
clipping, 145
close box, 74
Close command, 74
closing a path, 27
coils, 280
color, 143
    blending, preventing banding, 370-371
    custom, 79, 144
    delete, 80
    edit, 80
    gradations, 34
    monitor, 76
    on screen, 122
    palette, 122
    preview image, 133
    separations, 360-369
    trapping, 372-373
Color Macintosh preview mode, 133
column design, 157
    design name, 158
    column width, 94
Column graph tool, 48
columns and rows of text, 188
commands, 55-159
    choosing, 55
comments, 148
compatibility modes, 133
compound lines, 212-218
compound paths, 102, 146
    as masking objects, 102
    convert back, 128
concentric shapes, 38
condense type, 151
constrain angle, 106, 120
continuous patterns, 202
control panel accessory, 74
control panel technique for managing artwork, 236
Convert-direction-point tool, 46
Copy command, 77
corner points, 26
corner radius, 30, 121
corners, 147
cover page, 127

Create Outlines command, 76, 78, 102, 262, 344, 346
Cricket Draw, 117
crop marks, 136
    release, 129, 136
    replace, 136
cubes, 282-288
cursor key distance, 121
    in preferences dialog box, 12
curves, 24-26
Custom Color command, 79-81
custom colors, 80, 144
custom colors library, 80
Cut command, 81
    alternatives to, 81
cylinders, 347

D

dash pattern, 149
dashed lines, 240
data entry area, 87
data series for graphing, 88
data window for graphs, 50
date format, 75
default flatness, 374-386
default tools, 129
defaults in Startup file, 81, 84, 86, 117
Define Graph Design command, 82-84
Delete-anchor-point tool, 46
Densitometer, 364-365
depth, 283
descriptive notes, 148
desktop pattern, 75
Detroit area map, 304
Detroit Free Press, 317, 321
diagrams, 304-323
dialog box entries, 56-59
Direct-selection tool, 9
direction lines, 24-25
disk space, 132
dividing equally, 168
dotted lines, 240
downloadable fonts, 112
drawing curves, 25
drawing ovals, 31
drawing straight lines, 24
DrawOver, 356-359
drop shadows, 290-293, 315, 317
    behind graph elements, 93

INDEX

E
Earth Surface Graphics, 309
Edit menu, 62
editing a path, 27
ellipses, 31
    with numerically specified dimensions, 32
emulsion options, 363
Encapsulated PostScript (EPS) importing, 117
end caps, 147
endpoints, connecting, 71, 98
enlargement, 111
EPS format, 132-133
EPSF header, changing, 374-386
    including, 132
    omitting, 132
EPSF Riders file, 374-386
expand type, 151

F
fan, 324
File menu, 63
file name, 135
fill options, 142-143
filling with text, 18
fills and patterns, 192-211
    blending colors or grays, 192
    paint palettes, 194
    patterns: method 1: discrete objects, 196-201
    patterns: method 2: continuous symmetry, 202-205
    patterns: method 3: continuous asymmetry, 206-211
Fit in Window command, 84
Fit in Window, using hand tool, 16
flatness, 147
    in EPSF Riders file, 374-386
flip, 112
floor plans, 212, 236, 316
flower petals, 294
flowers, 331
font, 150
Font command, 85-86
Font dialog box, 86
font size, 140, 150
Font Size dialog box, 100, 141
font substitution, 111
fonts downloadable, 112
FreeHand (Aldus), 117, 134
Freehand to Pen tool shortcut, 22

freehand tolerance, 21, 121
Freehand tool, 20-22
Fuller, D. L., 309

G
gradual changes of color or pattern, 34
    preventing banding, 370-371
graph axis options, 92
Graph Axis Style dialog box, 92
Graph Column Design dialog box, 157
graph data cell style, 90
Graph Data command, 87-90
graph data import, 89
graph data transpose, 89
graph data window, 50, 87
graph design, 82, 157, 159
    creating, 83
    deleting, 83
    editing, 83
Graph menu, 63
Graph Style command, 90-94
graph tools, 48
graph type, 91
graphics smoothing, 112
graphing visually, 49
graphing with numerically specified dimensions, 49
graphs, editing, 50
grids, 170-179
    page layout, 176
    perspective, 174
    quadrille rules, 170
Group command, 95
grouped paths, 95
Grouped-column graph tool, 48
guides, 139
    convert, 104
    delete, 104
    objects, 103

H
halftone screen options, 364
hand, 346
Hand tool, 15-17, 85
    changing magnifications, 16
hand-drawn looks, 242-247, 340
hanging punctuation, 152
header (PostScript), 132
Help button, 127

407

INDEX

hidden (invisible) objects, 140
hidden notes, 178
Hide command, 96, 230
Hide (see Show/Hide)
highlights, 296
holes in solid objects, 102-103, 262
horizontal scale, 151

I
IBM PC preview mode, 133
illustrations, 324-351
Illustrator, 66
Illustrator 1.1, 134
import text, 97
Import Text command, 20, 97
importing EPS files, 117
importing Illustrator files into other applications, 132
include placed images option, 118
indentation, 151
inline type, 218
instructions as part of artwork, 178
invert, 112
invisible objects, 140
isometric view, 288

J
Japan fan, 324
Join command, 71, 98-99
joins, 147

K
kerning, 153
   auto, 151
keyboard shortcuts, 55
   for the toolbox, 6
kimono, 328
Knight-Ridder Graphics Network, 317
knockout, 145, 372-373

L
labels in graphs, 87, 93
landmarks, 323
layering, 72
layering techniques, 212-239
   compound lines, 212-217
   control panel technique for managing artwork, 236
   inline type, 218

masking, 220
masking a mask, 224
overlays, color separations, 226
overlays, layers, 228
overlays, separate documents, 232
pasting in layers, 234
layers rearrange, 234
layers sequence, 239
leaders (between tabs), 240
leading, 141, 151
   auto, 151
   increment, 100
   leading before, 152
Leading command, 99-100
legends in graphs, 88, 93
   rotating, 158
letter spacing, 141-142
line breaks, text 88
Line graph tool, 48
line, scatter graphs options, 94
line spacing, text 99
line weight, 146
   scaling, 119
lines, 24-26
   brushed ink look, 246
   dashed lines, 149, 240
   dotted lines, 240
   hand-drawn looks, 242-248
   parallel curves, 248
   stippled effect, 246
   techniques, 240-251
Link command, 100-101
linked columns, 101
lists within a dialog box, 57
Lock command, 101-102, 228

M
MacDraw, 69, 356-359
MacLink, 133
MacPaint, 68
MacWrite, 97
magnification, 13
Make Compound command, 102-103, 262
Make Guide command, 103
Make Text Wrap command, 104
manual feed option, 127
maps, 212, 236, 304-323
marker design, 159
masking, 136, 145, 220, 324, 330
masking a mask, 224

INDEX

Measure dialog box, 47
measure distances, 183
Measure tool, 47, 106
measurement system, 139
measuring with a point, 180
memory available, 66
memory limitations, 66
menus, 60-65
messages, 57
Microsoft Word, 97
miter joins, 146-147
Monitors icon, 76
mouse operations, 3
Move command, 105-106
Move dialog box, 28, 105, 181
moving objects, 11-13
MS-DOS, 133
MultiFinder, 68, 75

N

negative printing, 364
New command, 106
New Window command, 108
None (include EPSF header) preview mode, 132
None (omit EPSF header) preview mode, 132
notes (PostScript), 148
notes, in artwork, 178

O

Object-selection tool, 10
objects transparent, 262
Open command, 110
open path, 27
open windows, 159
organization charts, 258
orientation, 363
outline fonts, 78
output resolution, 121
Oval dialog box, 32
Oval tool, 31
oval tools, 31-33
oval width and height, 32
overlays
   color separations, 226
   layers, 228
   separate documents, 232
overprint, 145, 372-373

P

Pacific Century Charts and Map, 308
packaging design, 286
page breaks, 48, 123
page frame, 123
page layout applications, 132
page layout specifications, 176
page numbers, 123, 126
page orientation, 111, 363
Page Setup command, 111
page size, 362
page spread, 123
Page tool, 48
PageMaker, 69, 117, 132-133
Paint menu, 64
paint palettes, 194
Paint Style dialog box, 142
PANTONE® colors, 79-80, 144
paper cassette option, 127
paper size, 111
paper source, 127
paragraph alignment, 152
paragraph spacing, 152
parallel curves, 248
Paste command, 113
Paste in Back command, 113
Paste in Front command, 114
pasting in layers, 234
Path-type tool, 17
paths, 24-26
   splitting, 44
pattern, 136, 144, 324, 326
Pattern command, 115-117
   continuous asymmetry, 206-211
   continuous symmetry, 202-205
   delete, 116
   discrete objects, 196-201
   edit, 116
   style, 211
   transformation, 119
   preview and print, 119
Pen tool, 24-28
perspective, 174, 286
PICT format, 106, 133
   converting to Illustrator, 356-359
   copy an Illustrator file into, 77
Pie graph tool, 48
pie graphs options, 94

INDEX

Pixel Paint, 117
Place Art command, 117
placed images, 118
    Encapsulated PostScript (EPS) images, 120
point text, 17
polygons, 264
Pontiac Silverdome Chart, 316
pop-out menus, 58
portrait, 336
poster, 344
PostScript code
    changing, 374-386
    notes, 148
PostScript fonts, 85
PPD files, 361
Preferences command, 118-124
preview and print patterns, 119
Preview Illustration command, 124
preview image, 132
preview modes, 131
Preview pop-up menu, 132
Preview Selection command, 125
print area, 112
Print command, 126
printed pages, 48
printer fonts, 78
printing negatives, 364
printing to disk, 368
process color, 143
process color separations, 360-369
progressive colors, 122
projecting caps, 147
punctuation, 152
puzzle pieces, 270

Q
QuarkXPress, 69, 132
Quit command, 127

R
radial symmetry, 266-269
radially symmetrical object, 40
radio buttons, 59
RAM, 110
RAM cache, 75
Rectangle dialog box, 30
rectangle
    drawing visually, 29
    with numerically specified dimensions, 29

Rectangle tool, 28
rectangle tools, 28-31
rectangular buttons, 59
rectangular text, 18
Redo (see Undo), 128
reduction, 111
Reflect dialog box, 40
Reflect tool, 40, 252, 348
reflect tools, 40-42
Reflect-dialog tool, 40
reflecting by a specified amount, 41
reflecting visually, 41
Release All Guides command, 128
Release Compound command, 128
Release Cropmarks command, 129
Release Text Wrap command, 129
repeating graph designs, 158
Reset Toolbox command, 129
reversed, 112, 146
ribbons, 350
Riders file (EPSF), 374-386
roads, 212
Rotate dialog box, 39
rotate legend, 158
Rotate tool, 264, 266-277, 294
rotate tools, 38-40
rotating by a specified amount, 39
rotating visually on the screen, 38
rough sketch, scanned, 340
round caps, 147
round joins, 147
rounded corners, 30
Rounded-rectangle tool, 28
RTF (Rich Text Format), 97
ruler guide, 139, 166
ruler units, 124
rulers, 139, 166

S
Save As command, 131
Save As dialog box, 130-131
Save command, 130
Scale dialog box, 37
scale graph design, 158
scale line weight, 119
Scale tool, 36, 277, 294
scale tools, 36-38
Scale-dialog tool, 36
scaling objects by a specified percentage, 37

INDEX

scaling objects visually, 36
scanned image as template, 304, 316
scanned map as template, 308
scanned portrait, 336
Scatter graph tool, 48
schematic drawings, 212
Scissors tool, 44-45, 270, 318, 344
screen angle, in EPSF Riders file, 374-386
screen colors, 122
screen frequency, in EPSF Riders file, 374-386
scroll bars, 15
scrolling lists, 57
scrolling with the hand tool, 15
see-through object, 103
Select All command, 135
selecting objects, 8-11
    guide objects, 104
    text, 19
Selection tool, 9
selection tools, 9-13
Send to Back command, 135
separations, color printing, 360-369
Separator, 227, 360-369
Set Cropmarks command, 136
shaded effect, 154
shading, 293, 338
shading effects, 296
shadow, 290
shapes (closed paths), 252-280
    arrows, 252
    charts: selecting and modifying, 254
    holes in solid objects, 262
    organization charts, 258
    polygons, 264
    radial symmetry: method 1, 266
    radial symmetry: method 2, 268
    shared borders, 270
    stars, 272-277
    symmetrical designs, 268
shared borders, 270
Shear tool, 288, 310
shear tools, 42-44
shearing by a specified amount, 43
shearing visually, 43
Show All command, 137
show placed images option, 118, 120
Show/Hide Clipboard command, 137
Show/Hide Rulers command, 139
Show/Hide Toolbox command, 139

Show/Hide Unpainted Objects command, 140
size, 150
Size command, 140
sliding column designs, 158
smoothing, 111
snap to point, 119
space before paragraphs, 152
space between words and letters, 141, 152
spacing guides, 182
spacing options, 152
Spacing Options command, 141
spheres, 347
split long paths on save/print option, 120
splitting a path, 44
spot color, 80
spot color separations, 360-369
springs, 280
squared rules, 170
Stacked-column graph tool, 48
stars, 272-277
Startup file, 81, 84, 86, 117, 158
stippled effect, 246
straight line of an exact length, 28
street map, 320
streets composed of white lines on black lines, 322
streets drawn as wide black lines, 322
stroke, 142, 145
Style command, 86
Style command (Paint menu), 142-149
Style command (Type menu), 150-152
SuperPaint, 359
switch XY values in graph, 90
symmetrical designs, 40, 154, 266, 268
symmetrical pattern, 202

T

tabular text, 188, 240
techniques, 163-299
template, 106
    adding to existing artwork, 111
    changing, 111
Template Only command, 153
text, 17-20
    alignment, 152, 184-189
    columns, 101, 188
    convert to outlines, 78
    entries in dialog boxes, 57
    format, 150

INDEX

hidden, 178
import, 97
labels, 307
leading, 99
  on a curved path, 190
paths, 101
size, 140, 150
smoothing, 112
techniques, 184-191
wrap, 104-105, 129
three-dimensional effects, 280-299, 306
  coils, 280
  cubes, 282-287
  drop shadows, 290-293
  flower petals, 294
  highlights, 296
  perspective, 174
  springs, 280
tick marks, 93
tile full pages, 123, 136
tile imageable areas, 136
tiling, 48
tint adjustment chart, 365
toolbox, 139
  overview, 4-7
  reset, 129
  shortcuts, 5
tools, 3-51
TOPS, 133
tracing bitmaps, 22-23
  tracing part of a shape, 23
traced portrait, 336
tracking/kerning, 151
Tracking/Kerning command, 142, 153
transfer function, 364
Transform Again command, 154, 165, 171, 185, 273, 277, 294
Transform Pattern Style dialog box, 144, 200, 205, 211
transform pattern tiles, 119
transparencies, 226, 228
trapping, 372-373

type (see also text)
  along a path, 19
  attributes, 150
  condense, 151
  expand, 151
  inline, 218
  outlines as a masking object, 103
  overlap, 219
  preferences, 122
Type menu, 64
Type Preferences dialog box, 122
Type Style dialog box, 150
type tools, 17-20

U

Undo/Redo command, 155
Ungroup command, 155
uniformly scaled columns, 158
unit of measure, 124, 139
Unlink command, 156
Unlock All command, 156
unpainted objects, 140
Use Column Design command, 157-158
Use Marker Design command, 159

V

Van Pelt John, 317, 321, 337, 341
Ventura Publisher, 133
vertical shift, 151
vertically scaled columns, 158
View menu, 65

W

warnings, 57
Washington, D.C. street map, 320
weight, 146
Window menu, 65
window names, 159
window tiles, 159
word spacing, 141

Z

zoom tools, 13-15